Introduction to Mediaeval Latin Studies

A Syllabus and Bibliographical Guide

by

Martin R. P. McGuire, Ph. D.

Professor of Greek and Latin
The Catholic University of America

The Catholic University of America Press

Washington, D. C. 20017

1964

FLORENTIAE VXORI CARISSIMAE

PREFATORY NOTE

The purpose of this work is to give the beginning graduate student a comprehensive, solid, and up-to-date orientation in a field that presents special difficulties by its very vastness, to say nothing of other problems. The SYLLABUS and SELECT BIBLIOGRAPHY are broader in scope than their titles might indicate, for they include references to, or even initial orientation in, a number of other disciplines -- e.g., Classical, Patristic, Celtic, Germanic, Romance, Byzantine, and Islamic Studies -- insofar as these disciplines have connections with Mediaeval Latin Studies. The writer firmly believes that, despite the demands and fruitful results of specialization, the closest possible union should be maintained between Mediaeval Latin Studies and all other disciplines that are concerned with the scholarly investigation of Mediaeval civilization in its various aspects.

The SYLLABUS is not a manual. The topical outlines are intended primarily to highlight points which are important and which should be examined in the detailed expositions listed in the Bibliography following each topical outline. The period of Late Latin, i.e., from c. 200 to 500 A.D., has been treated rather fully, because a good knowledge of Late Latin is fundamental for a proper understanding of Mediaeval Latin and its characteristic features. The period from c. 1100 to the close of the Middle Ages is treated only sketchily in the SYLLABUS. The 12th century is dealt with thoroughly and systematically in De Ghellinck's L'Essor de la littérature latine du XIIe siècle, which includes the 13th century to c. 1225, and it would not be possible to cover the writers of the period from c. 1225 to c. 1500 without greatly increasing the size of the present work. However, the Later Middle Ages are adequately covered in the Bibliographies in the SYLLABUS and in the SELECT BIBLIOGRAPHY. Originally, it was planned to deal in some detail with Mediaeval Latin versification, but this difficult subject is now covered in excellent fashion in the easily available monograph of D. Norberg, Introduction à l'étude de la versification latine médiévale (Stockholm 1958).

The SELECT BIBLIOGRAPHY is intended to give the graduate student a systematic introduction to a number of disciplines in which, sooner or later, he will have to acquire a working familiarity. When a full title of a work is not given in the SYLLABUS, it can be run down quickly through the INDICES following the SELECT BIBLIOGRAPHY. All bibliographical items have been chosen from the scholarly point of view. Hence, books and articles have been listed exclusively on the basis of scientific merit; the language in which they are written was ignored as a factor in their selection.

The SYLLABUS and SELECT BIBLIOGRAPHY represent the latest revised form of the notes and bibliography which the writer has assembled and repeatedly reworked as he has gained in knowledge and experience since inaugurating the course, Introduction to Mediaeval Latin Studies, at The Catholic University of America in 1929. The course has been given annually on a two-semester basis since that time, and for many years it has been offered in Summer Session.

It would no longer be possible to identify all the sources from which he has derived information, and which have served to stimulate or shape his own thinking. However, he remembers vividly the enthusiasm engendered by his first reading of L. Traube's Einleitung in die lateinische Philologie des Mittelalters and wishes to acknowledge his indebtedness to that brilliant and delightfully written sketch. He is gratefully conscious, too, of the special help received from the works of P. Lehmann, C. H. Haskins, K. Strecker, F. Blatt, E. Löfstedt, M. Grabmann, J. De Ghellinck, M. L. W. Laistner, H. I. Marrou, P. Courcelle, C. Mohrmann, E. A. Lowe, and B. Bischoff. The SYLLABUS and SELECT BIBLIOGRAPHY are not without original features in organization, emphases, and selection of references, but the writer has not really been too much concerned with what is original and what has been borrowed or adapted from others. He hopes rather that the SYLLABUS and SELECT BIBLIOGRAPHY will furnish guidance to graduate students in Mediaeval Latin Studies and related disciplines and encourage them to persevere in a field that needs many new, but well-qualified, workers.

TABLE OF CONTENTS

I. MEDIAEVAL LATIN STUDIES AND THEIR SCOPE

Mediaeval Latin Studies are concerned with the investigation of Western Mediaeval culture in so far as that culture is represented, conditioned, or influenced by works written in the Latin language. They are concerned, therefore, but in no narrow or exclusive sense, with the study of language and style, with literary history and literary forms, and with the transmission of Ancient and Mediaeval Latin texts to the invention of printing. (This definition is adapted from Lehmann.)

The relation of Mediaeval Latin Studies to other disciplines: Mediaeval History, Patristic and Mediaeval Philosophy, Theology, and Law, Classical Scholarship, Celtic, English, Germanic, and Romance Studies, Byzantine, Islamic, and Slavic Studies

The origin and history of the term "Middle Ages"

The history of Mediaeval Latin Studies and their development into a distinct and independent discipline in the last decades of the nineteenth century

Readings

On the nature and scope of Mediaeval Latin Studies, see especially: Lehmann, Erforschung des Mittelalters 1:4-5; Franceschini, "Limiti e compiti di una nuova disciplina"; Lind, Medieval Latin Studies, Their Nature and Possibilities. See also the other pertinent works listed in my SELECT BIBLIOGRAPHY 1. General Introductions, Bibliographical Guides, etc.

On the history of the term "Middle Ages," see especially: Lehmann, "Vom Mittelalter und von der lateinischen Philologie des Mittelalters"; id., Erforschung des Mittelalters 1:49-55; Gordon, Medium Aevum and the Middle Age: Falco, "Medioevo". See also the other studies listed in my SELECT BIBLIOGRAPHY 1.

On the history of Mediaeval Latin Studies and their development into an independent discipline, see, especially: Lehmann, "Vom Mittelalter und von der lateinischen Philologie des Mittelalters" 11-25 (translation by M.R.P. McGuire available in typescript); Rumpf, L'étude de la Latinité médiévale; Faral, "L'orientation actuelle des études relatives au latin médiéval". See also the other pertinent works listed in SELECT BIBLIOGRAPHY 1.

On the development of Mediaeval Studies in general in the United States, see: C. W. David, "American Historiography of the Middle Ages, 1884-1934," Speculum 10 (1935) 125-137; M. R. P. McGuire, "Mediaeval Studies in America: A Challenge and an Opportunity for American Catholics," Catholic Historical Review 22 (1936) 12-26; F. N. Robinson, "Anniversary Reflection," Speculum 25 (1950) 491-501 (on the occasion of the 25th annual meeting of the Mediaeval Academy of America).

II. BIBLIOGRAPHY OF MEDIAEVAL LATIN STUDIES

General and special works, collections of texts, works on language and style, dictionaries, periodicals, bibliographical orientation in related disciplines

The SELECT BIBLIOGRAPHY which forms a part of this SYLLABUS will furnish the student a broad systematic bibliographical introduction to Mediaeval Latin Studies and related disciplines. See also: Paetow, Guide to the Study of Medieval History passim, but especially 483-493; Lind, Medieval Latin Studies 38-44; Strecker-Palmer, Introduction to Medieval Latin, passim; Raby, Christian Latin Poetry 469-489; id., Secular Latin Poetry 2:361-399; De Ghellinck, "La littérature latine du moyen âge," Les Études Classiques 7 (1938) 492-515; id., "Aperçu bibliographique," L'essor de la littérature latine au XIIe siècle 1:19-32 (not confined to the twelfth century, but an excellent bibliographical introduction to the whole field of Mediaeval Latin Studies); Bossuat, "Aperçu des études relatives au latin médiéval," Mémorial...Marouzeau (Paris 1943) 256-270

For full bibliographical data on the works listed and for other works, see SELECT BIBLIOGRAPHY 1.

For quarterly or annual surveys and reviews of new publications, see especially: Analecta Bollandiana; L'Année Philologique; Archivum Latinitatis Medii Aevi (Bulletin du Cange); Progress of Medieval and Renaissance Studies in the United States and Canada (biennally); Publications of the Modern Language Association; Recherches de théologie ancienne et médiévale, with Bulletin; Revue Bénédictine; Revue du moyen âge latin; Revue d'Histoire Ecclésiastique; Revue des Études latines; Romania; Speculum; The Year's Work in Modern Language Studies; Zeitschrift für deutsches Altertum und deutsche Literatur; Zeitschrift für romanisch Philologie; Quarterly Check-List of Medievalia.

For full bibliographical data on the periodical publications listed and for a large number of others which deal in whole or in part with Mediaeval Latin Studies, see SELECT BIBLIOGRAPHY 13. Periodicals.

III. LATIN WRITING IN THE MIDDLE AGES

We shall begin our work proper with a survey of Latin writing in the Middle Ages, because Latin writing, as Traube once observed, is the clearest evidence of the unbroken connection between Antiquity and Modern Times.

a. Landmarks in the history of Paleography and Diplomatics

Mabillon and his Libri sex de re diplomatica (1681). On the controversy between the Bollandist Papebroch and the Maurists which occasioned Mabillon's treatise, see especially H. Leclercq, "Mabillon," DACL 10.1:427-723, especially 498-515. Mabillon's classification of hands: Saxon, Lombard, Merovingian, and Gothic, and his erroneous opinion on their origins

Montfaucon's Paleographia Graeca (1708)

Scipio Maffei and his discovery of Early Mediaeval Mss in Verona (1713); his recognition of the unity of Latin writing and of majuscule, minuscule, and cursive script

The Nouveau Traité de diplomatique by the Maurists Toustain and Tassin (1750-1765). It was only in the course of their work that they came to see that Scipio Maffei was right, so that the Nouveau Traité represents a kind of compromise between the teachings of Mabillon and Maffei. Toustain and Tassin, however, were the first to recognize the half-uncial as a distinct script and to derive the insular hand from it. Furthermore, they gave us the technical terms: capitalis, uncialis, semi-uncialis, minuscula.

Progress since the Nouveau Traité

The development of practical paleography and the founding of institutes; the influence of the Monumenta Germaniae historica (founded in 1819) and similar projects in the development of paleography

The École des Chartes (1821)

The Institut für österreichische Geschichtsforschung (1854; reorganized 1878); the work of Theodor von Sickel

The Palaeographical Society founded by Westwood and Bradshaw (1873)

The Pontificia Scuola Vaticana founded under Leo XIII (1886)

The great impetus given to paleography through the development of photography

The unsatisfactory method of dating Mss in the earlier history of paleography. See P. Lehmann, "Einteilung und Datierung nach Jahrhunderten," Aus der Geisteswelt des Mittelalters, Studien und Texte Martin Grabmann 1:31-51 (Bäumkers Beiträge..., Supplementband 3, 1935).

The pioneer work of Léopold Delisle in determining the place and date of composition of Mss. See especially his "Mémoire sur l'école calligraphique de Tours au IXe siècle," Mémoires de l'Académie des Inscriptions et des Belles-Lettres 32 (1885).

The epoch-making achievements of L. Traube in the field of historical (genetic) paleography and his wide and fruitful influence as a teacher; his American pupils, Rand, Beeson, Clark, Lowe, and their important contributions to paleography by their own research and through their numerous pupils

The necessity of cataloging completely all mediaeval Mss and of investigating all mediaeval centers of culture systematically

On mediaeval and modern catalogues of Mss, see IV infra.

The descriptive and historical study of abbreviations of various kinds. Abbreviation by suspension and by contraction; the value and limitations of works like Cappelli, Lexicon abbreviaturarum

Lists of incipits or initia and their value

The new impetus given to paleographical studies through the development of microfilm

Bibliography

A detailed history of Latin paleography remains to be written. The best sketch of the subject to the beginning of the present century is that of L. Traube, "Geschichte der Paläographie," Vorlesungen und Abhandlungen 1 (Munich 1909) 1-80. See also L. Traube, Einleitung in die lateinische Philologie des Mittelalters 5-31, especially 5-19.

As typical examples of paleographical investigations as developed in accordance with the basic ideas and method of Traube, see, e.g., Rand, Studies in the Script of Tours; C. H. Beeson, Lupus of Ferrière as Scribe and Text Critic; L. W. Jones, Script of Cologne.

On abbreviations, see: R. Cagnat, Cours d'épigraphie latine (4th ed. Paris 1914) 399-473; Steffens-Coulon, Paléographie latine xxix-xl; A. Cappelli, Lexicon abbreviaturarum; Martin, The Record Interpreter. A Collection of Abbreviations...
L. Traube, Nomina Sacra; W. M. Lindsay, Notae Latinae: An Account of Abbreviations in Latin Mss. of the Early Minuscule Period (c. 700-850), with Supplement (Abbreviations in Latin Mss. of 850 to 1050 A.D.), by Doris Bains; E. M. Thompson, Introduction to Greek and Latin Palaeography 75-91; M. Prou, Manuel de paléograph 106-165; M. Laurent, De abbreviationibus et signis scripturae Gothicae; L. Schiaparelli, Avviamento allo studio delle abbreviature latine nel medioevo.

As representative collections of incipits, see: M. Vattasso, Initia patrum aliorumque scriptorum ecclesiasticorum latinorum ex Mignei Patrologia et ex compluribus aliis libris collecta; A. G. Little, Initia operum latinorum quae saeculis XIII, XIV, XV attribuuntur; L. Thorndike and P. Kibre, A Catalogue of Incipits of Mediaeval Scientific Writings in Latin.

For full bibliographical data on the works cited and for further pertinent bibliography, see SELECT BIBLIOGRAPHY 10 A and D (near end).

b. The main phases in the development of Latin writing

In the history of Greek writing – and it must be kept in mind that the Latins borrowed their alphabet from the Greeks – we note the following kinds of letters: 1) Capitals, or majuscule letters, which are characterized by their same height and by their being confined to the square or circular form; 2) the Uncial, i.e., a majuscule letter which exhibits a freer form in general and a more pronounced rounding; 3) the Majuscule-Cursive, a script marked by a certain flowing, rapid character and by the connection of the individual letters; 4) the Minuscule-Cursive, which developed from the majuscule-cursive; 5) the Literary Minuscule, which exhibits a mixture of uncial and cursive and which does not become a fully developed script before the ninth century A. D. It may be observed that the minuscule letters in which our Greek classics are printed only acquired their present form in the period from the ninth to the fourteenth century A. D.

We distinguish similar phases in the development of Latin writing. The dissolution of the Roman Empire into national States, however, exercised a marked influence on the development of Latin writing. Accordingly, the Roman forms of writing to the end of Antiquity should be distinguished from the forms of writing which subsequently developed out of the Roman scripts.

A. The Roman Scripts

The Roman scripts exhibit the following kinds of letters:

1) Majuscule Capitals, which we find at first in inscriptions and later in a freer and lighter form in Mss. The characteristic feature of this kind of writing is that the letter forms consist essentially of straight lines. This script falls into two main divisions: Capitalis Quadrata and Capitalis Rustica. In the Capitalis Quadrata the letters are mostly square, as broad as they are high. In the Capitalis Rustica the letters are mostly higher than they are broad, and they are less regularly formed (hence the name "rustic"), the lines being slightly undulated. The Capitalis Rustica flourished well into the sixth century A. D. and continued to be used much longer in titles, etc. The Scriptura Capitalis is very easy to read, since it is essentially the same as our ordinary printed Latin capital. Cf. Thompson 272-284.

Examples of the Capitalis Quadrata: Thompson, 275, No. 82; Ehrle, Plate 1; Steffens, Plates 12a, 12b; Lowe, Codices Antiquiores, passim.

Examples of the Capitalis Rustica: Thompson 276-282, Nos. 82-86; Ehrle, Plates 2 and 3; Steffens, Plate 19; Lowe, op. cit.

See also: E. Hübner, Exempla scripturae epigraphicae Latinae a Caesaris dictatoris morte ad aetatem Iustiniani (Berlin 1885); A. E. and J. S. Gordon, Album of Dated Latin Inscriptions. 1, Rome and the Neighborhood, Augustus to Nerva (Berkeley 1958); Mallon-Marichal-Perrat, L'écriture latine de la capitale romaine à la minuscule (1939)

2) The Uncial, which developed from the Capital, is distinguished from the latter by its more rounded forms. It is characterized particularly by the form of the letters a, d, e, h, m. This kind of writing was already in use, it seems, in the third century A. D. and flourished until the beginning of the ninth century. Cf. Thompson 284-297; Lowe, op. cit.

Examples: Steffens, Plates 17, 18, 21a, 21b; Thompson, Nos. 87-94; Ehrle, Plates 4 and 5; Lowe, op. cit.

3) The Majuscule-Cursive, or the old epistolary script. It is characterized by rapid form, by fondness for the connection or ligature of adjoining letters, and by the unequal heights of the latter. Cf. Thompson 310-339; H. B. Van Hoesen, Roman Cursive Writing (Princeton 1915). On the development of Roman cursive scripts, the following references are especially important: Mallon-Marichal-Perrat, L'écriture latine de la capitale romaine à la minuscule; Marichal, "L'écriture latine et l'écriture grecque du Ier au VIe siècle," Antiquité classique 19 (1950) 113-144; Mallon, Paléographie romaine (1952)

Examples: Thompson, Nos. 101-114; Steffens, Plates 3 and 9; Van Hoesen, passim; Mallon-Marichal-Perrat, Plates IVff.

4) The Minuscule Cursive, which developed out of the earlier cursive in the third and fourth centuries. The form of the individual letters becomes even more fluent, the ligatures increase in number and in variety of forms, and the writing adapts itself to the "four-line system."

Examples: Steffens, Plates 13, 22, 25b; Thompson, Nos. 112 and 113; Mallon-Marichal-Perrat, passim.

5) The Half-Uncial, a script which is between majuscule and minuscule and exhibits a mixture of capital, uncial, and cursive elements. It flourished in the period from the fifth to the ninth century and was particularly preferred by ancient Christian writers. Cf. Thompson 298-309.

Examples: Thompson, Nos. 95-100, Ehrle, Plates 5, 6, 7; Steffens, Plates 14, 17, 20, 23c; Lowe, Codices antiquiores.

B. The Post-Roman Scripts

After the fall of the Roman Empire there developed from the Roman scripts the various minuscule scripts which are usually called the National Hands (or Scripts). These are the Old Italian, the Montecassino-Beneventan, the Merovingian, and the Visigothic — all derived chiefly from the minuscule cursive; and the Irish-Anglo-Saxon Script, based on the Half-Uncial.

1) The Old Italian Script. Cf. the references given under Majuscule-Cursive and Minuscule-Cursive, supra.

Examples: Steffens, Plates 25b, 27, 33, 34, 42, 48a; Ehrle, Plate 10; Thompson, No. 114.

2) The Montecassino-Beneventan Script. Cf. E. A. Lowe, The Beneventan Script (1914); Thompson 348-355.

Examples: Steffens, Plates 42a, 68, 75; Ehrle, Plates 11, 12, 13, 17; Thompson, Nos. 120-123, Lowe, op. cit.

3) The <u>Merovingian Script</u>. Cf. Thompson 355-367.

Examples: Steffens, Plates 25a, 28, 29, 37, 38, 40, 43, 44, 39a, 59; Ehrle, Plates 18, 19; Thompson, Nos. 124, 125.

4) The <u>Visigothic Script</u>. Cf. Thompson 341-347, and, especially, C. U. Clark, <u>Collectanea Hispanica</u>, in Transactions of the Connecticut Academy of Arts and Sciences (1920).

Examples: Steffens, Plates 35, 36, 49b, 66b; Ehrle, 25, 26; Thompson, Nos. 115-118; Clark, <u>op. cit</u>.

5) The <u>Irish-Anglo-Saxon Script</u>. Cf. Thompson 371-402.

Examples: Steffens, Plates 21a, 26, 30-32, 50, 54, 57a, 65, 71a, 83a; Ehrle, 21-24; Thompson, Nos. 134-151.

6) The <u>Carolingian Minuscule</u>. In the second half of the eighth century a minuscule script was developed in France - most probably first at Corbie - which was based chiefly on the half-uncial. This new minuscule, which we call the Carolingian Minuscule, is distinguished for its "orderliness, simplicity, clarity, and dignity." Superior to all earlier minuscules, it soon replaced them except in Spain, South Italy, Ireland, and England. Even in England it gained ascendance, at least as the hand employed in Latin documents, in the tenth century. It supplanted the Visigothic Script in Spain in the twelfth century, and the Beneventan Script of South Italy in the thirteenth. In Ireland, the Irish hand has persisted in an unbroken tradition down to the present time. There are many disputed points in the early history of the Carolingian Minuscule, but it is now certain that it originated in France, not Italy, and that it was already being used at Tours before the coming of Alcuin. Cf. Thompson 367-403ff., but especially, E. A. Lowe, "Handwriting," in Crump and Jacob, <u>Legacy of the Middle Ages</u> 216-222.

Examples: Steffens, Plates, 45, 47, 51-53, 55, 56, 60, 61, 63, 64, 66a, 67, 69, 70, 71b, 74, 77, 78-85, 87; Thompson, Nos. 131-133 and 152ff.; Ehrle, Plates 29-35.

7) The <u>Gothic Minuscule</u>. In the twelfth and thirteenth centuries there gradually evolved out of the Carolingian Minuscule a script that had little in common with the Carolingian script of the ninth century. This new script, which is characterized by its straight lines, sharp turns, and pointed angles, is called the <u>Gothic Minuscule</u>. It spread over Europe and in part took on national forms. Cf. Steffens-Coulon xx-xxiii; Thompson 424ff.; Lowe, <u>op. cit</u>. 222-224. See also B. Bischoff, G. I. Lieftinck, G. Battelli, <u>Nomenclature des écritures livresques du IX au XVIe siècle</u> (Paris 1954).

Examples: Steffens 86, 89, 92, 113, 115a; Ehrle, 36-46; Thompson, Nos. 167ff; Bischoff-Lieftinck-Battelli, <u>op. cit</u>.

8) <u>The Humanistic Script and the Modern Gothic Script</u>. From the fifteenth century on we note two kinds of writing in Western Europe: the <u>Humanistic Script</u>,

based on the Carolingian Minuscule of the ninth and tenth centuries, and the Modern Gothic Script, based on the Gothic Minuscule of the late Middle Ages. The Humanists had no taste for the Gothic Minuscule of their time and they sought to replace it by a deliberate imitation of the Carolingian Minuscule. Their script is called Scriptura humanistica (littera antiqua horum temporum, lettera antica nuova, antica). The Gothic script, however, continued to be used and developed. It was only gradually supplanted by the Humanistic Script in Spain, France, and England, and it remained the dominant script in Germany. The German script today is simply a further developed form of the Modern Gothic Script of the fifteenth century. Cf. Steffens-Coulon xxiii-xxviii; Lowe, op. cit. 224-226; Thompson 512-570 (chiefly concerned with England); and, especially, B. L. Ullman, The Origin and Development of Humanistic Script (Rome 1960).

Examples of Humanistic Script: Steffens, Plates 114, 115b, 124a (Books); 116a, 116b, 117, 118a, 123b (Cursive); 116c, 122 (Chancery); Ehrle, Plates 47-50; Ullman, op. cit.

Examples of Modern Gothic Script: a) French Gothic Cursive: Steffens, Plates 119a, 119b, 123a; b) English Gothic Cursive: Steffens, Plates 120, (cf. Plate 115a); Thompson, Nos. 240ff.; c) German Gothic Cursive: Steffens, Plates 118b, 121, 124a, 124b.

N.B.:   The scripts of documents are, in general, closely connected with the literary or book-hands. In the former, however, there is frequently to be noted a fondness for greater effect, for certain old forms, for ornament, and for elaborate abbreviation forms. Cf. Thompson 490 ff. See also C. Johnson and F. J. H. Jenkinson, English Court Hand A. D. 1066 to 1500 (Oxford 1915).

The early printers, naturally, turned to the Modern Gothic or Humanistic Script for their type models, and thus our Roman type today is essentially the Carolingian Minuscule as adapted by the Humanists.

The spread of the Latin form of writing in the modern world: the adoption of the Latin alphabet, e.g., in Turkey.

Bibliography

The following works in particular are recommended to those who have had no formal training in Latin paleography and who may wish to acquire some proficiency in this discipline by private study:

E. A. Lowe, "Handwriting" in Crump and Jacob, Legacy of the Middle Ages; H. Leclercq, "Paléographie," DACL 13.1:610-736; E. M. Thompson, Introduction to Greek and Latin Palaeography: M. Prou, Manuel de paléographie latine et française; G. Battelli, Lezioni de paleografia (3rd ed. 1949; the most up-to-date manual); B. Bischoff, Paläographie (2nd ed. revised Berlin 1956; Sonderdruck from W. Stammler, ed., Deutsche Philologie im Aufriss); F. Steffens, Paléographie latine.

For a new and epoch-making approach to the study of Latin paleography, which, among other things, stresses the essential relationship between paleography and epigraphy, see J. Mallon, Paléographie romaine (Madrid 1952); id., "Paléographie romaine", in L'Histoire et ses méthodes (Paris 1961; Encyclopédie de la Pléiade) 353-584. See the important reviews by C. Higounet in Revue des Études anciennes 56 (1954) 235-241, and by A. Dain, Latomus 15 (1956) 398-404. See also R. Marichal, "Paléographie précaroline et papyrologie, L'écriture latine du Ier au VIe siècle: Les sources," Scriptorium 4 (1950) 116-142; F. Masai, "Paléographie et codicologie," ibid. 279-293.

For facsimiles, see especially, Thompson, passim and 577-583; Steffens, op. cit.: Ehrle and Liebaert, Specimina Codicum Latinorum; J. Kirchner, Scriptura Latina libraria a saeculo primo ad finem medii aevi LXXVII imaginibus illustrata (Munich 1955); Lowe, Codices Latini antiquiores; Umbrae codicum occidentalium, edd. G. Battelli, B. Bischoff, et al. (Amsterdam 1960 ff). For further collections of facsimiles, see Paetow, Guide 35-38; Bretholz, Lateinische Paläographie 36-40; Leclercq, op. cit., col. 732-736; Battelli, Lezioni, etc.

The standard manuals of Diplomatics are: A. Giry, Manuel de diplomatique; H. Bresslau, Handbuch der Urkundenlehre für Deutschland und Italien; A. de Boüard, Manuel de diplomatique française et pontificale. For a good sketch (with bibliography), see G. Tessier, "Diplomatique", in L'Histoire et ses méthodes (Paris 1961; Encyclopédie de la Pléiade) 633-676. See also R. L. Poole, Lectures on the History of the Papal Chancery down to the Time of Innocent III.

On the influence of the late Mediaeval and Renaissance styles of writing on the early printers, see "History of Printing," in H. B. van Hoesen and F. K. Walter, Bibliography, Practical, Enumerative, Historical (New York 1928) 259-315.

For recent and current bibliography in the field of Latin paleography, see: R. J. Dean, "Latin Paleography 1929-1943," Progress of Mediaeval and Renaissance Studies in the United States and Canada, No. 18 (1944) 6-18; Strecker-Palmer, Introduction to Medieval Latin 131-136; the section, "Paléographie, histoire de l'écriture et des manuscrits," in L'Année philologique; Scriptorium. International Review of Manuscript Studies.

For full bibliographical data on works cited throughout III, LATIN WRITING IN THE MIDDLE AGES, and for additional bibliography, see SELECT BIBLIOGRAPHY 10A.

IV. MEDIAEVAL BOOKS AND THEIR PRODUCTION. MEDIAEVAL
LIBRARIES. MEDIAEVAL AND MODERN CATALOGS OF MSS.

These topics could be dealt with after the sections on language and literature, as is done, e.g., in Strecker's Introduction. The student, however, will have a better understanding of Mediaeval Latin and of Mediaeval Latin literature if he has some preliminary information on the mediaeval book and its production, dissemination, and care, on the small holdings of mediaeval libraries, on the destruction and scattering of mediaeval collections, and on the mediaeval and modern catalogs of mediaeval Mss. Such information will be valuable also as background for understanding certain features of mediaeval education and the conditions under which it was conducted.

The difficulty of producing and reproducing books before the invention of printing and the relative scarcity of books in Antiquity and the Middle Ages as compared with Modern Times

Writing materials: papyrus (until the eleventh century A. D.); parchment and vellum; paper not used in the West much before the twelfth century A. D.

Writing implements: the stilus, reed and quill pens; inks – black, red, silver and gold

The roll and codex – the problem of making citations from a roll

The codex the typical form of the mediaeval book

The make-up of the mediaeval book – arrangement of leaves, gatherings, bindings, ornamentation

The monastic scriptoria and their procedures; the monastic scribes

The rise of the universities and the growing demand for books; the rise of professional lay scribes; the official control of their work; the pecia; the stationarii and librarii

Mediaeval libraries: the libraries of pagan and Christian Antiquity; Cassiodorus, and the rise of monastic and cathedral libraries in the Early Middle Ages; the libraries of Monte Cassino, Bobbio, St. Gall, Lindesfarne, Canterbury, York, Fleury, Cluny, St. Riquier, Corbie, Tours, Fulda, Reichenau, Corvey, Spanheim; the growth of royal and college libraries in the later Middle Ages; arrangements and rules in mediaeval libraries

Catalogs of mediaeval libraries and their significance for the cultural history of the Middle Ages

The destruction of mediaeval libraries and the wide dispersion of such books as survived

Modern catalogs of mediaeval Mss: the work accomplished to date in the various countries; the great amount of cataloging still to be done; the unsatisfactory character of the earlier catalogs of Mss; Catalogi catalogorum

Bibliography

On books and their production and dissemination, see: Kenyon, Books and Readers in Ancient Greece and Rome; Hall, Companion to Classical Texts, ch. I,

"The Ancient Book", 1-21; ch. III, "The Text of Latin Authors in Ancient Times," 53-64; ch. IV, "The History of Latin Texts from the Age of Charlemagne to the Italian Renaissance," 94-107; ch. IX, "The Nomenclature of Mss. with the Names of Former Possessors," 286-357; Thompson, Introduction to Greek and Latin Palaeography 8-74; H. Hunger, "Antikes und mittelalterliches Buch - und Schrift-wesen," in H. Hunger, O. Stegmüller, et al., Geschichte der Textüberlieferung der antiken und mittelalterlichen Literatur 1 (Zurich 1961) 25-71; D. Diringer, The Hand-Produced Book (New York, 1953), especially chs. IV, V, VI, VII, X, and XI ("Inks, Pens, and Other Writing Tools"); id., The Illuminated Book; McCown, "Codex and Roll"; C. H. Roberts, "The Codex," Proceedings of the British Academy 40 (1955) 169-204; Milkau, Handbuch der Bibliothekswissenschaft 1, especially chs. IV, V, IX, X, and XI; De Ghellinck, Patristique et Moyen Age 2, "Diffusion et trans-mission des écrits patristiques," 181-377; Weitzmann, Illustration in Roll and Codex; Bardy, "Copies et éditions du Ve siècle"; Marrou, "La technique de l'édition à l'époque patristique"; Destrez, La pecia dans les manuscrits universitaires du XIIIe au XIVe siècle; Rashdall-Powicke-Emden, Universities of Europe in the Middle Ages 1 (1936) 184-190, 421-423 (on peciarii, stationarii and librarii).

On mediaeval libraries, see: the article "Libraries" in Encyclopedia Britan-nica; the articles "Biblioteca" in the Enciclopedia Italiana and Enciclopedia Cat-tolica; the article "Bibliothèques" in Cabrol-Leclercq, DACL; Thompson, The Medieval Library; Milkau, Handbuch der Bibliothekswissenshaft 3, chs. I, II, III, IV, V; De Ghellinck, Patristique et Moyen Age 2: 259-289; id., "Progrès récents et tendances actuelles en histoire des bibliothèques," Revue d'Histoire ecclésias-tique 38 (1942) 156-168; Laistner, Thought and Letters in Western Europe, A. D. 500 to 900, ch. IX, "Libraries and Scriptoria"; Lesne, Les livres, "Scriptoria" et Bibliothèques du commencement du VIIIe siècle à la fin du XIe siècle.

On mediaeval and modern catalogs of Mss, see: James, The Wandering and Homes of Manuscripts; P. O. Kristeller, Latin Manuscript Books before 1600. A List of the Printed Catalogues and Unpublished Inventories of Extant Collections (new ed. revised New York 1960); Seymour de Ricci-Wilson, Census of Medieval and Renaissance Mss in the United States and Canada, with Supplement (1963); Becker, Catalogi bibliothecarum antiqui; Gottlieb, Ueber mittelalterliche Biblio-theken; Manitius, Handschriften antiker Autoren in mittelalterlichen Bibliotheks-katalogen; Lehmann, Mittelalterliche Katalogen Deutschlands und der Schweiz; id., "Quellen zur Feststellung und Geschichte mittelalterlicher Bibliotheken". See also the additional bibliography in Strecker-Palmer, Introduction to Medieval Latin 121-126.

On the Institut de Recherches et d'Histoire des Textes in Paris, see: J. Vielliard and M. Th. Boucrel, "La recherche des manuscrits latins," Mémorial... Marouzeau (Paris 1943) 442-457. See also Centre National de la Recherche Sci-entifique, Publications de l'Institut de Recherche et d'Histoire des Textes, Bulle-tin d'information, No. 1 (1952) (Paris 1953).

For photostats and microfilms see Strecker-Palmer, op. cit. 136-139. For the collection of microfilms of Vatican Mss in process of being assembled at St. Louis University, see the periodical Manuscripta.

For full bibliographical data on the works listed <u>supra</u> and for further bibliography, see SELECT BIBLIOGRAPHY 10C, <u>The Ancient and Mediaeval Book and the Diffusion and Transmission of Texts</u>, and 10D, <u>Mediaeval Libraries</u>, <u>Mediaeval and Modern Catalogs of Mss</u>, <u>Incipits</u>.

For current bibliography on mediaeval and modern catalogs of Mss., etc., see especially <u>Scriptorium</u>, and <u>L'Année Philologique</u>, s. v. "Paléographie: histoire de l'écriture et des manuscrits."

N.B.: The student will find the great majority of the printed mediaeval and modern catalogs of Mss available in our great libraries — Library of Congress, Harvard, Yale, Princeton, etc.

On the incunabula, so many of which are important for Mediaeval Latin Studies, see: Van Hoesen and Walter, <u>Bibliography, Practical, Enumerative, Historical</u> (New York 1928), ch. XIII, "History of Printing," 316-372, especially 316-336; Milkau, <u>Handbuch der Bibliothekswissenschaft</u> 1, ch. VI, "Buchdruck und Buchillustration bis zum Jahre 1600," by M. Husing; L. Hain, <u>Repertorium bibliographicum</u> (4 vols. Stuttgart 1826-1838), with <u>Supplements</u> by Burger (1891) and Copinger (1895); <u>Gesamtkatalog der Wiegendrucke</u> (Leipzig 1925 ff.): M. B. Stillwell, <u>Incunabula in American Libraries</u> (New York 1940).

V. THE ORIGINS AND CONSTITUENT ELEMENTS OF EARLY MEDIAEVAL LATIN

1. Some General Preliminary Notions

Latin as a spoken and written universal language in the West during the period of the Roman Empire

Greek as a universal language in the East and West before Latin and beside Latin — Old Babylonian and Aramaic as universal languages in the East before Greek

The adoption of Latin as the official language of the Catholic Church in the West and the spread of Latin as the universal language of religion and culture in the West during the Middle Ages

The conversion of Ireland, Britain, the Franks, Germany, Bohemia, Scandinavia, Poland, Hungary, and their subsequent entrance into the domain of Latin culture

The strong religious and cultural unity of Western Christendom as contrasted with the collapse of religious and cultural unity in the East even before the coming of Islam and the significance of this fact

The extent to which Mediaeval Latin may be considered a "living language"

Arabic as a universal language beside Latin from the Early Middle Ages

French and, to a lesser degree, Italian as universal languages from the age of the Crusades to the close of the Middle Ages

The rise of the vernacular languages and literatures beside Latin, and their increasing rivalry with Latin in the Late Middle Ages

The decline of Latin as a universal language from the Late Middle Ages: the neglect of the auctores in the universities, the triumph of the vernacular languages and literatures, the Humanists, the Reformation, the secularization of culture, the rise of science, and the changed content and philosophy of education since the last quarter of the nineteenth century, as factors in this decline

The unsatisfactory situation as regards the knowledge of Latin and interest in Latin, even in Catholic circles, at the present time – the recent Roman pronouncements on the study of Latin

French as a universal language of culture in the seventeenth and eighteenth centuries

The spread of English as a universal language in the nineteenth and twentieth centuries

The failure of artificial international languages like Esperanto to win general acceptance and its causes

The practical impossibility of making Latin again an international language of scholarly intercourse

Bibliography

A number of the points dealt with above were suggested by a reading of L. Traube, Einleitung in die lateinische Philologie des Mittelalters 31-46, especially 31-35, and C. Mohrmann, "Die Rolle des Lateins in der Kirche des Westens" in her Études sur le latin des chrétiens 2 (Rome 1961) 35-62. See also, F. Skutsch, "Die lateinische Sprache," in P. Hinneberg ed., Die Kultur der Gegenwart 1.8: Die griechische und lateinische Literatur und Sprache (3rd ed. Berlin 1912) 523-565, especially 547-562; Devoto, Storia della lingua di Roma 343-365; Baumgartner, Die lateinische und griechische Literatur der christlichen Völker 229-241; P. Lehmann, "Vom Leben des Lateinischen im Mittelalter," Erforchung des Mittelalters 1:62-81; Raby, Secular Latin Poetry in the Middle Ages 2:341-348; De Ghellinck, L'éssor de la littérature latine au XIIe siècle 2:312-321; G. E. Ganss, S. J., "A Historical Sketch of the Teaching of Latin," in his St. Ignatius' Idea of a Jesuit University (Milwaukee 1954) 208-248, especially 215 ff.

On the concern of the Church for improving the knowledge of Latin among the clergy, see the Apostolic Constitution, Sedes Sapientiae, issued by Pius XII in 1936, the "Letter to Local Ordinaries on the Proper Study of Latin," issued by the Sacred Congregation of Seminaries and Universities in 1958 (for an English translation, with accompanying comments, see M. R. P. McGuire, ed., Teaching Latin in the Modern World [Washington 1960] 246-257), and the Apostolic Constitution, Veterum Sapientiae, issued in 1962.

2. The History of the Latin Language to the End of the Second Century A.D., with Emphasis on Its Relation to the Development of Latin Literature

A. The Preliterary Period (to 240 B.C.)

The place of Latin among the Italic dialects

Our fragmentary knowledge of Latin before the second half of the third century B.C.

B. The Period of Early Latin: From the Beginnings of Formal Latin Literature to the Social War (240-90 B.C.)

The rise of a formal Latin literature against the background and under the influence of the earlier and contemporary Greek literature

The rise of a Latin literary language and the beginning of the cleavage between the conservative, Hellenized language of literature and the spoken language of the masses; the nature of this cleavage and the danger of exaggerating it, at least in this period

Characterization of the Latin of Ennius, Plautus, Terence, Cato, Luciliu and of the inscriptions of this period

C. Latin in the Golden Age of Latin Literature: From the End of the So-cial War to the Death of Augustus – the Ciceronian and Augustan Ages (88 B.C. – 14 A.D.)

The spread of Latin throughout Italy and, through colonization, in Africa Spain, and Gaul

The Hellenization of Roman education in the last two centuries of the Republic

The Greek influences on Latin style in prose and poetry – Asianism, Atticism, Alexandrianism

The classical prose style of Cicero and Caesar and its characteristics

The style of Sallust, Asinius Pollio, and Livy

The poetic style of Catullus, Lucretius, Horace, Vergil, and Ovid

The Latin of inscriptions in this age

The artificial character of the literary language in this period as contrasted with the spoken language of the masses

The spoken Latin of the educated class – our limited knowledge of the spoken Latin of all classes in the Classical Period

D. Latin in the Silver Age of Latin Literature: From the Death of Augustus to the Death of Hadrian (14 A. D. – 138 A. D.)

The vital role of the provinces in the Latin literature of the Empire – Spain, Africa, Gaul

Education in the Early Empire – the supremacy of rhetoric

The full identification of poetry with rhetoric from the close of the Augustan Age – the significance of this identification of poetry and rhetoric for the Middle Ages

The entrance of colloquial elements into the literary Latin of the Silver Age and the question of provincialisms - the critical investigation of Livy's Patavinitas and of Africitas and its results

The growing tendency towards abstract expression and the great number of abstract substantives added to the Latin vocabulary during the Silver and Late Periods

The growth of individualism and subjectivism and the breaking down of the barriers between the language of prose and that of poetry

The custom of reading all written material aloud in Antiquity and in the Middle Ages and the influence of this practice on the use of rhetorical devices in all types of literary composition

The style of Lucan, Seneca, Tacitus, and Suetonius

Quintilian and his place in the history of Latin style

The precious evidence furnished by Petronius and the inscriptions of Pompeii for the spoken Latin of the Early Empire

The exhaustion of pagan Latin literature – Apuleius, Ammianus Marcellinus, Ausonius, and Claudian (the last two perhaps nominal Christians) the only really outstanding representatives – apart from the great Jurists – of pagan Latin literature after Suetonius

E. The Period of Archaism: The Age of the Antonines (138 - 192 A.D.)

Archaism as a literary movement from Sallust on

The culmination of this movement in Fronto, Gellius, and Apuleius

The creative genius of Apuleius and the peculiar features of his language and style

The importance of the Archaists for our knowledge of Early Latin

The revival of Greek literature under Hadrian and the Antonines and the new enthusiasm for Greek and Greek literature in the West in this period

The truly Roman style of the great Jurists of the second and early third century and its comparative freedom from rhetorical turgidity and bombast

Bibliography on A – E

Palmer, The Latin Language 59-147; Meillet, Esquisse 73-238; Devoto, Storia della lingua di Roma 72-274; Skutsch, "Die lateinische Sprache," 523-565; Stolz-Debrunner, Geschichte der lateinischen Sprache (3rd ed. Berlin 1953) 62-99; W. Kroll, "Die Entwicklung der lateinischen Schriftsprache," Glotta 22 (1933) 1-27. See also: Norden, Die antike Kunstprosa 156-367 and 573-605; Duff, A Literary History of Rome from the Origins to the Close of the Golden Age (3rd ed. London 1953), especially ch. III, "The Latin Language - Its History and Qualities," 18-38; id., A Literary History of Rome in the Silver Age, especially ch. I, "Prologue," and ch. II, "Roman Education under the Empire," 1-41, and the "Conclusion," 650-658; A. Gwynn, Roman Education from Cicero to Quintilian (Oxford 1926); H. I. Marrou, A History of Education in Antiquity (New York 1956) 229-298; M. L. Clarke, Rhetoric at Rome. A Historical Survey (London 1953) 1-138; Baldwin, Ancient Rhetoric and Poetic 224-247; id., Medieval Rhetoric and Poetic 1-125; Raby, Secular Latin Poetry 1:1-47; M. Bernhard, Der Stil des Apuleius von Madaura (Stuttgart 1927). On the language of the great Roman jurists, see F. Schulz, Roman Legal Science (Oxford 1948) 96-98 and 258-261.

On reading all written matter aloud in Antiquity and later, see J. Balogh, "Voces paginarum. Beiträge zur Geschichte des lauten Lesens und Schreibens," Philologus 82 (1927) 84-109 and 202-240

The standard reference works in the field of Latin literature, Schanz-Hosius-Krueger, Römische Literaturgeschichte, and Teuffel-Kroll-Skutsch, Geschichte der römischen literatur, cover the Latinity of all writers and literary types and give pertinent bibliography.

Studies on the Latinity of Latin authors appearing after the publication of the respective volumes of Schanz-Hosius may be controlled through J. Cousin, Bibliographie de la langue latine 1880-1948, and Marouzeau's L'Année philologique. For full bibliographical data on the works listed above and for further bibliography, see SELECT BIBLIOGRAPHY 4 and 11A.

3. The Period of Late Latin (c. 200 A.D. - c. 500 A.D.) – The Age of Transition from Antiquity to the Middle Ages

General Observations

The decline of pagan literature and learning from the later part of the Silver Age on

The decline of the knowledge of Greek in the West from the end of the second century A.D. and its importance for the subsequent history of Western culture

The supremacy of rhetoric in Roman education under the Empire and the predominantly pagan character of the public schools to the end of Antiquity

The rise of Christianity and its final triumph; the moral and intellectual problems facing Christians in an environment of pagan education, literature, and tradition

The spread of Christianity in the West as well as in the East and the rise of a great Christian literature in Latin beside that in Greek

The highly conservative character of the later literary Latin

The general decline in culture, however, and the considerable influence exercised by the speech of the masses on late literary Latin

The gradual evolution of the spoken language of the masses into Primitive Romance

Early Mediaeval Latin essentially a continuation of the literary Latin employed especially by Christian writers in the last centuries of Antiquity

Early Mediaeval Latin, therefore, a fusion of Christian, "Classical" (pagan or secular), and popular elements

The necessity of analysing these three elements for obtaining an adequate understanding of Early Mediaeval Latin and of Early Mediaeval culture in general

A. The "Classical" Element (i.e., the Continued Production, Study, and Influence of the Pagan or Secular Literature)

The decline of the knowledge of the Greek language and literature in the West from the end of the second century and the rise of a translation literature of pagan as well as of Christian works

General characterization of pagan or secular Latin literature after the middle of the second century A.D. – the few outstanding names except in the field of law

The importance, however, of the work of grammarians, editors, and compilers for the Middle Ages – Servius, Donatus, Marius Victorinus, Martianus Capella, Nonius Marcellus, Macrobius, Priscian

Roman education under the Empire and its organization – the rise of rhetorical schools in the provinces – Africa, Spain, Gaul

The establishment of a fixed curriculum of "liberal" arts – Cicero, Varro, Vitruvius, Quintilian, Martianus Capella, Augustine, and Cassiodorus

The preoccupation with form and style rather than with content in the study of literature in the schools of the Empire

The pronounced pagan character of the schools of rhetoric and the persistence of the pagan tradition to the end of Antiquity

The attitude of the Christians to pagan literature and education – theoretical views and the practical compromise (see B. The Christian Element)

The highly artificial and bombastic literary style in the second half of the fifth and in the sixth century – Apollinaris Sidonius, Ennodius, Cassiodorus

The great importance of imitatio in the literature of Antiquity and the Middle Ages – the modern emphasis on strict originality, or at least on formal acknowledgment of borrowed material, foreign to the theory and practice of ancient and mediaeval writers

"Higher" imitatio: the elaboration or general treatment of a theme based on the handling of a similar or different theme by an earlier writer – Prudentius' use of Vergil, and Einhard's use of Suetonius in this way

"Lower" imitatio: the borrowing of words, phrases, even sentences, from earlier writers – the common form of imitatio; the marked verbal influence of Vergil on all subsequent epic poetry, even on a great poet like Prudentius; the verbal influence of Cicero and Vergil on Ambrose and Augustine; the verbal influence of Suetonius on Einhard; the extremes of such borrowing as evidenced in a writer like Rhabanus Maurus

The roll and the book in relation to free and exact reproduction of the words and thoughts of preceding writers (see also IV supra)

The allegorical method of interpretation among the pagans – the influence of the Stoics

Christian use of the allegorical method in interpreting Scripture and other works also (see C. The Christian Element)

The influence of the Latin grammarians in developing a bent in mediaeval writers for the strange and the unusual in their imitating and borrowing

N.B.: The glossaries, their origin and their use, will receive formal treatment later under the section on Dictionaries.

The Hisperica Famina and other examples of highly artificial or bizarre forms of Latin in Late Antiquity and the Early Middle Ages

Final Remarks on the "Classical" Element

Given the fact that the Church in the West adopted Latin as her official language and was for centuries the highest and even the sole source of intellectual culture, the pagan Latin literature, which was such a basic part of the Latin cultural tradition, could not be neglected or repudiated without impairing the development of the Christian Latin culture itself. The great bulk of what we call secular Latin literature and learning was pagan in origin, and Latin Christians felt that this secular literature and learning was an essential part of their cultural inheritance. Hence, they strove as best they could during a long period of general political upheaval and cultural decline to preserve much of the pagan literature along with what was specifically Christian in their intellectual tradition.

This striving to preserve should be thought of, not in terms of the benefits to be conferred on generations of the distant future, but in terms of their own immediate experience and needs. In spite of their severe pronouncements on the dangers and slight worth of pagan writings, men like Jerome, Augustine, and Gregory the Great were Romans by tradition and sympathy. They were deeply shocked by the decline and disappearance of Roman political authority in the West, and they could not conceive of any intellectual culture except a Greek or Latin culture. In fact, the idea of the permanence of the Roman Empire and of the dominance of Rome was so deeply rooted in the West, particularly in Italy, that even in the late sixth century men still refused to accept the harsh truth that the Roman Empire in the West had long passed away. In those chaotic centuries of Late Antiquity and the Early Middle Ages, when men had no thought of creating a new culture but were looking backward because all about them they saw only confusion and darkness, it is not surprising, after all, to find Cassiodorus and Isidore citing pagan and Christian writers side by side in their attempt to salvage what they could from the wreck of the ancient intellectual culture. The intellectual work of Late Antiquity and the Early Middle Ages was almost entirely one of preservation and transmission in the face of great difficulties. The splendid creative achievement of the Middle Ages was to come much later.

Bibliography on A. The Classical Element:

The decline of the knowledge of Greek in the West: McGuire, "The Decline of the Knowledge of Greek in the West from about A.D. 150 to the Death of Cassiodorus: A Reexamination of the Phenomenon from the Viewpoint of Cultural Assimilation," Classical Folia 13.1 (1959) 3-25; Marrou, Saint Augustin et la fin de la culture antique 27-46; Bardy, La question des langues dans l'Église ancienne 1: 155-229; Courcelle, Les Lettres grecques en Occident de Macrobe à Cassiodore; De Labriolle, "La connaissance du grec," in Fliche and Martin, Histoire de l'Église 4: 570-572

Pagan or secular literature from the end of the second to the sixth century A.D.: Schanz-Hosius-Krueger, Römische Literaturgeschichte 3-4; Wright and Sinclair, History of Later Latin Literature 1-121 (very brief); Norden, "Die lateinische Literatur im Uebergang vom Altertum zum Mittelalter"; E. K. Rand, "The Latin Literature of the West from the Antonines to Constantine," CAH 12:571-610.

Marius Victorinus, Aelius Donatus, and Priscian as representative grammarians: Schanz-Hosius-Krueger, op. cit. 4. 1:149-165; 4. 2:221-238. The extant works of most of the Latin grammarians are available in Keil, Grammatici Latini. There are good editions of Nonius Marcellus by Müller and by Lindsay, and of Martianus Capella by Dick. The best edition of Isidore of Seville's Etymologiae is by Lindsay. There is an edition of Lindsay's text with a Spanish translation (BAC Series). See SELECT BIBLIOGRAPHY 11 A (near end).

Roman education in the Early and Late Empire and the domination of rhetoric: Gwynn, Roman Education from Cicero to Quintilian; Duff, A Literary History of Rome in the Silver Age 23-41, 42-81, and 387-421; F. H. Colson, Quintilian: Institutiones oratoriae 1 (Cambridge 1924), with excellent introduction and commentary; M. F. Clarke, Rhetoric at Rome. A Historical Survey (London 1953) 139-164; D. L. Clark, Rhetoric in Greco-Roman Education; E. R. Curtius, European Literature and the Latin Middle Ages, especially 36ff. and 62-75; Raby, A History of Secular Latin Poetry in the Middle Ages 1: 1-116, an excellent treatment of ancient rhetoric and poetics to the end of the fourth century A.D.; Marrou, Histoire de l'éducation dans l'antiquité 313-415 (Engl. Trans. 229-313); id., Saint Augustin et la fin de la culture antique, passim; Leclercq, "École," DACL, with good bibliography; R. R. Bolgar, The Classical Heritage and Its Beneficiaries (Cambridge [Engl.] 1954) 13-58; R. M. Martin, "Arts libéraux (septs)," in Baudrillart-Vogt-Rouziès, Dictionnaire d'histoire et de géographie ecclésiastiques 4:827-843; Haarhoff, Schools of Gaul: A Study of Pagan and Christian Education in the Last Century of the Western Empire

The highly artificial style of the late fifth and sixth century: Sister Genevieve Marie Cook, The Life of Saint Epiphanius by Ennodius (Washington 1942; CUA Studies in Mediaeval and Renaissance Latin Language and Literature 14); A. Loyen, Sidoine Apollinaire et l'esprit précieux en Gaule aux derniers jours de l'Empire (Paris 1943; with good bibliography)

Imitatio and literary borrowing in general: Baldwin, Ancient Rhetoric and Poetic, and Medieval Rhetoric and Poetic (check s.v. imitatio in the indices); Atkins, Literary Criticism in Antiquity 2 (check s.v. "imitation" in the index); J. F. D'Alton, Roman Literary Theory and Criticism (London 1931) 426-434 and 558-559; R. McKeon, "Literary Criticism and the Concept of Imitation in Antiquity," Modern Philology 34 (1936-1937) 1-35; Curtius, European Literature and the Middle Ages, passim (check through index); E. Stemplinger, Das Plagiat in der griechischen Literatur (Leipzig 1912); Traube, Einleitung in die lateinische Philologie des Mittelalters 70-73. On the influence of Vergil on Saint Ambrose, see: Sister M. Dorothea Diederich, Vergil in the Works of St. Ambrose (Washington 1931; CUA Patristic Studies 29); on Prudentius: Brother Albertus Mahoney, Vergil in the Works of Prudentius (1934; CUA Patristic Studies 39); I. Rodriguez-Herrera, Poeta Christianus. Prudentius' Auffassung vom Wesen und von der

Aufgabe der christlichen Dichters (Munich 1936): C. Schwen, Vergil bei Prudentius (Leipzig 1937). On the influence of Ovid on Prudentius, see: Sister Marie Ligouri Ewald, Ovid in the Contra Orationem Symmachi of Prudentius (Washington 1942; CUA Patristic Studies 66); Sister Isaac Jogues Rousseau, "The Influence of Ovid on the Psychomachia of Prudentius" (unpublished CUA Master's Dissertation 1954). All the studies listed present excellent examples of "higher" as well as of "lower" imitatio. On Einhard's use of Suetonius, see: Laistner, Thought and Letters 273-275; on the practice of Rhabanus Maurus, ibid. 301-307. As exemplary modern critical editions of ancient or mediaeval works in which imitations or unacknowledged borrowings have been identified, see, e.g.: R. A. B. Mynors, Cassiodori Senatoris institutiones (Oxford 1937); M. L. W. Laistner, Bedae Venerabilis Expositio Actuum Apostolorum et retractio (Cambridge [Mass.] 1939; Med. Acad. of Am. Publ. No. 35); Brother Charles Henry Buttimer, Hugonis de Sancto Victore Didascalicon de studio legendi (Washington 1939; CUA Studies in Mediaeval and Renaissance Latin 10. On the sources of Hugh of St. Victor's Didascalicon see also the additions made by J. Taylor in his The Didascalicon of Hugh of St. Victor. A Mediaeval Guide to the Arts. Translated from the Latin with an Introduction and Notes (New York 1961). See also the monographs of Fanning, Sullivan and Nelson in the CUA series); A. Steiner, Vincent of Beauvais, De eruditione filiorum nobilium (Cambridge [Mass.] 1938; Med. Acad. of Am. Publ. No. 32).

Indices and concordances of ancient Latin writers: P. Faider, Répertoire des index et lexiques d'auteurs latins (Paris 1926); J. Cousin, Bibliographie de la langue latine 1880-1948 (Paris 1951) 279ff. See also: H. and B. Riesenfeld, Repertorium lexicographicum Graecum. A Catalogue of Indices and Dictionaries to Greek Authors (Stockholm 1954).

Fortleben: For tracing the continued study and influence of ancient Latin writers, both pagan and Christian, see, especially, the treatment of the particular author in Schanz-Hosius-Krueger, Römische Literaturgeschichte, under the section entitled "Fortleben." The influence of ancient writers on mediaeval, and of earlier mediaeval on later mediaeval, authors can be checked to some extent through the indices in Manitius, Geschichte der lateinischen Literatur des Mittelalters. New studies appearing on the continued study and influence of ancient writers can be controlled through L'Année Philologique under the names of the individual writers, and under the section, "Survie et influence d'auteurs anciens."

N.B.: On the allegorical treatment of themes and on the allegorical method of interpretation, see the references given in the Bibliography on C. The Christian Element.

The Hisperica famina and other bizarre forms of Latin: Laistner, Thought and Letters 137 and 176-177; F. J. H. Jenkinson, The Hisperica famina (Cambridge 1908); E. K. Rand, "The Irish Flavor of Hisperica famina," in Studien zur lateinischen Dichtung des Mittelalters. Ehrengabe für K. Strecker (Dresden 1931) 134-142; M. Niedermann, "Les dérivés latins en - osus dans les Hisperica famina," ALMA 23 (1954) 75-101. On Virgilius Maro, see also: Manitius, Geschichte der lateinischen Literatur des Mittelalters 1.119-127; Kenney Sources for the Early History of Ireland 1:143-145; D. Tardi, "Sur le vocabulaire de Virgile le grammairien," ALMA 3 (1927) 22-27. See also: W. Süss, "Ueber antike Geheimschreibenmethoden und ihr Nachleben," Philologus 78 (1923) 142-175.

The idea of the continuance of the Empire and the eternity of Rome: F. Lot, La fin du monde antique et le début du moyen âge 284-297; F. Schneider, Rom und Romgedanke im Mittelalter (Munich 1926); P. E. Schramm, Kaiser, Rom und Re-novatio (Leipzig 1929); R. Folz, L'idée d'empire en Occident du Ve au XIVe siècle (Dijon 1953); A. Graf, Roma nelle memorie e nelle immaginazioni del medio evo (2 vols. Turin 1882-1883)

The attitude of the Romans, Christians as well as pagans, towards the bar-barian peoples in the fourth, fifth, and sixth centuries: P. de Labriolle, "L'Église et les Barbares," in Fliche and Martin, Histoire de l'Église 4:353-396, especially 353-367. The chapter includes a good treatment of the term Romania and its background.

The process of the transmission of the ancient Latin literature, both pagan and Christian, to the Middle Ages: Hall, Companion to Classical Texts 53ff.; Traube, Einleitung in die lateinische Philologie des Mittelalters 121-137; Norden, "Erhaltung und Überlieferung der römischen Literatur," in Gercke-Norden, Einleitung in die Altertumswissenschaft 1.4 (3rd ed. Leipzig 1927; also available in revised form in E. Norden, Die römische Literatur 5th ed. Leipzig [1954] 146-154); De Ghellinck, "Diffusion et transmission des écrits patristiques," in Pat-ristique et moyen âge 2:181-377; H. Hunger, O. Stegmuller, et. al., Geschichte der Textüberlieferung der antiken und mittelalterlichen Literatur. 1:Ueberliefe-rungsgeschichte der antiken Literatur (Zurich 1961).

For full bibliographical data on works listed on the "Classical" Element, and for further bibliography, see SELECT BIBLIOGRAPHY 4, 9, 10C, 11A and C.

B.   The Popular Element

The spread of Latin as a spoken language in Italy and in the Roman provinces outside of Italy

The relations between the spoken Latin of all classes and the literary language from the time of Plautus to the end of the second century A.D.

The terms sermo cottidianus, sermo urbanus, sermo plebeius, sermo vulgaris, Vulgar Latin, Umgangssprache, and their precise significance

Our very limited knowledge of the spoken Latin of the masses in the Golden and Silver Ages

The considerable influence exercised by the spoken Latin on literary Latin from c. 200 A.D.

Early Christian written or literary Latin especially influenced by the spoken Latin of the masses

The spread of Christianity in the West and the permeation of the Latin of the masses with Christian terminology – the marked influence of Christianized spoken Latin on Primitive Romance

The question of African Latin, Spanish Latin, Gallic Latin – theoretical views and the actual evidence; the attempts to localize and date the Peregrinatio Aetheriae on the basis of language alone and their lack of success

The influence of the Celtic and Germanic languages on Vulgar Latin and Primitive Romance vocabulary

The special influence of the spoken language of the masses on the literary Latin in the regions included in Romania during the last centuries of Antiquity and to the beginning of the Carolingian Age

The question of the date when spoken Latin ceased to be Latin and began to be Primitive Romance: the theory of F. Lot that spoken Latin was becoming Primitive Romance in the sixth and early seventh centuries; the theory of H. F. Muller that spoken Latin did not become Primitive Romance before the dissolution of the Empire of Charlemagne; the more recent treatment of the question by Norberg, Mohrmann, and L. R. Palmer

Strictly speaking, there are no extant texts of Vulgar Latin, but rather texts and inscriptions which reflect merely certain characteristic features of spoken Latin.

Bibliography on B.   The Popular Element

The spread of Latin as a spoken language and on the relations between the spoken Latin and the literary Latin (see also 2 A-E supra): Palmer, The Latin Language 148-180; the section "Vulgärlatein und Romanisch, Umgangssprache, Schriftsprache," in Leumann-Hofmann, Lateinische Grammatik 9-11; J. B. Hofmann, Die lateinische Umgangssprache (3rd ed. Heidelberg 1951); Devoto, Storia della lingua di Roma 275-307; Stolz-Debrunner, Geschichte der lateinischen Sprache (3rd ed. 1953) 99-113; G. Rohlfs, Sermo Vulgaris Latinus. Vulgärlateinisches Lesebuch (Heidelberg 1951); C. Battisti, Avviamento allo studio del latino volgare (Bari 1949); K. Vossler, Einführung ins Vulgärlatein. Herausgegeben von H. Schmeck (Munich 1955); Strecker-Palmer, Introduction to Medieval Latin 28-31 (the note on "Vulgar Latin" especially valuable); J. Sofer, "Reichssprache und Volkssprache im römischen Imperium," Wiener Studien 65 (1950-51) 138-155; C. Mohrmann, "Les formes du latin dit vulgaire," in her Etudes sur le latin des chrétiens 2 (Rome 1961); id., Latin vulgaire. Latin des chrétiens. Latin médiéval (1955); J. Svennung, Untersuchungen zu Palladius und zur lateinischen Fach-und Volkssprache (Uppsala 1935); W. Baehrens, Sprachlicher Kommentar zur vulgärlateinischen Appendix Probi (Halle [Saale] 1922); J. B. Hofmann, "Beiträge zur Kenntnis des Vulgärlateins," Indogermanische Forschungen 43 (1928) 80-122; D. Norberg, Syntaktische Forschungen auf dem Gebiete des Spätlateins und des frühen Mittellateins (Uppsala 1943); V. Väänänen, Introduction au latin vulgaire (Paris 1964)

The influence of the spoken Latin on Christian written or literary Latin, and on the Christianization of the spoken Latin of the masses in late Antiquity: See the references to L. R. Palmer, Schrijnen, Mohrmann, and Devoto given in the Bibliography on C. The Christian Element. See also: Löfstedt, Philologischer Kommentar zur Peregrinatio Aetheriae; id., Late Latin (Oslo 1959) 11-38; B. Linderbauer, S. Benedicti Regula Monachorum herausgegeben und philologisch erklärt; A. H. Salonius, Vitae Patrum. Kritische Untersuchungen über Text, Syntax und Wortschatz der spätlateinischen Vitae Patrum (B. III, V, VI, VII) (Lund 1920); F. Blatt, Die lateinischen Bearbeitungen der Acta Andreae et Matthiae apud anthropophagos mit Kommentar (Giessen 1930; Beihefte zur Zeitschrift für die Neutestamentliche Wissenschaft 12)

The influence of the Celtic and Germanic languages on Vulgar Latin and Primitive Romance, and of Vulgar Latin on Celtic and Germanic: Meyer-Lübke, Einführung 37-57, and the Spanish translation 71-102; E. Gamillscheg, Romania Germanica (3 vols. Berlin 1934-1936); H. Rosenfeld, "Buch, Schrift, und lateinisch Sprachkenntnis bei den Germanen vor der christlichen Mission," Rheinisches Museum 95 (1952) 193-209; K. Jackson, Language and History in Early Britain (Edinburgh 1953), especially, ch. II, "Britons and Romans under the Empire," 76-121; ch. IV, "The British Loanwords in Irish," 122-148; ch. V, "The Early Christian Inscriptions," 149-193; "The Vulgar Latin Accent," 267-271

The chronology of Vulgar Latin: H. Muller, A Chronology of Vulgar Latin (Halle 1929; Beihefte zur Zeitschrift für romanische Philologie 78); F. Lot, "A quelle époque a-t-on cessé de parler latin?", ALMA 6 (1931) 97-159; Palmer, The Latin Language 175-180; D. Norberg, Syntaktische Forschungen aus dem Gebiete des Spätlateins und des frühen Mittelalters (Uppsala 1943) 11-25

Vulgar Latin and its relation to Primitive Romance: E. Löfstedt, "Spätlateinische und romanische Sprachentwicklung," Syntactica 2 (Lund 1933) 373-405; Stolz-Debrunner, op. cit. 113-119; id., Late Latin (Oslo 1959) 1-38; Norberg, op. cit. supra; Meyer-Lübke, Einführung in das Studium der romanischen Sprachwissenschaft (3rd ed. Heidelberg 1920; Spanish translation by A. Castro, Introducción a la lingüística romanica [Madrid] 1926); E. Bourciez, Éléments de linguistique romane (4th ed. Paris 1948); C. H. Grandgent, An Introduction to Vulgar Latin (Boston 1907; largely antiquated); H. F. Muller and P. Taylor, A Chrestomathy of Vulgar Latin (Boston 1942; to be used with care); C. H. Grandgent, From Latin to Italian. An Historical Outline of the Phonology and Morphology of the Italian Language (Cambridge [Mass.] 1927); M. K. Pope, From Latin to Modern French with Especial Consideration of Anglo-Norman Phonology and Morphology (new ed. Manchester [England] 1951); W. Meyer-Lübke, Romanisches etymologisches Wörterbuch (3rd ed. Heidelberg 1935); W. D. Elcock, The Romance Languages (London 1960) 17-169. See also: F. Brunot, Histoire de la langue française 1 and 2 (Paris 1905 ff). For an historical sketch of research in the field of Vulgar Latin to 1915, see K. von Ettmayer, "Vulgärlatein," in W. Streitberg, Geschichte der indogermanischen Sprachwissenschaft 2. 1 (Strassburg 1916) 231-280; an English translation by M. R. P. McGuire is available for private use). See also the systematic critical surveys of studies in the field of Vulgar and Late Latin by Th. Bögel in Bursiansjahresbericht: 1921-1924, 201 (1924) 143-196, and 205

(1925) 1-49; 1925-1936: ibid. 240 (1940) 256-412. There is a copious bibliography in C. Battisti, Avviamento allo studio del latino volgare, listed supra. See also the section "Latin post-classique, latin vulgaire et bas-latin," in Cousin, Bibliographie de la langue latine, 1880-1948, 26-31. For annual bibliography, see the journal Glotta, and L'Année philologique under the section "Latin et dialectes italiques." Studies on the Latinity of individual authors are listed under their respective names.

For full bibliographical data on works listed supra and for further bibliography, see SELECT BIBLIOGRAPHY 11 A and 7 B.

C.   The Christian Element

Christianity first preached in the West in Greek

Greek the sole, then the predominant, liturgical language at Rome to the later fourth century

Latin-speaking converts in Italy, Africa, Spain, and Gaul, and the need of a Christian religious terminology in Latin and of translations of the sacred writings of Christianity into Latin

The great majority of converts from the lower classes and the strong influence of the spoken Latin of the masses on early Christian written or literary Latin

The special influence exercised by Greek on Christian Latin owing to the fact that the sacred writings of Christianity were in Greek and that a Christian religious terminology was long established in Greek when Latin Christians were faced with the problem of creating a Christian terminology in Latin

Hence the very large number of words and meanings in Christian Latin borrowed from or inspired by Christian Greek, a considerable group of words being mere transliterations: apostolus, angelus, ecclesia, evangelium, presbyter, baptisma, etc.

The application of the principles and methods of general linguistics by J. Schrijnen and C. Mohrmann, the founders and chief representatives of the Nijmegen School, to the investigation of the origin and development of Christian Latin and its importance

Their penetrating and convincing evaluation of the work of the first Latin translators of the Scriptures and of Tertullian's role in the development of Christian Latin

The Latin translations of the Bible before St. Jerome — the enigmatic Itala and the unfortunate use of this term to include all Latin translations of the Bible before Jerome's Vulgate

St. Jerome's Vulgate and its significance in the history of Western culture

The works of the Ancient Christian and Mediaeval writers permeated with the phraseology, thought, and imagery of the Latin Bible; hence an intimate knowledge of the Latin Bible indispensable for students of Early Christian and Mediaeval Latin language and literature. The Latin Bible and a concordance to the Latin Bible must always be at hand.

The allegorical method of interpretation and its predominance in Christian Antiquity and in the Middle Ages

The attitude of Christians to pagan education, literature, and learning – Tertullian, Clement of Alexandria, St. Basil, St. Gregory Nazianzen, St. John Chrysostom, St. Jerome, St. Augustine, Cassiodorus, St. Gregory the Great, Isidore of Seville

The absence of a fully developed system of Christian education before the Middle Ages and the necessity of attending pagan schools and employing pagan literature and learning in Christian intellectual training and apologetic; the study of pagan literature regarded as a propaedeutic for Christian studies, especially Biblical studies

St. Basil's Address to Young Men on the Study of Pagan Literature the clearest and most systematic patristic statement of the proper attitude to be taken towards pagan literature – its importance for the preservation of ancient Greek literature in Byzantine times, and in the controversies over the place of the pagan Classics in education from the Renaissance to the last century

The lack of a similar, clear statement in the West and the continuance of conflicting views throughout the Middle Ages – St. Basil's work apparently not translated from the Greek before the Renaissance (Lionardo Bruni)

The place of and attitude towards the pagan Classics in the early monastic schools – the School of Lerins, St. Benedict, Cassiodorus, St. Gregory the Great – the great significance of Cassiodorus and his work in the history of Western culture

N.B.: The role of the Irish and Anglo-Saxon monks in the preservation of ancient Classical literature will be taken up in VI infra.

The development of a great Christian literature in Latin from Tertullian and Minucius Felix to Gregory the Great

The dependence of Christians in the West on Greek Christian literature before St. Augustine – the numerous translations from the Greek to the end of Antiquity

The nature and scope of Christian Latin literature in prose and verse — literature in the service of religion

The strong influence of the contemporary pagan school tradition and literary taste on the language and style of Christian writers — the rise of Christian humanism and its character

Early Christian Latin literature an integral part of the Latin literature of Antiquity — the unhappy choice of the term "national" to designate the Late pagan or secular Latin literature as opposed to the Christian Latin literature

The building up of a rich Latin terminology in dogmatic and moral theology, asceticism, canon law, and ecclesiastical administration

Ambrose, Jerome, Augustine, Prudentius, Cassiodorus, Boethius, and Gregory the Great as "Founders of the Middle Ages" not only in thought but also in language and style

The towering figure of St. Augustine in late Antiquity and throughout the Middle Ages

Bibliography on C.   The Christian Element

The replacement of Greek by Latin as a liturgical language in the West: C. Mohrmann, Liturgical Latin: Its Origins and Character (Washington 1957); L. Eisenhofer, Handbuch der katholischen Liturgik 1 (Freiburg im Br. 1932) 149-159; H. Leclercq, "Langues liturgiques," DACL 8.1:1297-1312; Th. Klauser, "Der Uebergang der römischen Kirche von der griechischen zur lateinischen Liturgie-sprache," Miscellanea G. Mercati 1 (Rome 1946) 467-482; and, especially, the two following studies: G. Bardy, "Le latinisation de l'Église d'Occident," in his La question des langues dans l'Eglise ancienne. 1 (Paris 1948) 81-121; C. Mohr-mann, "Les origines de la latinité chrétienne à Rome, Vigiliae Christianae 3 (1949) 67-106, and 163-183. See also the treatment of this problem in J. A. Jungmann, Missarum Sollemnia (2nd ed. Vienna 1949; check through the lemma, "Griechisch in der römischen Liturgie," in Register B.)

The rise and character of Christian Latin: Palmer, The Latin Language 181-205; C. Mohrmann, Études sur le latin des chrétiens.1 (Rome 1958) especially, "Altchristliches Latein. Entstehung und Entwicklung der Theorie der altchrist-lichen Sondersprache," 3-19; "Quelques traits caractéristiques du latin des chrétiens, 21-50; "Le latin langue de la chrétienté occidentale," 51-81; "La langue et le style de la poésie latine chrétienne," 151-168; id., "How Latin Became the Language of Early Christendom," Studies 40 (1951) 277-288; id., "Les emprunts grecs dans la latinité chrétienne," Vigiliae Christianae 4 (1950) 193-211; id., "Le dualisme de la latinité mediévale," REL 29 (1951) 330-348; id., "Medieval Latin and Western Civilization," American Benedictine Review 10 (1959) 45-66; McGuire, "The Origin, Development, and Character of Christian Latin," in M. R. P. McGuire, ed., Teaching Latin in the Modern World (Washington 1960) 37-55. See also: J. Schrijnen, Charakteristik des altchristlichen Latein (Nijmegen 1932; English trans.

by M. R. P. McGuire available for private use); id., "Le Latin devenu langue com-mune," REL 12 (1934) 96-116; G. Devoto, "L'età cristiana," Storia della lingua de Roma (2nd ed. Bologna 1944) 309-341; E. Löfstedt, "Zur Entstehung der christ-lichen Latinität," Syntactica 2 (Lund 1933) 458-473; id., Late Latin (Oslo 1959) 68-119; J. de Ghellinck, "Latin chrétien ou langue des chrétiens," Les Études Classiques 8 (1939) 449-478; id., "Langue latine des chrétiens. Quelques aperçus récents," ibid. 13 (1944) 286-296; A. Blaise, Manuel du latin chrétien (Strasbourg 1955). For additional bibliography see: Vigiliae Christianae, Strecker-Palmer, Introduction to Medieval Latin 22-28, and L'Année philologique under the heading, "Latin et dialectes italiques"

The Old Latin versions and the Vulgate: Robert-Tricot, Guide to the Bible 1 (2nd ed. revised New York 1960) 637-664 (with bibliography 674-676); Dom B. Botte, "Itala," in Pirot-Robert-Cazelles, Dictionnaire de la Bible, Supplément 4 (1949) 777-782; id., "Latines (versions) antérieures à s. Jérôme," ibid. 5 (1952) 334-347; De Labriolle-Bardy, Histoire de la littérature latine chrétienne (Paris 1947) 61-83; F. Stummer, Einführung in die lateinische Bibel (Paderborn 1928). On the history of the Vulgate in the Middle Ages, see also: S. Berger, Histoire de la Vulgate pendant les premiers siècles du moyen âge (Paris 1893); H. Glunz, History of the Vulgate in England from Alcuin to Roger Bacon (Cambridge [Eng-land] 1933); F. Stegmüller, Repertorium Biblicum Medii Aevi (5 vols. Madrid 1940-1955)

The new Vatican edition of the Vulgate: Robert-Tricot, op. cit. 1:664. Since 1926 to date (1964) the following books have been published: Genesis (1926), Ex-odus and Leviticus (1929), Numbers and Deuteronomy (1936), Josue, Judges, and Ruth (1939), 1 and 2 Samuel (1944), 1 and 2 Kings (1945), Malachy (1945), Para-lipomenon (1948), Esdras, Tobias, and Judith (1950), Esther and Job (1951), Psalms (1953), Proverbs, Ecclesiastes, Canticle of Canticles (1957). For the Vul-gate New Testament, see, especially: Wordsworth-White, Novum Testamentum Domini Nostri Iesu Christi Latine secundum editionem sancti Hieronymi (3 vols. Oxford 1889-1954)

The Old Latin texts: Dom P. Sabatier, Bibliorum Sacrorum Latinae versiones antiquae seu Vetus Itálica (3 vols. in 6 Paris 1743); Vetus Latina: Die Reste der altlateinischen Bibel nach Petrus Sabatier neu gesammelt und herausgegeben von der Erzabtei Beuron. 1, Bonifatius Fischer, Verzeichnis der Sigel für Handsch-riften und Kirchenschriftsteller (Freiburg im Br. 1949; 2nd ed. 1963); 2, Genesis (1951-1955); 26, Epistulae Catholicae, Apocalypsis (1956 ff); 24, Epistulae ad Ephesios, Philippenses, Colossenses (1962 ff. For a detailed, critical evaluation of the "New Sabatier," including a valuable comparison with the "Old Sabatier," see B. M. Peebles in CBQ 16 [1954] 210-225); J. Wordsworth and others, Old-Latin Biblical Texts (7 vols. Oxford 1883-1923.); Dom R. Weber, Les anciennes versions latines du deuxième livre des Paralipomènes (Rome 1945); id., Le Psautier ro-main et les autres anciens Psautiers latins (Rome 1953); A. Jülicher, Das Neue Testament in altlateinischer Ueberlieferung. 1, W. Matzkow, Matthäus - Evangel-ium (Berlin 1938); 2, id., Marcus - Evangelium (1940); 3, id., Lukas - Evangelium (1954); id., and K. Aland, 4, Johannes - Evangelium (1963)

The language of the Old Latin and the Vulgate: H. Rönsch, Itala und Vulgata (2nd ed. Marburg 1875; old, but still useful); F. Kaulen, Sprachliches Handbuch zur biblischen Vulgata (2nd ed. Freiburg im Br. 1904; largely antiquated); W. E. Plater and H. J. White, A Grammar of the Vulgate (Oxford 1926; rather superficial and almost entirely descriptive); and, especially, the following: P. W. Hoogterp, Étude sur le latin du Codex Bobiensis (k) des Evangiles (Wageningen 1930); W. Süss, "Das Problem der lateinischen Bibelsprache," Historische Vierteljahrschrift 27 (1932) 1-39; id., Studien zur lateinischen Bibel. 1, Augustins Locutiones und das Problem der lateinischen Bibelsprache (Tartu 1932); W. Matzkow, De vocabulis quibusdam Italae et Vulgatae quaestiones lexicographicae (Berlin 1933); M. Sainio, Semasiologische Untersuchungen über die Entstehung der christlichen Latinität (Helsinki 1940). See also the studies of C. Mohrmann listed supra.

Biblical concordances: F. Dutripon, Concordantiae Bibliorum Sacrorum Vulgatae editionis (Paris 1838, and several times reprinted); Peultier-Étienne-Gantois, Concordantiarum universae Scripturae Sacrae thesaurus (Paris 1899; in the series Cursus Scripturae Sacrae, edd. Cornely, Knabenbauer, Himmelauer). For further information on Biblical concordances, see: E. Mangenot, "Concordances de la Bible," Vigouroux, Dictionnaire de la Bible 2: 892-905; J. Schmid, "Bibelkonkordanz," in Lexicon für Theologie und Kirche (new ed.) 2: 360-363.

Jewish and Christian allegorical interpretation of Scripture: Robert Tricot, Guide to the Bible 1: 678-709 (with good bibliography, 775-780); J. Bonsirven, G. Bardy, M. Jugie, C. Spicq, "Interprétation (Histoire de)," Pirot-Robert-Cazelles, Dictionnaire de la Bible, Supplément 4 (1949) 561-627; B. Smalley, The Study of the Bible in the Middle Ages (2nd ed. Oxford 1952); C. Spicq, Esquisse d'une histoire de l'exégèse latine du moyen âge (Paris 1944; actually covers from the eighth to the fourteenth century); L. F. Hartman, "St. Jerome as an Exegete," in A Monument to St. Jerome, ed. F. X. Murphy (New York 1952) 35-81; M. Pontet, L'exégèse de S. Augustin prédicateur (Paris 1946); R. E. McNally, S. J., The Bible in the Early Middle Ages (Westminster [Md.] 1959); M. L. W. Laistner, "Antiochene Exegesis in Western Europe in the Middle Ages," Harvard Theological Review 40 (1947) 19-31; M. D. Chenu, O. P., "Les deux âges de l'allégorie scripturaire au moyen âge," Recherches de théologie ancienne et médiévale 18 (1951) 19-28; H. De Lubac, S. J., Exégèse médiévale. Les quatre sens de l'Écriture (4 vols. Paris 1959-1964; in progress). The student of Patristic and Mediaeval literature will often find the copious commentaries of Cornelius a Lapide (1587-1637) very useful, for they continue the mediaeval tradition to such a large degree and, in their emphasis on allegorical interpretation, they furnish a wealth of quotations from the Fathers and mediaeval commentators. Complete editions: 12 vols. (Turin 1838ff.); 20 vols. (Lyons 1865ff.); 22 vols. (Paris 1859ff.). See also E. Mangenot, "Allégories Bibliques," DTC 1 (1902) 833-836, especially section II: "Recueils d'interprétations allégoriques," 835-836.

Allegorical interpretation outside the Bible: T. Klauser, ed., Reallexikon für Antike und Christentum, "Allegorese," 1:283-293 (with bibliography); Schmid-Stählin, Griechische Literaturgeschichte 2. 2 (6th ed. Munich 1924; check through the index, 1507, s. v. "Allegorische Erklärung"); De Labriolle-Bardy, Histoire de la littérature latine chrétienne (check s. v. "Allégorie" in index); J. Pépin, Mythe et allégorie. Les origines grecques et les contestations judéo-chretiennes (Paris 1958); E. Curtius, European Literature and the Latin Middle Ages (New York 1952; check through the index s.v. "Allegoresis In," "Allegorical Figures In"); J. Seznec, The Survival of the Pagan Gods, The Mythological Tradition and Its Place in Renaissance Humanism and Art (New York 1953), especially 84-121. On the Psychomachia of Prudentius and its influence, see: Raby, A History of Christian Latin Poetry 61-63; De Labriolle-Bardy, op. cit., 716-720. On Fulgentius' allegorical interpretation of Vergil, see Schanz-Hosius-Krueger, 4. 2:198-200; H. Liebeschütz, Fulgentius Metaforalis. Ein Beitrag zur Geschichte der antiken Mythologie im Mittelalter (Leipzig 1926). See also D. Comparetti, Virgilio nel medio evo (new ed. by G. Pasquali, 2 vols. Florence 1937-1941). On the allegorical interpretation of Ovid in the Middle Ages, see: E. K. Rand, Ovid and His Influence (New York 1926) 108-167; L. K. Born, "Ovid and Allegory," Speculum 10 (1934) 362-379. For a good sketch of Dante's use of allegory see, e.g., E. Gardner, "Dante," in the Catholic Encyclopedia.

The history of ancient Christian Latin literature: In addition to the general works of Schanz-Hosius-Krueger and Teuffel-Kroll-Skutsch listed under The "Classical" Element, supra, see the following works: Bardenhewer, Geschichte der altkirchlichen Literatur; Moricca, Storia della letteratura latina cristiana; De Labriolle-Bardy, Histoire de la littérature latine chrétienne; Altaner, Patrologie (English trans. New York 1960); Cayré, Précis de patrologie. Histoire et doctrine de Pères et Docteurs de l'Eglise (1 and 2 go down to St. Francis de Sales); and, especially, J. Quasten, Patrology 1 (Utrecht 1950); 2 (1953); 3 (1960; to be completed in five volumes). On Christian Latin poetry, see, especially: C. Mohrmann, "La langue et le style de la poésie latine chrétienne" (see supra, The rise and character of Christian Latin); Raby, A History of Christian Latin Poetry from the Beginnings to the Close of the Middle Ages (with excellent bibliography). See also his A History of Secular Poetry in the Middle Ages.

For hagiography in Antiquity, see: H. Delehaye, S. J., Les passions des martyr et les genres littéraires (Brussels 1921); id., Les légendes hagiographiques (3rd ed. Brussels 1927); id., L'oeuvre des Bollandistes à travers trois siécles, 1615-1915 (2nd ed. with bibliography brought up to date, Brussels 1959); R. Aigrain, L'hagiographie, ses sources, ses méthodes, son histoire (Paris 1953). For full bibliographical data on the histories of literature, etc., listed supra, and for further bibliography, see SELECT BIBLIOGRAPHY 4.

Translations from the Greek, in addition to the translations of the Bible: McGuire, "The Decline of the Knowledge of Greek in the West from c.150 to the Death of Cassiodorus. A Reexamination of the Phenomenon from the Viewpoint of Cultural Assimilation," Classical Folia 13.1 (1959) 3-25; Bardy, La question des langues dans l'Eglise ancienne. 1, ch. V, "Traducteurs et adapteurs au IVe siècle," 231-289; F. Blatt, "Remarques sur l'histoire des traductions latines," Classica et Mediaevalia 1 (1938) 217-242; Courcelle, Les lettres grecques en Occident de Macrobe à Cassiodore (see also the important review-article on this work by B. Altaner, "Der Einfluss und das Fortleben der griechischen Literatur im Abendland vom Ende des 4. bis in die zweite Hälfte des 6. Jahrhunderts," Theologische Revue 48 [1952] 41-50); Siegmund, Die Ueberlieferung der griechischen christlichen

Literatur in der lateinischen Kirche bis zum zwölften Jahrhundert. See also: Laistner, Thought and Letters 238-250; B. Bischoff, "Das griechische Element in der abendländischen Bildung des Mittelalters," Byzantinische Zeitschrift 44 (1951) 27-55; S. Lundström, Uebersetzungstechnische Untersuchungen auf dem Gebiete der christlichen Latinität (Lund 1955); L. Szymanski, The Translation Procedure of Epiphanius – Cassiodorus in the Historia Tripartita Books I and II (Washington 1963; CUA studies in Medieval and Renaissance Latin 24); R. Weiss, "Lo studio del greco all'abbazia di San Dionigi durante il medio evo," Rivista di storia della Chiesa in Italia 6 (1952) 426-438; id., Greek in Western Europe before the Renaissance (in press, March 1964). For full bibliographical data on the works listed, see SELECT BIBLIOGRAPHY 6. Much information on the translation literature is available in the standard histories of Greek and Latin literature – Christ-Schmid-Stählin, Schanz-Hosius-Krueger, Bardenhewer, Manitius, and Krumbacher – and in the Patrologies, but it is incomplete, widely scattered, and difficult to control. An annotated list and guide, Mediaeval and Renaissance Latin Translations and Commentaries, which includes Latin translations made in Antiquity, is now being prepared under the editorship of Professor Paul O. Kristeller of Columbia University and is being published by the Catholic University of America Press (Vol. 1, Washington 1960).

The Christian attitude to pagan literature, learning, education, and culture in general: De Labriolle-Bardy, Histoire de la littérature latine chrétienne 1: 1-53; De Labriolle, "La culture chrétienne," in Fliche-Martin, Histoire de l'Eglise 3: 405-428; id., "La culture chrétienne en Occident," ibid., 4: 559-572; McGuire, "Mediaeval Humanism," Catholic Historical Review 38 (1953) 397-409; Laistner, Christianity and Pagan Culture in the Later Roman Empire (Ithaca 1951); G. Ellspermann, The Attitude of the Early Christian Writers towards Pagan Literature and Learning; G. Bardy, "Aux beaux temps de l'humanisme chrétien (380-430)," La France franciscaine 22 (1939) 101-130; C. Dawson, "The Classical Tradition and Christianity," in his The Making of Europe 48-66; id., "The Study of Christian Culture," "The Christian East and the Oriental Background of Christian Culture," and "The Christian West and the Fall of the Empire," in Medieval Essays (New York 1954) 1-52; E. A. Quain, S.J., "St. Jerome as a Humanist," in F. X. Murphy, ed., A Monument to St. Jerome (New York 1952) 203-232; W. Jaeger, Humanism and Theology (Milwaukee 1943); C. Foligno, Latin Thought and Letters during the Middle Ages (Oxford 1929), especially ch. I, "Rome and the Middle Ages," ch. II, "The Salvage," ch. III, "The Christian Contribution," and ch. IV, "Summaries," 1-52; F. Ozanam, La civilisation au cinquième siècle (3rd. Paris 1873), especially the chapter "Comment les lettres entrèrent dans le Christianisme"; E. Norden, Die antike Kunstprosa 659-693; H. Leclercq, articles, "Écoles," and "Lettres Classiques," in DACL. See also, especially, Marrou, Saint Augustin et la culture antique, with Retractatio; id., Histoire de l'éducation dans l'antiquité 416-461 (English trans. 314-350); Courcelle, Les lettres grecques en Occident; C. N. Cochrane, Christianity and Classical Culture (New York 1944); R. R. Bolgar, The Classical Heritage and Its Beneficiaries 45-58; H. Hagendahl, The Latin Fathers and the Classics (Göteborg 1958). For St. Basil's Address to Young Men on the Study of Pagan Literature, see the translation, with introduction, by R. J. Deferrari and M. R. P. McGuire in Deferrari, St. Basil: The Letters 4 (London and New York 1934; Loeb Classical Library) 363-435. On the place of and on controversies about pagan and Christian Greek and Latin Classics in education down to our own times, see: "Klassiker, Ghristliche griechisch-lateinische," in E. Roloff, Lexikon der Pädagogik 2 (Freiburg im Br. 1913) 1295-1298, and "Klassiche Studien," ibid. 1315-1317 (with good bibliography); H. Musurillo, S.J., "Christian Latin in the High School and College," in McGuire, ed., Teaching Latin in the Modern World (Washington 1960) 56-68. On the "Gaume Controversy," see: J. M. Campbell, The Greek Fathers (New York 1929) 144-145; Musurillo, art. cit., 65-66. For full bibliographical data on the works listed supra, see SELECT BIBLIOGRAPHY 9.

The influence of the pagan school tradition and literary taste on the language and style of Christian writers: See the references given supra under A. The "Classical" Element, and also, especially: Norden, Die antike Kunstprosa 573-656; Marrou, Saint Augustin et la culture antique 1-327, and the pertinent comments in his Retractatio; M. L. Clarke, Rhetoric at Rome (London 1953) 148-157; the pertinent volumes on language and style in the Catholic University of America Patristic Studies, and Studies in Mediaeval and Renaissance Latin Language and Literature (with good bibliographies in each volume); J. Finaert, L'évolution littéraire de Saint Augustin (Paris 1939; of special importance from the viewpoint of content and method). For current bibliography, see L'Année philologique under the names of the individual writers, under "Histoire littéraire," and under "Latin et dialectes italiques."

Christian interpolations, forgeries, etc.: On the old charge of Christian interpolations or suppressions in pagan texts and its refutation, see: Traube, Einleitung in die lateinische Philologie des Mittelalters 67-68; F. W. Hall, Companion to Classical Texts (Oxford 1913) 182-183 and 188-189. On interpolatio ecclesiastica, Christian forgeries, etc., see: Traube, op. cit., 69-70; De Ghellinck, Patristique et moyen âge 2:348 ff.; G. Bardy, "Faux et fraudes littéraires dans l'antiquité chrétienne," Revue d'Histoire Ecclésiastique 32 (1936) 5-23 and 275-302.

Major collections of Christian and Early Medieval Latin writers and works: See SELECT BIBLIOGRAPHY, 3 A. The indispensable guide to the best available editions of Ancient and Early Mediaeval Christian Latin writers and works is Dom E. Dekkers, Clavis Patrum Latinorum (Steenbrugge and The Hague 1951; Sacris Erudiri 3 ([1951]; new ed. revised and enlarged 1961). On the new Corpus Christianorum in course of publication, see the latest prospectus: Corpus Christianorum (Brepols, Turnhout [Belgium] 1963). For a large number of corrections in assignment of authorship of texts, etc., in Migne, Patrologia Latina, see P. Glorieux, "Pour revaloriser Migne. Tables rectificatives," Mélanges de Science religeuse, IXe année (1952) Cahier supplémentaire. See also A. Hamman, Patrologia Cursus completus a J. P. Migne editus ... Series Latina. Supplementum (Paris 1958ff.; to be completed in 4 vols.). On Migne and his work, see H. Leclercq, "Migne (Jacques-Paul)," DACL 11.1: 941-957.

Indices to the Ancient Christian writers: See the editions of their works in Migne PL, in CSEL, MGH (Auctores antiquissimi), and in the Corpus Christianorum. The indices in Migne are primarily theological; those in the CSEL, chiefly philological; those in the MGH, historical or philological; those in the Corpus Christianorum, theological and philological. The references in the indices in Migne are, ordinarily, not to the columns in the Migne volumes themselves, but rather to the pages of the original edition reprinted by Migne. Such page numbers appear in boldface within the Migne columns. The following works, which are in part concordances, will often prove very helpful: Bartholomaeus of Urbino (died 1350), Divi Ambrosii Milleloquium (2 vols. Lyons 1556); id., Milleloquium Sancti Augustini (Lyons 1555; Paris 1645. See V. A. Fitzpatrick, M.S.SS.T., "Bartolomaeus of Urbino: The Sermons Embraced in His Milleloquium S. Augustini" [Catholic University of America Master's diss. 1954]); D. Lenfant, O. P., Concordantiae Augustinianae sive collectio omnium sententiarum quae sparsim reperiuntur in omnibus S. Augustini operibus ad instar concordantiarum Sacrae Scripturae (Paris 1656-1667; reprinted 1963). For a systematic list of indices to Latin authors, including the Christian, see P. Faider, Répertoire des index et lexiques d'auteurs latins (Paris 1926). This list is supplemented by that in Cousin, Bibliographie de la langue latine 1880-1948 (Paris 1951) 279ff. Cousin also furnishes bibliography on the history of important words, groups of words, or concepts, ibid. 308ff. For current bibliography see the pertinent sections in L'Année philologique. See also SELECT BIBLIOGRAPHY 11 B.

The role of St. Ambrose, St. Jerome, St. Augustine, and other great Ancient Christian writers as "founders of the Middle Ages": See, e.g.: E. K. Rand, Founders of the Middle Ages (Cambridge [Mass.] 1928); A Monument to Saint Augustine, by M. C. D'Arcy, S.J., M. Blondel, C. Dawson, E. Gilson, and others (London 1930; reprinted 1945); A Monument to Saint Jerome, edited by F. X. Murphy, C.SS.R. (New York 1952); E. Portalié, article, "Augustinisme (Développement historique de l')", DTC 1.2:2501-2561; E. Gilson, Introduction à l'étude de Saint Augustin (2nd ed. Paris 1943) 299-323; J. de Ghellinck, "Diffusion, utilisation et transmission des écrits patristiques," Patristique et moyen âge 2 (Brussels 1947) 181-377.

VI. LATIN IN THE PRE-CAROLINGIAN PERIOD: FROM BOETHIUS AND CASSIODORUS TO ALCUIN (c. 500 - c. 780)

In this period there is a general decline of the late literary Latin after Boethius and Cassiodorus throughout Romania, but especially in Gaul. On the other hand, we note the adoption and enthusiastic cultivation of literary Latin by the Irish monks and their Anglo-Saxon pupils, and the first phase of their activities as teachers and promoters of the Latin language, literature, and learning on the European continent, both within and beyond the borders of the old Romania. Owing to the disintegration of the Roman Empire in the West, the presentation of material on a regional basis is justified on a scientific as well as a practical basis.

A. Italy

Boethius (c. 480-524) and the great influence of his own writings and of his translations from the Greek in the Middle Ages; the classical qualities of his Latinity. N. B. Boethius' translations from the Greek as well as the translation work of Cassiodorus will be treated in VIII, THE KNOWLEDGE OF GREEK IN THE WEST IN THE MIDDLE AGES.

St. Benedict (died 547) and the universal influence of his Rule; the language and style of St. Benedict; the history of the text of the Rule

Arator (fl. 545) and his epic, De actibus Apostolorum; the language and style of Arator; the great influence of Arator in the Early Middle Ages

Cassiodorus (c. 490-c. 583); the highly rhetorical and bombastic character of his language and style; the influence of the Variae on the chancery style of the Middle Ages; the more attractive style of portions of the Institutes, the Commenta Psalterii, and the Complexiones; his role in the diffusion of St. Jerome's version of the Scriptures

The Latinity of the compilers of the Corpus iuris civilis prepared under Justinian

Jordanes (516-573); the inferiority of Jordanes' Latinity as compared with that of Cassiodorus

Pope Gregory the Great (590-604) and his great influence in the Middle Ages; his Letters, Pastoral Rule, Dialogues, Moralia, and Homilies; his elaborate use of allegorical exegesis; his emphasis on miracles, prophecies, and visions in the Dialogues and its marked effect on mediaeval literature; the language and style of Gregory; his attitude to pagan literature — the letter to bishop Desiderius and its interpretation. Gregory's Latin shows, actually, that he had a good training in the liberal arts and that he could write with a sure control of language — apart from the orthographical confusion characteristic of his age — and with a feeling for style in the better sense.

The Liber Diurnus and the Liber Pontificalis

The generally low level of Latin culture in Italy after St. Gregory — some intellectual activity at certain monastic centers but no outstanding names before the Carolingian Age

B. Africa

Dracontius (fl. 490) and the reflection of the pagan and Christian traditions in his poetry; the influence of Vergil and Ovid in his works. In spite of his tendency toward mere rhetorical embellishment, he possessed the lyric feeling of a true poet

The Latinity of the poet Corippus (fl. 550) and of the prose writers Fulgentius of Ruspe (467-552) — and Fulgentius the Mythographer, Junilius (died 552), Primasiu of Hadrumentum (died c. 558), and Victor of Tunnuna (died after 556)

The decline and end of Latin culture in Africa

C. Spain

Martin of Bracara (c.515-c.580); his knowledge and use of Seneca; his De correctione rusticorum and its historical and linguistic importance; its influence on St. Caesarius of Arles and St. Pirmin of Reichenau

Leander (before 549-600 or 601), elder brother of St. Isidore, and archbishop of Seville; the Latinity of his De institutione virginum and In Laudem Ecclesiae

St. Isidore of Seville (c.560-636) and his encyclopedic learning; his great influence in the Middle Ages; the Etymologiae or Origines; his theological and other works; the library of Seville; Isidore's language and style

The Latinity of John of Biclaro (died c. 621), of St. Braulio, bishop of Saragossa (died c. 651), and of St. Eugenius III (647-657), St. Ildefonsus (657-667), and St. Julian (680-690), archbishops of Toledo

The Latinity of the acta of sixth and seventh century Spanish church councils — the artificiality of Latin style in seventh century Spain

The Latinity of the Vitas sanctorum patrum Emeritensium and of the Vita sancti Fructuosi

The coming of the Mohammedans (711) and the relatively few Spanish contributions to Mediaeval Latin literature and learning from this time until the end of the eleventh century

The Latinity of Paul Albar of Cordoba (first half of the ninth century)

D. Gaul

St. Avitus, Bishop of Vienne (494-518); the classical qualities of his epic style in spite of his preoccupation with rhetorical embellishment in his prose style and its reflection of the preciosity of his model, Sidonius Apollinaris

St. Caesarius of Arles (c. 470-543) and the clear, familiar style of his sermons; his deliberate avoidance of the preciosity cultivated by the contemporary rhetoricians and writers of Gaul; the influence of St. Augustine on the content and style of his sermons; perhaps after Augustine the greatest popular preacher of the Ancient Latin Church (Altaner)

Venantius Fortunatus (c. 530-c. 600); an outstanding figure in an age and region of semi-barbarism; Raby's characterization:

> "It is far truer, therefore, to regard Fortunatus, not as the last of
> the Romans, but as the first of the medieval poets. His hymns are
> steeped in Catholic spirit, in Catholic symbolism and mysticism. The
> form may be Classical at bottom, but in his use of rime and even more
> in the quality of his inspiration he is in the great line of liturgical poets
> who were the creators of a new tradition, a tradition out of which was

to issue the lyrical poetry of the modern world. Further, in his secular verses, he expresses the spirit of a new civilization, which was being raised on the ruins of the Gallo-Roman past." (Christian Latin Poetry 94).

Gregory of Tours (538-594), the lumen generale of the Merovingian Age; his education; his prefaces in the Historia Francorum and their interpretation; the wide divergences from Classical norms in Gregory's orthography, vocabulary, and syntax – "hardly a line which could pass as having been written in the Classical Period or in the best Classical tradition" (Bonnet 751); the great influence of Gregory in the field of hagiography

The Latin of the Merovingian charters, formulae, etc.; the intention of the writers to write "correct" Latin, not to reproduce the spoken language of their time; the Latinity of the acta of church councils and saints' lives in Merovingian Gaul; the Latin of the Chronicle of the so-called Fredegarius (first half of the eighth century) and of the Liber historiae Francorum (727-737); the generally low and lethargic state of Latin culture in Gaul in the period from c.600 to 750

The enigmatic Virgilius Maro and his bizarre Latinity (see V 3A near end supra)

E. The Irish and the Anglo-Saxons

The state of Latin culture in Britain in the fifth and sixth centuries; Gildas and the Hisperica famina; the artificial language and style of both

St. Patrick and the conversion of Ireland; the Latinity of St. Patrick's Confessio and Epistola

The development of excellent monastic schools in Ireland and the interest in pagan as well as Christian Latin literature; no Greek taught in Ireland, however, before the end of the seventh century

N.B.:   The source and extent of the knowledge of Greek among Irish scholars in the seventh, eighth, and ninth centuries will be taken up later in VIII. THE KNOWLEDGE OF GREEK IN THE WEST IN THE MIDDLE AGES.

Latin learned as a foreign tongue by the Irish and the Anglo-Saxons from books and written from the first in a book script, the half-uncial; the modification of the script by the Irish and in turn by the Anglo-Saxons; insular Latin in general quite superior in grammatical correctness to the contemporary Latin of the Continent but of a pronounced artificial or "hot-house" character – St. Bede's Latin the great exception

The continued interest in and cultivation of their vernaculars as literary languages by the Irish and Anglo-Saxons, and later by the Germans; the large number of Old Irish, Old English, and Old High German glosses, but the small number of Romance glosses

The early missionary zeal of the Irish monks and the conversion of Scotland; Iona founded by St. Columba (Columkille) c. 565; the exclusive use of the term Scotus in the sense of "Irish" down to the eleventh century

The great missionary activity of St. Columbanus (c. 530-615) on the Continent; the founding of Luxeuil, Bobbio, and St. Gall; the Latinity of the extant works of Columbanus; the constant flow of Irish monks to the Continent after Columbanus and their numerous monastic foundations; the founding of Reichenau (724) by St. Pirmin; the question of Pirmin's origin; the Latinity of his Scarapsus

The Latinity of the De duodecim abusivis saeculi (written in Ireland in the seventh century) and of the works of Adamnan (abbot of Iona 679-705)

The coming of St. Augustine (597) and the gradual conversion of England; the Irish foundations of Lindisfarne (635) and Malmesbury (c. 650)

The significance of the work of the Greek ecclesiastics Theodore of Tarsus (Archbishop of Canterbury 669-690) and Hadrian in England; the rapid development of the School of Canterbury

St. Wilfrid and St. Benedict Biscop; the founding of Wearmouth (674) and Jarrow (682)

Aldhelm (c. 639-709) and his training at Malmesbury and Canterbury; the library resources of these two centers at the time; the works of Aldhelm and the highly artificial and involved character of his Latin

St. Bede (c. 672-735), one of the greatest and most influential of mediaeval writers — theologian, exegete, historian, grammarian, and computist; the classical qualities of his Latinity

St. Boniface (675-754), the most illustrious of the numerous Anglo-Saxon missionaries to the Continent; his great work as a missionary and as an organizer of the Church in Germany; the Latinity of his Letters

The Latinity of Irish and Anglo-Saxon canonical collections, penitentials, hymns, and saints' lives of the pre-Carolingian Age: L. Bieler, The Irish Penitentials with an Appendix by D. A. Binchy (Dublin 1963; Script. Lat. Hibern.); the Latin Hymns of the Antiphonary of Bangor and the Liber hymnorum; the hymns of Aldhelm; Jonas' Life of Columbanus (written in 641 — Jonas trained at Bobbio); the lives of St. Patrick by Tírechán and Muirchú (c.670 - c.700); Bede's Life of St. Cuthbert, Willibald's Life of St. Boniface, etc.

F. The Latin of Early Mediaeval Liturgies

The Latinity of the continental and insular liturgies of the Pre-Carolingian Age — the Roman, Milanese, Mozarabic, Gallican, and Celtic liturgies

Bibliography on VI. LATIN IN THE PRE-CAROLINGIAN PERIOD

The general historical background: Shorter Cambridge Medieval History 1: 1-200 and 283-312; J. Gaudemet, L'Église dans l'Empire romain (IVe - Ve siècles) (Paris 1958); Stein-Palanque, Histoire de Bas-Empire (2 vols. Bruges 1949-1958); Lot-Phister-Ganshof, Les destinées de l'Empire en Occident de 395 à 888 (Paris 1928; Glotz, Histoire générale: Histoire du Moyen Age 1); De Labriolle-Bardy-Bréhier-De Plinval, De la mort de Théodose à l'élection de Grégoire le Grand (Paris 1937; Fliche-Martin, Histoire de l'Église 4); Bréhier and Aigrain, Grégoire le Grand, les États barbares, et la conquête arabe (597-757) (Paris 1938; same series 5); F. Lot, La fin du monde antique et le début du moyen âge (new ed. Paris 1952); S. Dill, Roman Society in Gaul in the Merovingian Age (London 1926); E. Salin, La civilisation mérovingienne d'après les sépultures, les textes et le laboratoire. 1, Les idées et les faits (Paris 1950); 2, Les sépultures (1952); 3, Les techniques (1957); 4, Les croyances. Conclusions. Index général (1959)

Histories of Latin literature: Laistner, Thought and Letters 83-185, (excellent); Wright and Sinclair, History of Later Latin Literature (London 1931; brief and rather superficial); De Labriolle-Bardy, Histoire de la littérature latine chrétienne (to Isidore); Altaner, Patrologie (to Isidore); Cayré, Précis de patrologie 2: 195-274; De Ghellinck, Littérature latine au moyen âge 1:5-83 (excellent); Gilson, History of Christian Philosophy in the Middle Ages (New York 1955) 95-109 and 601-606; Ueberweg-Geyer, Geschichte der patristischen und scholastischen Philosophie (11th ed. Berlin 1928) 131-140; Raby, Christian Latin Poetry 72-153; id., Secular Latin Poetry 1. 117-177 (excellent bibliographies in both volumes); U. Sessini, Poesia e musica nella latinità cristiana del III al X secolo, edited by G. Vecchi (Turin 1949); M. R. James, "Learning and Literature to the Death of Bede," CMH 3: 485-513. The standard reference histories of Latin literature covering this period in whole or in part are: Schanz-Hosius-Krueger (to St. Gregory the Great); Teuffel-Kroll-Skutsch (to St. Boniface); Bardenhewer (to St. Isidore); Moricca (to St. Gregory the Great); Manitius, Geschichte der lateinischen Literatur des Mittelalters 1 (Munich 1911) 1-242.

N.B.: For the best editions of Latin texts of authors and collections in this period, the indispensable guide is Dekkers, Clavis Patrum Latinorum.

Schools and learning: In addition to the works listed supra, see especially: Marrou, Histoire de l'éducation dans l'antiquité 416-461, especially 435-461 (English translation 314-350, especially 330-350); R. R. Bolgar, The Classical Heritage and Its Beneficiaries (Cambridge [England] 1954) 13-58; and 91-106; Sandys, History of Classical Scholarship 1 (3rd ed. 1921) 216-275 and 441-470; Roger, L'enseignement des lettres classiques d'Ausone à Alcuin; Leclercq, "École," DACL 4.2: 1730-1883, especially 1796-1883; id., "Lettres Classiques," ibid., 8.2: 2885-2942, especially 2910-2942; Norden, Die antike Kunsprosa 631-693; N. K. Chadwick, Poetry and Letters in Early Christian Gaul (London 1955); P. Riché, Éducation et culture dans l'occident barbare. VIe — VIIIe siècles (Paris 1962); M. Deansley, "Medieval Schools to c. 1300," CMH 5. 765-779, especially 765-772.

N.B.: Riché is the most important work for this period.

A. Italy

Boethius: A. P. McKinlay, "Stylistic Tests and the Chronology of the Work of Boethius," Harvard Studies in Classical Philology 18 (1907) 123-156; F. di Copua "Il 'cursus' nel De consolatione philosophiae e nei trattati teologici di Severino Boezio," Didaskaleion 3 (1914) 268-303; L. Cooper, A Concordance of Boethius (Cambridge [Mass.] 1928); L. Alfonsi, "Studi boeziani," Aevum 25 (1951) 132-146, 210-229; K. Dienelt, "Sprachliche Untersuchungen zu Boethius' Consolatio philosophiae," Glotta 29 (1941) 98-138. See also: H. R. Patch, The Tradition of Boethius. A Study of His Importance in Medieval Culture (New York 1935; with valuable bibliography); P. Courcelle, "Étude critique sur les commentaires de la Consolation de Boèce (IX - XVe siècles)," Archives d'histoire doctrinale et littéraire du Moyen Âge (1939) 5-140; M. H. Marshall, "Boethius' Definition of Person and Mediaeval Understanding of the Roman Theater," Speculum 25 (1951) 471-482.

St. Benedict: B. Linderbauer, O.S.B., S. Benedicti Regula Monachorum, herausgegeben und Philologisch erklärt (Metten 1922); R. Hanslik, S. Benedicti Regula (Vienna 1960; CSEL 75); C. Mohrmann, "La latinité de saint Benôit. Étude linguistique sur la tradition manuscrite de la Règle," Revue Bénédictine 62 (1952) 108-139 (reprinted in C. Mohrmann, Études sur le latin des chrétiens 1 [Rome 1958] 403-435); P. H. Koenders, O.C.R., Concordantiae Sanctae Regulae beatissimi ac Deo acceptissimi patris nostri Benedicti abbatis (Westmalle, Belgium, 1947); O. J. Zimmermann, O.S.B., "The Regula Magistri, the Primitive Rule of St. Benedict," American Benedictine Review 1 (1950) 11-36; P. Vandenbroucke, "Sur les sources de la Règle bénédictine et de la Regula Magistri," Revue Bénédictine 62 (1952) 216-273; P. B. Corbett, The Latin of the Regula Magistri, with Particular Reference to Its Colloquial Aspects (Louvain 1958; see also the constructive criticisms in reviews listed in APh 1959, 1960, and 1961). For the copious literature since 1930 on the Rule and on the relations of the Rule to the Regula Magistri, see the Revue Bénédictine, 1930 ff., and L'Année philologique, s.v., "Benedictus" and "Magistri Regula," and for an excellent critical summary of the problem and its present status, D. Knowles, "The Regula Magistri and the Rule of St. Benedict", in his Great Historical Enterprises. Problems in Monastic History (London 1963) 135-195. For the content and spirit of the Rule, see: Dom P. Delatte, Commentaire sur la Règle de St. Benôit (Paris 1914; English translation by Dom Justin McCann, New York 1925); Dom C. Butler, Benedictine Monachism. Studies in Benedictine Life and Rule (2nd ed. London 1924).

Arator: A. P. McKinlay, ed., Aratoris subdiaconi De actibus Apostolorum (Vienna 1951; CSEL 72, with valuable indices including a complete index verborum).

Cassiodorus: B. H. Skahill, The Syntax of the Variae of Cassiodorus (Washington 1934; CUA Studies in Mediaeval and Renaissance Latin Language and Literature 3); F. A. Bieter, The Syntax of the Cases and Prepositions in Cassiodorus' Historia Ecclesiastica tripertita (1938; same series, 6); Sister M. Gratia Ennis, The Vocabulary of the Institutiones of Cassiodorus with Special Advertence to the Technical Terminology and Its Sources (1939; same series, 9); O. J. Zimmermann, O.S.B., The Late Latin Vocabulary of the Variae of Cassiodorus, with Special Advertence to the Technical Terminology of Administration (1944; same series, 15); Sister M.

Josephine Suelzer, The Clausulae of Cassiodorus (1944; same series, 17); L. W. Jones, An Introduction to the Divine and Human Readings by Cassiodorus Senator. Translated with an Introduction and Notes (New York 1946; Columbia University Records of Civilization 40); id., "Notes on the Style and Vocabulary of Cassiodorus' Institutiones," Classical Philology 40 (1945) 24-31; id., "The Influence of Cassiodorus on Mediaeval Culture," Speculum 20 (1945) 433-442, and 22 (1947) 254-256; G. Bardy, "Cassiodore et la fin du monde ancien," Année théologique 6 (1945) 383-425; M. L. W. Laistner, "The Value and Influence of Cassiodorus' Ecclesiastical History," Harvard Theological Review 41 (1948) 51-67; A. J. Fridh, Études critiques et syntaxiques sur les Variae de Cassiodore (Göteborg 1950); id., Terminologie et formules dans les Variae de Cassiodore (Göteborg 1956); S. Lundström, "Zur Historia tripartita des Cassiodor," Lunds Universitets Årsskrift, N. F. Avd. 1. 49. 1 (1952); L. Traube, Index rerum et verborum to Mommsen's edition of the Variae (MGH, AA 12: 510-597; a model index of its kind). There is an excellent comprehensive article on Cassiodorus by Dom. M. Cappuyns, "Cassiodore (Senator)," in Baudrillart-DeMeyer-Van Cauwenbergh, Dictionnaire d'histoire et de géographie ecclésiastiques 1 (1949) 1349-1408 (with copious bibliography).

The Theodosian and Justinian Codes, the Barbarian Codes, and Canon Law: H. F. Jolowicz, Historical Introduction to the Study of Roman Law (new ed. Cambridge [Engl.] 1952) 484-512; F. Schulz, History of Roman Legal Science (Oxford 1946) 300-332; H. D. Hazeltine, "Roman and Canon Law in the Middle Ages," CMH 5. 697-764 (with good bibliography). See also: H. Leclercq, "Lois des Barbares," DACL 9.2 1947-2186; id., "Lois romaines," ibid., 2186-2273. For the standard editions of the Theodosian Code, of the Corpus iuris civilis, and of the Corpus iuris canonici, see SELECT BIBLIOGRAPHY 3A. For editions of the Barbarian Codes see MGH, Leges, and Fontes Iuris Germanici antiqui. There is an English translation of the Theodosian Code: C. Pharr, M. B. Pharr, and T. S. Davidson, The Theodosian Code and Novels and the Sirmondian Constitutions. A Translation with Commentary, Glossary and Bibliography (Princeton 1952). On language and style, see: Norden, Die antike Kunstprosa 581-582, 652-653, 946-947; Schulz, op. cit. 97-98, especially 258-261 and 328; H. Lévy-Bruhl, "Le latin et le droit romain", REL 2 (1924) 103-120; E. Albertario, Introduzione storica allo studio del diritto romano giustinianeo (Milan 1935) 50 ff.; W. Kalb, Roms Juristen nach ihrer Sprache dargestellt (Leipzig 1889); id., Wegweiser in die römische Rechtssprache (Leipzig 1912; the two studies by Kalb reprinted and published in one volume, 1962); S. Brasloff, "Beiträge zum Juristenlatein," Philologus, N. F. 40 (1931) 122-128; F. Pringsheim, "Die archäistische Tendenz Justinians," Studi Bonfante 1 (Milan 1930) 549-587; A. Berger, Encyclopedic Dictionary of Roman Law (Philadelphia 1953; with valuable bibliography); Heumann-Seckel, Handlexikon zu den Quellen des römischen Rechts (9th ed. Jena 1926); Vocabularium iurisprudentiae Romanae, edd. O. Gradenwitz, B. Kübler, and Others (Berlin 1903-1939; incomplete: a part of I, L, M, a part of P, and Q, have not been published.)

The Latinity of the Barbarian Codes and related works. See the indices to the following volumes in the MGH: Leges, Sect. I: Leges nationum Germanicarum. I, Leges Visigothorum, ed. K. Zeumer, Index rerum et verborum 493-569 (excellent) II. 1, Leges Burgundiorum, ed. L. R. de Salis, Index rerum et verborum 174-185; V. 1, Leges Alamannorum, ed. L. Lehmann, Index rerum et verborum 160-170;

V. 2, Lex Baiwariorum, ed. E. von Schwin, Index rerum et verborum and Glossarium verborum vernaculorum 474-489 (See also B. Krusch, Die Lex Bajuvariorum. Textgeschichte, Handschriften, Kritik und Entstehung [Berlin 1924]); Sect. III, Concilia: I, Concilia aevi Merovingici, ed. F. Maasen; Orthographica, lexica et grammatica 249-281. Fontes iuris Germanici antiqui: Leges Visigothorum antiquiores, ed. K. Zeumer; Index rerum et verborum 328-395 (excellent); Lex Ribuaria et Lex Francorum Chamavorum, ed. R. Sohm; Index rerum et verborum by K. Zeumer 124-146 (excellent). See also B. Löfstedt, Studien uber die Sprache der langobardischen Gesetze. Beiträge zur frühmittelalterlichen Latinität (Lund 1961).

Jordanes: E. Wölfflin, "Zur Latinität des Jordanes," Archiv für lateinische Lexikographie und Grammatik 11 (1900) 361-368; F. Werner, Die Latinität der Getica des Jordanes (Diss. Halle 1908); H. Kalén, Studia in Jordanem philologica (Diss. Uppsala 1939). See also Mommsen's indices to his edition of Jordanes (MGH, AA V.1 1882): III, Orthographica, and IV, Lexica et grammatica 167-200.

Gregory the Great: A. Sepulcri, "Le alterazioni fonetiche e morfologiche nel Latino di Gregorio Magno e del suo tempo," Studi Medievali 1 (1904) 171-234; Sister M. Borromeo Dunn, The Style of the Letters of St. Gregory the Great (Washington 1931; CUA Patristic Studies 32); J. F. O'Donnell, The Vocabulary of the Letters of St. Gregory the Great (Washington 1934; CUA Studies in Mediaeval and Renaissance Latin Language and Literature 2); Sister Ann Julia Kinniry, The Late Latin Vocabulary of the Dialogues of St. Gregory the Great. A Semasiological Study (1935; same series, 4); Sister Rose Marie Hauber, The Late Latin Vocabulary of the Moralia of St. Gregory the Great. A Morphological and Semasiological Study (1938; same series, 7); Sister Kathleen Brazzell, The Clausulae in the Works of St. Gregory the Great (1939; same series, 11); J. Seitz, Die Verwendungsweise der Abstrakta im Lateinischen, untersucht in den Dialogen Gregors des Grossen (Diss. Jena 1938); A. Ménager, "Les divers sens du mot contemplatio chez saint Grégoire le Grand," Vie spirituelle. Études et documents (1939) 59. 145-169; 60. 39-56; M. Walther, Pondus, dispensatio, dispositio. Werthistorische Untersuchungen zur Frommigkeit Papst Gregors des Grossen (Diss. Bern 1941); D. Norberg, In Registrum Gregorii Magni studia critica, 1-2 (Uppsala Univ. Årsskr. 1937.4, and 1939.7). There is an excellent Index rerum verborum grammaticae by L. Wenger to Ewald and Hartmann's edition of Gregory's Epistolae: MGH, Epistolae II: 515-600. On the use of formulae and on the development of the papal chancery style, see: R. L. Poole, Lectures on the History of the Papal Chancery down to the Time of Innocent III (Cambridge [Engl.] 1915); Bardenhewer, Geschichte der altkirchlichen Literatur 5 (1932) 288-290. See also the bibliography listed under Liber Diurnus.

The Liber Pontificalis: H. Leclercq "Liber Pontificalis," DACL 9.1: 354-460; L. R. Loomis, The Book of the Popes (Liber Pontificalis). Translated with an Introduction (New York 1916; Columbia University Records of Civilization); L. Duchesne, Liber Pontificalis: Texte, introduction et commentaire (2 vols. Paris 1886-1892; vol. 3, 1958) with Index covering all words discussed in the notes, etc., in 2. 575-646; N. Ertl, "Diktatoren frühmittelalterlicher Päpstbriefe," Archiv für Urkundenforschung 15 (1937) 61-66.

The Liber Diurnus: H. Leclercq, "Liber Diurnus Romanorum Pontificum,"
DACL 9.1: 243-344; A. de Boüard, Manuel de diplomatique française et pontificale
1 (Paris 1929) 138-142; W. M. Peitz, S. J., "Liber Diurnus, Beiträge zur Kenntnis
der ältesten päpstlichen Kanzlei vor Gregor dem Grossen," Sbb. Wien. Akad. d.
Wiss. Philos.-hist. Kl. 185. Bd. (1918) 1-140; E. Posner, "Das Register Gregors
I," Neues Archiv 43 (1922) 245-315 (against Peitz); W. M. Peitz, "Methodisches zur
Diurnus Forschung," Miscellanea Historiae Pontificiae 2 (Rome 1940); F. Di Capua,
"Analisi ritmica delle formule del Liber Diurnus," Studi dedicati alla memoria di
Paolo Ubaldi (Milan 1937) 345-361. There is a good Index grammaticae elocutionis
rerum by A. Haberda in R. von Sickel's edition of the Liber Diurnus (Vienna 1889)
141-220.

B. Africa

Dracontius: Raby, Christian Latin Poetry (2nd ed.) 471, and Secular Latin
Poetry 2. 357; F. Vollmer's excellent Indices nominum propriorum verborum, rei
grammaticae et metricae, rei orthographicae to his edition of Merobaudes, Dra-
contius, and Eugenius of Toledo, MGH, AA XIV (1905) 293-453 (only notabiliora for
Eugenius); C. Weyman, "Zu Dracontius," in his Beiträge zur christlichen lateinis-
chen Poesie (Munich 1926) 142-160; A. Hudson-Williams, "Notes on Dracontius,"
Classical Quarterly 33 (1939) 157-162, and 40 (1946) 92-100; id., "Notes on the
Christian Poems of Dracontius," ibid. 41 (1947) 95-108; A. M. Quatiroli, "Gli epilli
di Draconzio," Athenaeum 34 (1946) 160-187, and 35 (1947) 17-34; E. Rapisarda,
Draconzio, La tragedia di Oreste, testo e commento (Catania 1951).

Corippus: E. Appel, Exegetische kritische Beiträge zu Corippus mit besonderer
Berücksichtigung des vulgaren Elementes seiner Sprache (Diss. Munich 1904); A.
Welzel, De Claudiani et Corippi sermone epico (Diss. Breslau 1908); J. Partsch's
Index rerum verborum et locutionum to his edition of Corippus, MGH, AA III 2 (1879)
163-195.

Fulgentius, Bishop of Ruspe, and Fulgentius the Mythographer: O. Friebel,
Fulgentius der Mythograph und Bischof, mit Beiträgen zur Syntax des Spätlateins
(Paderborn 1911); A. A. Lapeyre, Saint Fulgence de Ruspé - Un évêque catholique
sous la domination vandale (Thèse Clermont-Ferrand, Paris 1929); H. Liebeschütz,
Fulgentius Metaforalis (London 1936). It is not definitely settled whether Fulgentius
the Mythographer and Fulgentius, Bishop of Ruspe, are the same person (Friedel's
position) or whether they are two different writers. However, it seems best to con-
sider them two different persons.

Junilius or Junillus: H. Kihn, Theodor von Mopsuestia and Junilius Africanus
als Exegeten (Freiburg im Br. 1880), especially 313 ff. On the respective roles of
teacher and pupil in the Instituta regularia divinae legis, see A. Rahlfs, "Lehrer und
Schuler bei Junilius Africanus," Nachrichten der Götting. Gesell. der Wiss. (1891)
242-246; M. L. W. Laistner, "Antiochene Exegesis in Western Europe during the
Middle Ages," Harvard Theol. Rev. 40 (1947) 19-31; T. McNamara, O.S.B., "The
Instituta regularia divinae legis of Junilius Africanus. A Translation with an Introduction and Commentary" (Catholic University of America unpublished Master's
diss. 1955).

There are, apparently, no formal studies on the Latinity of Primasius of Hadrumentum and Victor of Tunnuna. Mommsen published excellent critical editions of Victor of Tunnuna and his continuator John of Biclaro in the MGH (AA XI Chronica Minora 1894 63-206 and 207-220), but his indices do not cover vocabulary or grammar.

C. Spain

Martin of Bracara: E. Bickel, "Die Schrift des Martinus von Bracara, Formula honestae vitae," Rheinisches Museum 60 (1905) 505-551; C. W. Barlow ed., Martini episcopi Bracarensis Opera omnia (New Haven 1950; Papers and Monographs of the American Academy in Rome 12).

Isidore of Seville: J. Fontaine, Isidore de Séville et la culture classique dans l'Espagne wisigothique (2 vols. Paris 1959); J. Sofer, Die Vulgärismen und Romanismen in den Etymologiae des hl. Isidorus von Sevilla (Vienna 1924); id., "Lexikalische Untersuchungen zu den Etymologien des Isidorus von Sevilla," Glotta 16 (1928) 1-47; id., Lateinisches und Romanisches aus den Etymologiae des Isidorus von Sevilla (Göttingen 1930); Sister Patrick Jerome Mullins, The Spiritual Life according to St. Isidore of Seville (Washington 1940; CUA Studies in Mediaeval and Renaissance Latin Language and Literature 13; good on theological terminology and good bibliography). See also: W. M. Lindsay's index to his edition of Isidore's Etymologiae (Oxford 1911), and the Indices científicos in L. Cortés y Góngora and S. Montero Díaz, San Isidoro de Sevilla, Etimologías (Madrid 1951; a Spanish translation based on Lindsay's text with a good "Introducción general"). R. McNally, "Isidoriana", Theological Studies 20 (1959) 432-442
St. Braulio et al.: There are, apparently, no systematic studies on the Latinity of Leander of Seville, John of Biclaro, or Julian of Toledo. On Braulio, see the brief comments of C. H. Lynch in his Saint Braulio, Bishop of Saragossa (631-651). His Life and Writings (Washington 1938; CUA Studies in Mediaeval History, New Series 2. There is a Spanish edition of this monograph by C. H. Lynch and P. Galindo [Madrid 1950]). On Eugenius of Toledo, see Vollmer's Indices to his edition of Merobaudes, Dracontius, and Eugenius (cited under Dracontius supra). On Ildefonsus of Toledo, see Sister Athanasius Braeggelmann, The Life and Writings of Saint Ildefonsus of Toledo (Washington 1942; CUA Studies in Mediaeval History, New Series 4); V. Blanco Garcia, San Ildefonso de virginitate Mariae: Historia de su tradición manuscrita, texto y comentario gramatical y estilístico (Madrid 1937). On the Vita Sancti Fructuosi, see Sister Frances Clare Nock, The Vita Sancti Fructuosi: Text and Translation, Introduction, and Commentary (Washington 1946; CUA Studies in Mediaeval History, New Series 7). On the Fathers of Merida, see J. N. Garvin, C.S.C., The Vitas Sanctorum Patrum Emeritensium: Text and Translation with an Introduction and Commentary (Washington 1946; same series, 8. This is an outstanding contribution to our knowledge of Early Mediaeval Latin.)

The Latinity of Spanish Councils, etc.: J. Madoz, S.J., Le symbole du XIe concile de Tolède. Ses sources, sa date, sa valeur (Louvain 1938); Z. Garcia Villada, "La cultura literaria del clero visigodo," Estudios eclesiasticos 3 (1924) 250-263 and 356-369.

Paul Albar: C. M. Sage, Paul Albar of Cordoba: Studies of His Life and Writings (Washington 1943; CUA Studies in Mediaeval History, New Series 5).

N.B.:   For recent studies on early Spanish ecclesiastical writers, see the excellent critical survey by J. Madoz, S. J., Segundo decenio de estudios sobre patrística española (1941-1950) (Madrid 1951).

On the end of Christian Africa and on the long eclipse of Latin culture in Spain following the Mohammedan conquest, see: R. Aigrain, "La fin de l'Afrique chrétienne," in Fliche-Martin, Histoire de l'Église 5 (Paris 1938) 211-230; F. Lot, "L'Espagne chrétienne de 711 à 1037," in Lot-Phister-Ganshof, Les destinées de l'Empire en Occident de 395 à 888 (Paris 1928; Glotz, Histoire générale: Histoire du moyen âge 1) 740-763, especially 759-763. E. P. Colbert, The Martyrs of Cordoba (850-859): A Study of Sources (Washington 1962; CUA Studies in Med. Hist., N. S. 17).

D. Gaul

Avitus: H. Goelzer, Le latin de Saint Avit, évêque de Vienne (Paris 1909); id., "Remarques lexicographiques sur le latin de S. Avit," ALMA 3 173-195; R. Peiper, Indices scriptorum nominum et rerum, verborum et locutionum, in his edition of Avitus, MGH, AA VI 2 (Berlin 1883) 295-371. On preciosity in fifth and sixth century Gallic writers, see, especially, A. Loyen, Sidoine Apollinaire et l'esprit précieux en Gaule aux derniers jours de l'empire (Paris 1943).

Caesarius of Arles: G. Morin, "Quelques raretés philologiques dans les écrits de Césaire d'Arles," ALMA 11 (1936) 5-14; id., Index nominum et rerum and Index verborum et locutionum, in his Sancti Caesarii Arelatenses Sermones I 2 (2nd ed. Turnhout 1953; Corpus Christianorum, Series Latina 104) 1012-1103; A. Vaccari, "Volgarismi notevoli nel latino de S. Cesario de Arles (+543)," ALMA 17 (1943) 135-148; Mother Myrtle Wilkins, Word-Order in Selected Sermons of the Fifth and Sixth Centuries (Washington 1940; CUA Patristic Studies 60. Selected sermons of Caesarius are included); R. M. Frank, "An Etymology of Hágios in a Work of Caesarius of Arles," Traditio 8 (1952) 387-389; Sister M. Caritas McCarthy, The Rule for Nuns of Caesarius of Arles. A Translation with a Critical Introduction (Washington 1960; Studies in Mediaeval History, New Series 16)

Venantius Fortunatus: H. Elss, Untersuchungen über den Stil und die Sprache des Venantius Fortunatus (Diss. Heidelberg 1907); A. Meneghetti, "La latinità di Venanzio Fortunato," Didaskaleion (1916) 195-298, and (1917) 1-166 (also printed as a book, Turin 1917); S. Zwierlein, Venantius Fortunatus in seiner Abhängigkeit von Vergil (Diss. Würzburg 1926); D. Tardi, Fortunat, Étude sur un dernier représentan de la poésie latine dans la Gaule mérovingienne (Paris 1927); S. Blomgren, Studia Fortunatiana 1-2 (Uppsala 1933-1934); id., "De P. Papinii Statii apud Venantium Fortunatum vestigiis," Eranos (1950) 57-65; id., De Venantio Fortunato Lucani Claudianique imitatore," ibid. 150-156; A. F. Memoli, Il ritmo prosaico in Venanzio Fortunato (Mercato S. Severino [Italy] 1952); A. S. Walpole's commentary on the hymns of Fortunatus in his Early Latin Hymns (Cambridge [Engl.] 1922) 164-200; F. Leo's Indices grammaticae et elocutionis, rei metricae, locorum, to his edition of Fortunatus' poetry, MGH, AA IV.1 (1881) 389-427.

Gregory of Tours: O. M. Dalton, The History of the Franks by Gregory of
Tours. Translated with an Introduction (2 vols. Oxford 1927), especially 1. 20-39;
M. Bonnet, Le latin de Grégoire de Tours (Paris 1890); B. Krusch, Indices:
Orthographica, lexica et grammatica, to the edition of Gregory of Arndt and Krusch,
MGH, Script. rerum Meroving. I (1884) 912-963; S. Blomgren, "Ad Gregorium
Turonensem adnotationes," Eranos (1936) 25-40. See also the 2nd ed. of Gregory's
Historia by Krusch and Levison in MGH (1951), with Index 540-641.

Other Merovingian writers, Merovingian formulae, charters, etc.: Strecker-
Palmer, Introduction to Medieval Latin 28-34 (with valuable critical discussion of
Late Vulgar Latin and copious bibliography); H. F. Muller, L'époque mérovingienne,
essai de synthèse de philologie et d'histoire (New York 1945. See the critical re-
views by U. T. Holmes, Word 2 [1946] 87-90; H. Hatzfeld, Erasmus 1 [1946] 26-28;
and, especially, C. Mohrmann, Vigiliae Christianae 1 [1947] 186-190): A. de Boüard,
Manuel de diplomatique française et pontificale 1 (Paris 1929) 130-138; H. Leclercq,
"Formules," DACL 5.2: 1889-1948. See also the references given for the Barbarian
Codes, for Cassiodorus' Variae, for the Registrum of Gregory the Great, and for the
Liber Diurnus, under A supra); L. F. Sas, The Noun Declension System in Mero-
vingian Latin (Paris 1937); M. A. Pei, The Language of the Eighth Century Texts in
Northern France (New York 1924); P. Taylor, The Latinity of the Liber Historiae
Francorum (New York 1924). The last three studies reflect the theories of H. F.
Muller on the character of Merovingian Latin); J. Pirson, "Le Latin des formules
mérovingiennes et carolingiennes," Romanische Forschungen 26 (1909) 837-944;
F. Schramm, Sprachliches zur Lex Salica. Eine vülgarlat.-römische Studie (Diss.
Marburg 1911); A. Uddholm, Formulae Marculfi. Études sur la langue et le style
(Uppsala 1954; an excellent study with full bibliography); J. Vielliard, Le latin de
diplômes royaux et chartes privées à l'époque mérovingienne (Paris 1927; the best
comprehensive study of the Merovingian charters with good bibliography); H. W.
Martin, "A Brief Study of the Latinity of the Diplomata Issued by the Merovingian
Kings," Speculum 2 (1927) 258-267; id., "Some Phases of Grammatical Concord in
Certain Merovingian Charters," ibid. 4 (1929) 303-314; id., "A Contribution to the
Lexicography of Certain Merovingian Charters," Classical Philology 24 (1929)
245-257; O. Haag, Die Latinität Fredegars (Diss. Erlangen 1898); F. Müller-
Marquardt, Die Sprache der alten vita Wandregiseli (Halle 1912); P. W. Hoogterp,
"Les Vies des Pères de Jura. Études sur la langue," ALMA 9 (1934) 129-251; S.
Cavallin, Literarhistorische und textkritische Studien zur vita S. Caesarii Arelaten-
sis (Lund 1934); Vitae sanctorum Honorati et Hilarii episcoporum Arelatensium.
Rec. praef. indic. instr. S. Cavallin (Lund 1952); H. M. Rochais, Index verborum
asceticorum to his edition of Defensoris Locogiacensis Monachi Liber scintillarum
(Turnhout 1958; Corpus Christ., Series Latina 17) 257-307. See also the linguistic
indices to the following volumes in the MGH: Leges, Sect. V. Formulae Merovingici
et Karolini aevi, ed. K. Zeumer (Index rerum et verborum 745-752); Arbeonis
episcopi Fusingensis vitae sanctorum Hainrhammi et Corbiniani, ed. B. Krusch
(SS rer. German. in usum schol.; a critical edition with an introduction, notes, and
glossary. See also J. W. D. Skiles, The Latinity of Arbeo's Vita Sancti Corbiniani...
[Diss. U. of Chicago 1938]); SS rerum Merov. II, Fredegarii et aliorum chronica.
Vitae sanctorum, ed. id. (Lexica 557-575); III, Passiones vitaeque sanctorum aevi
Merovingici et antiquiorum aliquot, ed. id. (Lexica 674-684); IV, Passiones vitaeque
sanctorum aevi Merovingici, ed. id. (Lexica et grammatica 797-817); V, Passiones
vitaeque sanctorum aevi Merovingici, edd. B. Krusch and W. Levinson (Lexica et

grammatica 806-834); VI, Passiones vitaeque sanctorum aevi Merovingici, edd. idd. (Lexica et grammatica 653-675); VII, Passiones vitaeque sanctorum aevi Mero-vingici cum supplemento et appendice, edd. idd. (Lexica et grammatica 875-899).

N.B.: The indices to Vols. II - III by B. Krusch are too short, but the indices to Vols. IV - VII by W. Levison are good. See also the reprints from the MGH of Arndt's edition of the Epistulae and Vita of Desiderius, of Gundlach's ed. of the Epistulae Austrasicae, etc., contained in Corpus Christianorum, Se-ries Latina 117 (Turnhout 1958), with Index rerum et verborum 673-689.

Patristic and Early Mediaeval hagiography: H. Delehaye, S. J., Les passions des martyrs et les genres littéraires (Brussels 1921); id., Les légendes hagi-ographiques (4th ed. revised Brussels 1955; English trans. by D. Attwater, The Legends of the Saints [New York 1962]); R. Aigrain, L'hagiographie. Ses sources, ses méthodes, son histoire (Paris 1953); C. G. Loomis, White Magic. An Intro-duction to the Folklore of Christian Legend (Cambridge [Mass.] 1948. See also the review by M. R. P. McGuire, CHR 37 [1951] 179-180). For convenient control of the ancient and mediaeval vitae of individual saints, see Bibliotheca hagiographica Latina antiquae et mediae aetatis. For current bibliography, see, L'Année Phi-lologique, "Auteurs et Textes," s. v. "Vitae".

For the Latin of the Merovingian Age see also the works listed in the Bibliog-raphy on V B The Popular Element.

N.B.: The Thesaurus Linguae Latinae and Souter's Glossary stop at c. 600 A.D. but the dictionary of A. Blaise, Dictionnaire latin-français des auteurs chrétiens (Strasbourg 1954), includes the Merovingian period.

E.   The Irish and the Anglo-Saxons

General background: In addition to the general works listed supra at the be-ginning of the Bibliography on VI. LATIN IN THE PRE-CAROLINGIAN PERIOD, see: J. F. Kenney, The Sources for the Early History of Ireland. An Introduction and Guide. I: Ecclesiastical (New York 1929; Columbia University Records of Civilization); C. Gross, The Sources and Literature of English History from the Earliest Times to about 1485 (2nd ed. New York and London 1915; new edition in preparation); F. W. Bateson, Cambridge Bibliography of English Literature. 1, 600-1660 A.D. (Cambridge [England] 1940), and 5, Supplement (1957); R. I. Best, Bibliography of Irish Philology and of Printed Irish Literature (Dublin 1913); id., Bibliography of Irish Philology and Ms. Literature, 1913-1941 (ibid. 1942); W. Bonser, An Anglo-Saxon and Celtic Bibliography (450-1087) (2 vols. Berkeley 1957); J. Ryan, S.J., Irish Monasticism. Origins and Early Development (Dublin 1931); L. Bieler, Ireland, Harbinger of the Middle Ages (London 1963); L. Gougaud, OSB, Christianity in Celtic Lands. A History of the Churches of the Celts, Their Origin, Their Development, Influence and Mutual Relations (London 1932; with excellent bibliography xvii-lxii); P. H. Blair, Roman Britain and Early England 55 B.C.-A.D. 871 (London 1963); K. Jackson, Language and History in Early Britain (Edin-burgh 1953; of basic importance); E. S. Duckett, Anglo-Saxon Saints and Scholars (New York 1947); W. Levison, England and the Continent in the Eighth Century

(Oxford 1946); R. R. Bolgar, The Classical Heritage and Its Beneficiaries (Cambridge [England] 1954) 91-106; E. MacNeill, "Beginnings of Latin Culture in Ireland," Studies 20 (1931) 39-48 and 449-460; C. H. Slover, "Early Literary Channels between Britain and Ireland," University of Texas Bulletin No. 2648 (1926) 5-52 (Studies in English VI), and No. 2743 (1927) 5-111 (Studies in English VII); M. Esposito, "Notes on Latin Learning and Literature in Mediaeval Ireland," Hermathena 45 (1930) 225-260; 47 (1932) 253-271; 48 (1933) 221-249; 49 (1935) 120-165; 50 (1937) 139-183; H. Leclercq, "Irlande," DACL 7.2: 1461-1552; especially 1498-1512; J. W. Adamson, The Illiterate Anglo-Saxon (New York 1947); R. Aigrain, "L'Angleterre chrétienne et les églises celtiques," in Fliche-Martin, Histoire de l'Église 5 (1938) 277-328 (with good bibliography); id., "Le monachisme occidental," op. cit. 505-542 (includes St. Boniface); M. R. James, "Learning and Literature to the Death of Bede," CMH 3: 485-513, especially 501-513; P. Riché, Éducation et Culture..., 353-383 and 419ff. (The latest and best treatment of the subject)

On the bookish and artificial character in general of the Latin written by most Irish and Anglo-Saxon scholars, see, especially, Roger, L'enseignement des lettres classiques d'Ausone à Alcuin (Paris 1905) 202 to the end; Gougaud, op. cit. 250 ff.; L. Bieler, "Hibernian Latin," Studies 43 (1954) 92-95. See also the bibliography listed on the Irish Latin hymns infra.

N.B.: On the Hisperica Famina, Virgilius Maro, etc., see the Bibliography on V3A (near end) supra.

Gildas: Mommsen's critical edition of his Historia, in MGH, AA XVII Chronica Minora (Berlin 1898) 25-85: Kenney, op. cit. 150-152; Roger, op. cit. 223-227 and 251 ff.; Jackson, op. cit.

St. Patrick: L. Bieler, The Life and Legend of St. Patrick. Problems of Modern Scholarship (Dublin 1948. The Introduction contains a good survey of Patrician scholarship); id., "Libri Epistolarum Sancti Patricii Episcopi. Introduction, Text and Commentary. Part I: Introduction and Text" (Classica et Mediaevalia 11 (1949) 1-150 (published as a book, Dublin 1952. See the review of these two works by M. R. P. McGuire, Traditio 8 [1952] 449-455); id., Part II: "Commentary," Classica et Mediaevalia 12 (1950) 79-214 (published as a book, Dublin 1953); id., The Works of St. Patrick. St. Secundinus, Hymn on St. Patrick (Westminster, Md., 1953; Ancient Christian Writers 17); id., "Der Bibeltext des heiligen Patrick," Biblica 28 (1947) 31-58 and 236-263 (with bibliography); P. Grosjean, S.J., "St. Patrice d'Irlande et quelques homonymes dans les anciens martyrologes," Journal of Ecclesiastical History 1 (1950) 151-171; id., "Notes d'hagiographie celtiques 22. Paladius episcopus...qui Patricius," Analecta Bollandiana 70 (1952) 317-326; id., "Dominicati rhetorici," ALMA 25 (1955) 41-46; R. E. McNally, "St. Patrick 461-1961", CHR 47 (1961-1962) 305-324; D. A. Binchy, "St. Patrick and His Biographers," Studia Hibernica 2 (Dublin 1962) 7-173; C. Mohrmann, The Latin of Saint Patrick (Dublin 1961).

Latin and vernacular glosses: On the origin and character of Latin and vernacular glosses and glossaries, it will suffice here to refer to the brief but excellent treatment of the subject in Laistner, Thought and Letters 222-224. The Latin glossaries will be taken up in some detail later in connection with dictionaries. For the Irish glosses, see Whitley Stokes and J. Strachan, Thesaurus palaeohibernicus (2 vols. Cambridge [England] 1901 and 1903). For the Old English glosses, see especially: Th. Wright and R. Wülker, Anglo-Saxon and Old English Vocabularies (London 1884); A. Napier, Old English Glosses (Oxford 1900); W. M. Lindsay, The Corpus, Epinal, Erfurt, and Leyden Glossaries (London 1921). For German glosses see E. Steinmeyer and E. Sievers, Die althochdeutschen Glossen (5 vols. Berlin 1879-1922). For the Romance glosses, the Reichenau and Kassel Glosses, see W. Foerster and E. Koschwitz, Altromanisches Elementarbuch (Leipzig 1907) 2 ff.

Columbanus: F. O'Briain, art., "Colomban," DHGE 13 (1953) 313-320 (with good bibliography); Kenney, op. cit. 186-203; Raby, Christian Latin Poetry 138-140; G. S. M. Walker, "On the Use of Greek Words in the Writings of Columbanus," ALMA 21 (1949-1950) 117-131; id. ed., Columbani Opera (Dublin 1957; Scriptores Latini Hiberniae 2); P. F. Kendig, The Poems of Columbanus Translated into English with an Introduction and Bibliography (Diss. University of Pennsylvania 1949); C. B. Flaherty, SSC, "The Prose Letters of Saint Columban. A Translation with an Introduction and Commentary" (CUA unpublished Master's dissertation 1955).

St. Pirmin: Gall Jecker, OSB, Die Heimat des hl. Pirmin (Münster i.W. 1927; Beitr. z. Gesch. d. alten Mönchtums u. d. Benediktinerordens 13)

The De duodecim abusivis saeculi: See S. Hellmann's remarks in his edition, Pseudo-Cyprianus De XII abusivis saeculi, in Harnack-Schmidt edd., Texte und Untersuchungen zur Geschichte der altchristlichen Literatur 34.1 (Leipzig 1909); Kenney, op. cit. 281-282.

Adamnan: P. Geyer's introduction and index to his edition of the De locis sanctis, in CSEL 39, Itineraria Hierosolymitana saeculi IV-VIII (Vienna 1898); G. Brüning, "Adamnans Vita Columbae und ihre Ableitungen," Zeitschrift für keltische Philologie 11 (1917) 211-314; J. R. Fowler, Adamani Vita S. Columbae (Oxford 1894; 2nd ed. 1920), especially 167-173.

Irish and Anglo-Saxon canonical collections and penitentials: Kenney, op. cit. 199-200 and 235-250; H. Leclercq, "Pénitentiels," DACL 14.1: 215-251, especially 234-251; G. Le Bras, "Pénitentiels," DTC 12.1 (1933) 1160-1172; J. Lahache, "Pénitentiels," DDC 6 (1957) 1337-1343; T. P. Oakley, "The Origins of the Irish Penitential Discipline," CHR 19 (1933) 320-332; J. R. McNeill and H. M. Gamer, Medieval Handbooks of Penance and Selections from Related Documents (New York 1938; Columbia University Records of Civilization); L. Bieler, The Irish Penitentials. With an Appendix by D. A. Binchy (Dublin 1963).

The Antiphonary of Bangor and Irish Latin hymns: Kenney, op. cit. (Individual hymns may be checked through his Index, s.v. "Hymns"); Gougaud, op. cit. 313 ff.; Raby, Christian Latin Poetry 131-153 (with bibliography 473-475); F. E. Warren, The Antiphonary of Bangor (2 vols. London 1893 and 1895; Henry Bradshaw Society 4 and 10); J. H. Bernard and R. Atkinson, An Irish Liber Hymnorum (2 vols. London 1898. 1, Text and Introductions; 2, Translation and Notes; Henry Bradshaw Society 13-14).

Irish and Anglo-Saxon lives of saints and their Latinity: Kenney, op. cit. 288 ff. (Lives of individual saints may be checked through his Index under their respective names); E. S. Duckett, Anglo-Saxon Saints and Scholars (cited supra); B. Krusch, Ionae Vitae Sanctorum Columbani, Vedastis, Joannis in MGH, SS rer. Germ. in usum schol. (Berlin 1905; also edited by the same scholar in MGH, SS rer. Merov. IV [1902] 1-152, and in VII 2 [1920] 822-827); C. Plummer, Vitae Sanctorum Hiberniae (2 vols. Oxford 1910); id., Lives of Irish Saints (2 vols. Oxford 1922); W. G. Most, The Syntax of the Vitae Sanctorum Hiberniae (Washington 1946; CUA Studies in Medieval and Renaissance Latin Language and Literature 20. See also the valuable review of this work by J. Vendryes in Études Celtiques 4 [1940] 419-421); B. Colgrave, Two Lives of Saint Cuthbert. A Life by an Anonymous Monk of Lindisfarne and Bede's Prose Life. Texts, Translation, and Notes (Cambridge Engl. 1940); W. Levison, Vitae sancti Bonifatii, in MGH, SS rer. Germ. in usum schol. (Berlin 1905); with Index rerum et verborum 230-241.

Aldhelm: R. Ehwald's Indices verborum, rerum grammaticarum et metricarum, rei orthographicae, to his edition of Aldhelm, MGH, AA XV (Berlin 1919) 555-765. See also, Laistner, Thought and Letters 153-156; Roger, op. cit. 290 ff.; Raby, Christian Latin Poetry 142-145; E. S. Duckett, Anglo-Saxon Saints and Scholars 3-97; Riché, Éducation et Culture 422ff.

Bede: Laistner, Thought and Letters 156-166; Duckett, op. cit. 215-336; A. H. Thompson ed., Bede, His Life, Times and Writings. Essays in Commemoration of the Twelfth Century of His Death (Oxford 1935); Sister Thomas Aquinas Carroll, The Venerable Bede: His Spiritual Teachings (Washington 1946; CUA Studies in Mediaeval History, New Series 9; valuable for Bede's theological terminology); D. Ross Druhan, S.J., The Syntax of Bede's Historia Ecclesiastica (Washington 1938; CUA Studies in Medieval and Renaissance Latin Language and Literature 8); P. F. Jones, Concordance to the Historia Ecclesiastica of Bede (Cambridge 1929; Publications of the Mediaeval Academy of America 2); M. L. W. Laistner, Bedae venerabilis expositio actuum apostolorum et retractatio (Cambridge 1939; same series, 35); id., "Bede as a Classical Scholar," Transactions of the Royal Historical Society, 4th Series, 16 (1933) 69-94; id., "The Library of Bede," in Thompson, op. cit. 237-263; id. and H. H. King, A Hand-List of Bede Manuscripts (Ithaca 1943); C. Plummer, Venerabilis Baedae opera historica (2 vols. Oxford 1896); J. D. A. Ogilvy, Books Known to Anglo-Latin Writers from Aldhelm to Alcuin (670-804 A.D.) (Cambridge 1936; Publications of the Med. Acad. of America 23. See Laistner's critical review, Speculum 12 [1937] 127-129); C. W. Jones, Bedae Venerabilis opera de temporibus (Cambridge 1943; same series, 41); id., Bedae Pseudepigrapha. Scientific Writings Falsely Attributed to Bede (Ithaca 1939); id., "Bede as an Early Medieval Historian" Mediaevalia et Humanistica 4 (1946) 26-36; id., Saints' Lives and Chronicles in Early England, together with the First English Translation of the Oldest Life of Pope St. Gregory the Great by a Monk of Whitby and the Life of St. Guthlac of Crowland by Felix (Ithaca 1947); W. Jaager ed., Bedas metrische Vita sancti Cuthberti (Leipzig 1935); B. Gladysz, "Éléments classiques et post-classiques de l'oeuvre de Bède," Eos 34 (1933) 319-342; L. Whitbread, "A Study of Bede's Versus de die iudicii," Philological Quarterly 23 (1944) 193-221; F. P. Magoun, "Bede's Story of Caedmon: The Case History of an Anglo-Saxon Oral Singer," Speculum 30 (1955) 49-63.

St. Boniface: M. Tangl, Die Briefe des heiligen Bonifatius und Lullus, MGH, Epistolae Selectae I (Berlin 1916), with Wort-und Sachregister 301-314; P. Lehmann, "Die Grammatik aus Aldhelms Kreise," Historische Vierteljahrschrift 28 (1932) 758-771; Raby, Christian Latin Poetry 149-150; E. S. Duckett, op. cit. 339-455; Levison, (England and the Continent in the Eighth Century 70-93, and 290-294 ("St. Boniface and Cryptography").

F. The Latinity of the Ancient and Early Mediaeval Liturgies

General Background: F. Cabrol, OSB, The Books of the Latin Liturgy St. Loui, 1932); L. Eisenhofer, Handbuch der katholischen Liturgik 1 (Freiburg im Br. 1932) 31-39 and 57-126; F. Cabrol, "Léonien (Le Sacramentaire)," DACL 8.2: 2549-2573; id., "Gélasien (Le Sacramentaire)," ibid. 6.1: 747-777; id., "Grégorien (Le Sacramentaire)," ibid. 6.2: 1776-1796; P. Lejay, "Ambrosien (Rite)," ibid. 1.1: 1373-1442; L. Gougaud, OSB, "Celtiques (Liturgies)," ibid. 2.2: 2969-3032; id., Christianity in Celtic Lands 313-338; H. Leclercq, "Gallicane (Liturgie)," DACL 6.1: 473-593; F. Cabrol, "Mozarabe (La Liturgie)," ibid. 12.1: 390-491; H. Schmidt, "De lectionibus variantibus in formulis identicis sacramantariorum Leoniani, Gelasiani et Gregoriani," Sacris Erudiri 4 (1952) 103-173; A. Wilmart, OSB, "Bobbio (Missel de)," DACL 2.1: 939-962; F. Cabrol, "Missel," ibid 11.2: 1431-1468; id., "Missel Romain," ibid. 1468-1494; H. Leclercq, Messe," ibid. 11.1: 513-774; B. Botte and C. Mohrmann, L'ordinaire de la Messe (Paris 1953); J. A. Jungmann, S.J., Missarum Sollemnia. Eine genetische Erklärung der römischen Messe (2 vols. 2nd ed. Vienna 1949; 3rd ed. 1952; English trans. by F. A. Brunner, 2 vols. New York 1951-1955); P. Bruylants, OSB, Les oraisons du Missel Romain. Texte et histoire (2 vols. Louvain 1952); H. Leclercq, "Hymnes VI: Hymnographie dans l'Eglise latine," DACL 6.2: 2901-2938 (with a systematic classification of the contents of C. Blume and G. M. Dreves, Analecta hymnica medii aevi, and valuable bibliography); The Psalter Collects from V-VIth Century Sources, edited with Introduction, Apparatus Criticus, and Indexes by L. Brou from the Papers of A. Wilmart (London 1949; Henry Bradshaw Society 83. See also the review article by C. Mohrmann, Vigiliae Christianae 6 [1952] 1-19). See also the articles: "Messa, Enciclopedia Cattolica 8 (1952), especially, sect. III, "La Messa nella liturgia di ri romano," 792-808; "Messale," ibid. 831-841; "Sacramentario," 10 (1953) 1558-1569. The pertinent articles in the Catholic Encyclopedia were excellent for their time, but are now more or less antiquated.

Language and style: T. Klauser, "Der Uebergang der römischen Kirche von der griechischen zur lateinischen Liturgiesprache," Miscellanea Mercati 1 (Rome 1946) 467-482; G. Bardy, "La latinisation de l'Église d'Occident," in his La question des langues dans l'Eglise ancienne 1 (Paris 1948) 81-121; C. Mohrmann, "Les origines de la latinité chrétienne à Rome," Vigiliae Christianae 3 (1949) 67-109 an 163-183; id., "Quelques observations linguistiques à propos de la nouvelle version latine de Psauter," ibid. 1 (1947) 114-128 and 168-182; id., "Quelques observations sur l'évolution stylistique du canon de la messe romaine," Vigiliae Christianae 4 (1950) 1-19; id., "Le latin liturgique," La Maison-Dieu 23 (1950) 5-30; id., Liturgical Latin: Its Origins and Character (Washington 1957); J. A. Jungmann, op. cit. (check through the lemmata "Latein," "Sprache," and "Stilgesetze," in Register B); M. Feltoe, Sacramentarium Leonianum (Cambridge [Engl.] 1896; some discussion of language in the notes); P. Bruylants, OSB, "Concordance verbale du sacramentaire Léonien," ALMA 18 (1945) 51-376, and 19 (1948) 39-405; H. A. Wilson, "The Metrical Endings of the Leonine Sacramentary," Journal of Theological Studies 5 (1904) 386-395, and 6 (1905) 381-391 (somewhat antiquated now in method); id., The Gelasian Sacramentary. Liber Sacramentorum Romanae ecclesiae, with Introduction, Critical Notes and Appendix (Oxford 1894); id., A Classified Index to the Leonine, Gelasian, and Gregorian Sacramentaries according to the Text of Muratori's Lit. Rom. vet. (Cambridge 1892); id., The Gregorian Sacramentary under Charles the Great. Edited from Three MSS of the Ninth Century (London 1915; Henry Bradshaw Society 49); H. Lietzmann, Das Sacramentarium Gregorianum nach dem Aachener Urexemplar (Münster i.W. 1921; in the series, Liturgiegeschichtliche Quellen, ed. Kunibert Mohlberg, OSB), with good Wortregister 132-176; Dom M. Férotin, OSB, Liber Mozarabicus Sacramentorum (Paris 1912; Monumenta Ecclesiae liturgica, edd. F. Cabrol and H. Leclercq, 6), with good indices 969-1096; id., Le liber Ordinum en usage dans l'Église visigothique et mozarabe d'Espagne du cinquième au onzième siècle (Paris 1904; same series, 6), with excellent indices 551-800; A. Wilmart, E. A. Lowe, and H. A. Wilson, The Bobbio Missal. Notes and Studies (London 1924; Henry Bradshaw Society 61); R. E. Messenger, "Mozarabic Hymns in Relation to Contemporary Culture in Spain," Traditio 4 (1946) 149-177 (She calls attention to the importance of studying the language of Spanish hymns). The two following lists of definitions are useful: H. Leclercq, "Lexique Liturgique Grec," DACL 9.1: 1-14; "Lexique Liturgique (Latin)," ibid. 14-30.

N.B.:   Much more philogical work remains to be done on most of the Ancient and Early Mediaeval liturgical texts listed supra -- and the same holds for others not mentioned. Full indices like those prepared by Dom M. Férotin, or concordances like that prepared by Dom P. Bruylants, are indispensable tools not only for the historian of liturgy but also for the philologist and the cultural historian as well.

For control of new publications, see especially: L'Année Philologique (in section, "Auteurs et textes," s.v. Liturgica), Ephemerides Liturgicae, Liturgisches Jahrbuch, Recherches de théologie ancienne et mediévale, Revue Bénédictine, and Yearbook of Liturgical Studies.

VII. LATIN FROM THE CAROLINGIAN RENAISSANCE TO THE ITALIAN RENAISSANCE: FROM ALCUIN TO THE DEATH OF DANTE (c. 780-1321)

Some General Preliminary Notions

The assiduous study of the Latin grammarians, and the deliberate and systematic imitation of the ancient Pagan and Christian Latin writers in grammar and style as a result of the powerful impulse given to education and learning by Charlemagne

The establishment of a "correct" or standard Latin through school exercises and a school tradition

The formal cleavage between Late Vulgar Latin and Primitive Romance dialects, and the Latin of the school tradition

The flexibility of Carolingian and post-Carolingian Latin, however, as compared with the rigidity and narrowly Classical character of Renaissance Latin

The three factors stressed by F. Blatt as being responsible for certain changes in Mediaeval Latin in the Pre-Carolingian Age, but especially in the period from Charlemagne to Dante

a. The continued influence of the vernacular languages of Europe – Celtic, Germanic, Romance, Slavic, Hungarian – on the Latinity of writers using such vernaculars as their mother tongues

b. The transformation of society in the Middle Ages – new political, social, and economic institutions, etc., and the resulting need for and use of new Latin words or of old Latin words in new meanings

c. The development of mediaeval philosophy, science, and technology, and the necessity of creating an adequate technical and philosophical terminology in Latin

C. Mohrmann's penetrating analysis of the profane and Christian elements in Mediaeval Latin and of the dynamic and fruitful results of their interaction

Mediaeval Latin the universal language of religion, eccesiastical and civil administration, law, and literature throughout Western Christendom, and the significance of this fact for the history of Western civilization

Mediaeval Latin a "living" language during this period, but only within certain definite limits – no progressive modification of morphological structure, e.g., as in the case of the vernacular languages of Europe

Each mediaeval writer of the Carolingian Age and later must be studied individually from the viewpoint of his language, style, and models. No two writers of the same generation, no two writers even living at the same time in the same city necessarily write a Latin peculiar to their age and place, but reflect rather their respective school training and reading in the Classical, Patristic, or earlier Mediaeval authors. In general, the better trained a writer is and the more thoroughly versed he is in the Classical and Patristic literary tradition, the more international is the character of his Latinity. It is rather the imperfectly trained and careless writers who show the influence of their vernaculars in their Latin and thus indicate their original home or nationality.

The bent for rhetorical expression, even for the unusual and the bizarre, as already pointed out in an earlier section, the fondness for writing on all sorts of subjects in Latin verse, especially the hexameter, the extreme use of imitatio in many cases, etc., are all characteristic features of Mediaeval Latin from the Carolingian Age to the end of the Middle Ages and are to be explained in the last analysis by the fact that Latin, however thoroughly known and constantly employed, was always learned as a foreign language in school.

The general lack to date of detailed, scholarly studies on Mediaeval Latin in the period from the Carolingian Age to the Renaissance and the necessity of such studies.

The development of the vernacular languages of Europe beside and under the strong influence of the Mediaeval Latin language and literature, including, as it does, within its scope the transmission and cultivation of much of the pagan and Christian Latin literature of Antiquity — the influence of the vernacular literature on Mediaeval Latin literature especially in the late Middle Ages.

Bibliography

Strecker-Palmer, Introduction to Medieval Latin 20ff.; Traube, Einleitung 35-46; De Ghellinck, Littérature latine au moyen âge 1: 5-8 and 182-186; id., L'essor de la littérature latine au XIIe siècle 2: 312-321; E. Faral, "L'orientation actuelles des études relatives au Latin médiéval," Revue des études latines 1 (1923) 26-47; C. Mohrmann, "Le dualisme de la latinité médiévale," ibid. 29 (1951) 330-348 (reprinted in C. Mohrmann, Latin vulgaire. Latin des chrétiens. Latin médiéval [Paris] 1955 36-54); id., "Le latin médiéval," Cahiers de Civilisation Médiévale 1 (1958) 265-294 (the latest and best analysis of Mediaeval Latin as a language, with valuable bibliography); F. Blatt, "Sprachwandel im Latein des Mittelalters," Historische Viertejahrschrift 28 (1933) 22-52 (English translation by M. R. P. McGuire available in typescript for class use); R. Meister, "Mittellatein als Traditionssprache," in Liber Floridus. Mittellateinische Studien. Festschrift Paul Lehmann, edd. B. Bischoff and S. Brechter (Erzabtei St. Ottilien, [Bayern], 1950) 1-9; Raby, Christian Latin Poetry 452-456; id., Secular Latin Poetry 2: 341-348; P. Lehmann, "Vom Leben des Lateinischen im Mittelalter," in his Erforschung des Mittelalters 1 (Leipzig 1941) 62-81; A. Viscardi, Le origini (2nd ed. Milan 1950; Storia letteraria d'Italia 1) 238-296. See also the references given in the Bibliography on V 1 supra.

1. The Carolingian Renaissance: From the Accession of Charlemagne to the Death of Charles the Bald (768-877)

The intellectual activities of the Irish and Anglo-Saxon monks on the Continent in the seventh century and first half of the eighth, and the reforms of Pepin the Short

Charlemagne and the powerful impulse given to education and learning by his legislation and, especially, by his personal initiative, interest, and supervision; his primary purpose not the revival of ancient learning as such but rather the creation of an educated clergy – his Epistola de litteris colendis (c. 794-796), Admoniti generalis (789), and Epistola generalis (c. 780-800)

The Palace School at Aachen and its organization and development under Alcuin grammar the chief subject, but the rudiments of the other liberal arts also taught; the necessarily elementary character of the instruction given in Charlemagne's time; the importance of the Palace School in the history of European education

The reign of Charlemagne as the first phase – the preparatory phase – in the Carolingian Renaissance and the preponderant role of foreign scholars in this period: Peter of Pisa (died before 799) and Paulinus of Aquileia (died 802); Clement, Dungal, and Dicuil of Ireland; Alcuin; Paul the Deacon (died c. 800); Theodulph of Orleans (died 821)

Alcuin (c. 735-804) Charlemagne's "prime minister of intellectual affairs" and the significance of his work as an organizer, teacher, and writer, not only as head of the Palace School, but as abbot of St. Martin's of Tours; his excellent earlier training at the School of York, the leading cultural center of Europe in the second half of the eighth century; his scriptorium and his pupils at Tours

The second phase of the Carolingian Renaissance 814-877 and the fruition of Charlemagne's efforts in the achievements of a remarkable group of writers preponderantly of Frankish origin: St. Benedict of Aniane (c. 750-821), promoter of the ascetical life and monastic reform; Einhard (c. 770-840) and his Vita Caroli; Rhabanus Maurus (780-856), the Praeceptor Germaniae; Gottschalk (c. 805-869), theologian and poet; Hincmar of Rheims (c. 806-882), canonist and political theori Walafrid Strabo (809-849), the most gifted poet of the age; Paschasius Radbertus (died c. 860), Ratramnus (died after 868) of Corbie, and Jonas of Orleans (died 842), theologians; Amalarius of Metz (c. 780-850), liturgist; Christian of Stavelot (died after 880), exegete; Servatus Lupus of Ferrières (805-862), bibliophile and humanist; Heiric of Auxerre (c. 841-876) and Micon of St. Riquier (first half of the 9th cent.), philologists and grammarians; Florus of Lyons (died c. 860), poet and text critic

The Irish scholars active in the second phase of the Carolingian Renaissance: Smaragdus of St. Mihiel (died c. 830), philologist and grammarian; Sedulius Scott (died after 858), poet, theologian and grammarian: John the Scot (c. 815-877), theologian, philosopher, and Hellenist, the most original and brilliant mind of the Carolingian Age

The Spanish theologians Claudius of Turin (died c. 827) and Agobard of Lyons (769-840) and their role in the Carolingian Renaissance

The contemporary writers in Italy and Spain: the Romans, Anastasius the Librarian (c. 800-c. 880), historian and translator of Greek works, and John the Deacon (Hymonides, c. 825 – died before 882), historian and biographer; the Spanish polemists against Islam, Paul Albar of Cordoba (died c. 861) and Eulogius Archbishop of Toledo (died 859)

The coming of the Northmen to Ireland and England and the gradual decline of Irish learning and scholarly influence on the Continent from the close of the ninth century

A survey of Carolingian literature according to types (based chiefly on the brief but excellent exposition in De Ghellinck, Littérature latine au moyen âge 1: 132ff., and on Laistner, Thought and Letters in Western Europe 251-361)

a. Grammars, school manuals, treatises and commentaries of all kinds, copying of texts glossaries: Priscian the favorite grammatical authority of the Irish scholars and the most influential grammatical work in the Carolingian Age; Martianus Capella also a favorite author of the Scoti; the use and influence of the Ars Minor of Donatus; the Dicta or Disticha Catonis and its amazing vogue as a schoolbook from the ninth to the sixteenth centuries; the libraries and scriptoria of the Carolingian Age; the great majority of our extant works of ancient pagan and Christian writers preserved through the copies made in this period; the establishment of the text of the Latin Vulgate and of the Rule of St. Benedict in the Carolingian Age

b. Letters: their large number and variety; the high literary qualities of certain collections, especially the letters of Lupus of Ferrières; the need of detailed, comprehensive studies on the language and style of the letters of the Carolingian Age

c. Theological works: with the conspicuous exception of John Scotus, the theological writers of this period not original, but dependent on the Patristic writers, whom they quote copiously; the development of sententiae, and glossae or catenae; the use of the dialogue form and of dialectic in theological works; the penitentials and other canonical collections of the Carolingian Age; the literature of piety and devotion and its relative neglect to date

d. History: Einhard's Vita Caroli; no outstanding comprehensive historical work, however, produced in the Carolingian Age; saints' lives and annals the characteristic productions in the historical field; the Annales Mettenses priores (late 7th and early 8th cent.); Annales Laurissenses maiores or Royal Annals (741-829); Annales S. Bertiniani (741-882); Annales Fuldenses (651-814, and 742-822); the Historia or universal chronicle of Frechulf bishop of Lisieux (822-850); the Breviarium chronicorum of Ado of Vienne (874); the Gesta abbatum Fontanellensium (completed after 833); the Liber pontificalis of Ravenna by Agnellus (c. 805-854); Paul the Deacon's Historia Langobardorum and its continuation by Andrew of Bergamo (down to 877); the Historia Britonum ascribed to Nennius (written in 822); the Historiarum libri quattuor of Nithard of St. Riquier (died 844); the martyrologies of the Carolingian Age and the large number of vitae sanctorum, accounts of translationes of relics, and collections of miracula; the rewriting of earlier vitae by Walafrid Strabo, Jonas of Orleans, and Alcuin, among others

e.   Poetry and versification: the emphasis on prosody and poetical composition in the Carolingian schools and the intense interest in and continued practice of verse writing throughout life; the development of a knowledge of Latin and a richer vocabulary through verse composition; the verse form regarded as a natural means of written expression and hence employed in the treatment of the most varied subjects or incidents; the high esteem for poetical compositions in this age and later the copious extant poetical compositions of the Carolingian Age (those edited to date filling more than four quarto volumes in the MGH); the emphasis on classical prosody and the cultivation of various classical meters (e. g., by Theodulph of Orleans) beside the dominant hexameter and distich; the continued writing, however, of accentual verse, which had been developing steadily from the last centuries of Antiquity; the fondness for composing epitaphs after the fashion of Fortunatus and Pope Damasus; carmina figurata and in particular the De laudibus sanctae crucis of Rhabanus Maurus; the aenigmata or riddles in verse dear to the Anglo-Saxons, including St. Boniface; abecedarian poems; Theodulph of Orleans, Walafrid Strabo, Sedulius Scottus, and Gottschalk the true poets of the Carolingian Age

N. B.:   There is an excellent summary of the characteristic literary features and achievements of the Carolingian Age in De Ghellinck, op. cit. 1: 182-186.

On Latin grammar in the Carolingian Age, see also XII. THE LATIN GRAMMAR OF THE MIDDLE AGES. On the knowledge of Greek in this period, see VIII. THE KNOWLEDGE OF GREEK IN THE WEST IN THE MIDDLE AGES. On Latin glossaries, etc., of the Carolingian Age, see X DICTIONARIES OF MEDIAEVAL LATIN. On the verse technique of this period, see also XIII. MEDIAEVAL RHETORIC AND POETIC.

Bibliography on VII-1. The Carolingian Renaissance: From the Accession of Charlemagne to the Death of Charles the Bald (768-877)

The general background (see also the Bibliography on VI supra): C. Dawson, The Making of Europe (New York 1941) 189ff., very brief, but a masterly survey); CMH 2-3; Shorter Cambridge Mediaeval History 1: 297-387 and 379 ff.; Lot-Phister Ganshof, Les destinées de l'Empire en Occident de 395 à 888; L. Halphen, Les Barbares. Des grandes invasions aux conquêtes turques du XIe siècle (2nd ed.

Paris 1930; Halphen-Sagnac, Peuples et Civilisations 6); I. Hashagen, Europa im Mittelalter. Alte Tatsachen und neue Gesichtspunkte (Munich 1951) 1-110; E. Amann, L'époque carolingienne (736-888) (Paris 1937; Fliche-Martin, Histoire de l'Église 6); G. Schnürer, Kirche und Kultur im Mittelalter 1 (2nd ed. Paderborn 1927) 334 to end, and 2 (2nd ed. 1929) 1-119; E. Mühlbacher and J. Lechner, Die Regesten des Kaiserreichs unter den Karolingern (2nd ed. Innsbruck 1908). In addition to the treatments of monasticism contained in the general works listed, see also: H. Leclercq, art., "Monachisme," DACL 11.2 (1934) 1774-1947; David Knowles, The Monastic Order in England. A History of Its Development from the Time of St. Dunstan to the Fourth Lateran Council, 943-1216 (2nd ed. revised 1963. Cambridge [Engl.] There is a long and excellent introductory section on the development of monasticism from late Antiquity to the 10th century.).

Histories of Latin literature, philosophy, theology, and canon law: Laistner, Thought and Letters 189 to end (excellent); Wright and Sinclair, History of Later Latin Literature 137ff. (brief and rather superficial); De Ghellinck, Littérature latine au moyen âge 1: 81 to end (excellent); A. Baumgartner, Die lateinische und griechische Literatur der Christlichen Völker (3rd and 4th ed. Freiburg im Br. 1905) 292ff. (still valuable); M. Manitius, Geschichte der lateinischen Literatur des Mittelalters 1. 243 to end (indispensable as a work of reference); Raby, Christian Latin Poetry 154-201; id., Secular Latin Poetry 1: 178-521; De Wulf, History of Mediaeval Philosophy. Engl. trans. 1 (3rd ed.) 105-152; E. Gilson, La philosophie au moyen âge. Des origines patristiques à la fin du XIVe siècle (3rd ed. Paris 1947) 180-222 (in two sections, "La transmission de la culture latine," and "Jean Scot Érigène,"); id., History of Christian Philosophy in the Middle Ages 111-128 and 606-613; Cayré, Précis de Patrologie 2. 370ff. (very brief); Ueberweg-Geyer, Geschichte der patristischen und scholastischen Philosophie 141-180; M. Grabmann, Geschichte der scholastischen Methode 1 (Freiburg im Br. 1909) 178-214; id., Geschichte der katholischen Theologie seit dem Ausgang der Väterzeit (ibid. 1933) 25-28; H. D. Hazeltine, "Roman and Canon Law in the Middle Ages," CMH 5: 697ff.; P. Fournier and G. Le Bras, Histoire des collections canoniques en Occident 1 (Paris 1931) 1-201.

Schools, scriptoria, libraries, learning, culture in general (in addition to works listed supra): R. R. Bolgar, The Classical Heritage and Its Beneficiaries 91-129, especially 106-129; M. R. James, "Learning and Literature till Pope Sylvester II," CMH 3: 514-538; M. Deansley, "Medieval Schools to c. 1300," CMH 5: 765-779; E. Lesne, Les écoles de la fin du VIIIe siècle à la fin du XIIe (Lille 1940; Histoire de la propriété ecclésiastique en France 5); J. E. Sandys, A History of Classical Scholarship 1 (3rd ed. Cambridge [Engl.] 1921) 471-501; E. Norden, Die antike Kunstprosa 2 (4th reprint Leipzig 1923) 670-705; F. W. Hall, Companion to Classical Texts (Oxford 1913) 70-93; R. M. Martin, "Arts libéraux (sept)", DHGE 4 (1930) 827-843, especially 831-835; J. Koch, Artes Liberales. Von der antiken Bildung zur Wissenschaft des Mittelalters (Leiden-Köln 1959); De Ghellinck, "La Renaissance carolingienne," in his Le mouvement théologique du XIIe siècle (2nd ed. Brussels 1948) 9-37; W. J. Chase, The Ars Minor of Donatus, for 1000 Years the Leading Textbook of Grammar (1926; University of Wisconsin Studies in the Social Sciences and History

No. 11); id., The Distichs of Cato Translated from the Latin with Introductory Sketch (1922; same series, No. 7); Disticha Catonis, edd. M. Boas and J. Bot-schuyver (Amsterdam 1952); Gougaud, Christianity in Celtic Lands, ch. V, "The Irish Abroad," 129-184, and ch. VIII, sect. VI, "The Scots and the Carolingian Renaissance," 298-312; W. Levison, "Learning and Scholarship," in his England and the Continent in the Eighth Century (Oxford 1946) 132-173 (especially impor-tant for Alcuin); J. W. Thompson, The Mediaeval Library (Chicago 1939) 54-101; K. Christ, "Das Mittelalter," in Milkau-Leyh, Handbuch der Bibliothekswissenchaf 3, Geschichte der Bibliotheken (2nd ed. Leipzig 1955) 245-498; E. Lesne, Les Livres. Scriptoria et Bibliothèques du commencement du VIIIᵉ à la fin du XIᵉ siècle (Lille 1938; Histoire de propriété eccléstiastique en France 4); C. Foligno, Latin Thought during the Middle Ages (Oxford 1929) 68-86; F. B. Artz, The Mind of the Middle Ages A. D. 200-1500. An Historical Survey (3rd ed. revised New York 1958 179-222; A. C. Crombie, Medieval and Early Modern Science 1 (New York 1959) 1-32; L. Thorndike, History of Magic and Experimental Science. 1 (New York 1923 reprinted 1943) 551-691 (passim); G. Sarton, Introduction to the History of Science. 1, From Homer to Omer Khayam (Washington 1927) 503-618.

On the text of the Bible and on Biblical interpretation in this period, see the references given to Robert-Tricot, Berger, De Lubac, Glunz, McNally, Smalley, etc., in Bibliography on V C. The Christian Element.

On the text of the Rule of St. Benedict in the Carolingian Age, see the referenc given on St. Benedict in the Bibliography on VI A.

For hagiography and liturgy, see the references given in the Bibliography on VI D and F.

N. B.:   The student should gradually become thoroughly familiar with Paetow, Gross, Kenney, Dahlmann-Waitz, Potthast (and the Repertorium fontium historiae medii aevi, which is replacing it, Rome 1962ff.), Molinier, Wattenbach-Holtzmann, etc., which, for the mediaeval period at least, are as important for the history of literature as for history. See SELECT BIBLIOGRAPHY 1, and Paetow, Guide 8ff. For the period from c. 600 to the close of the Middle Ages we do not have a single, comprehensive annua bibliography in the field of Mediaeval Latin Literature. Marouzeau's L'Année philologique has a section, "Littérature médiévale," but this work can hardly be expected to cover the Middle Ages in any exhaustive fashion. Hence the student of Mediaeval Latin Literature must seek information on very recent publications in the various journals dealing in whole or in part with Mediaeval Studies. Two new bibliographical publications, the Quarter Check-List of Medievalia, and the International Guide to Medieval Studies are very helpful.

Editions of Mediaeval Latin texts of this period which deal in detail, or to some extent at least, with language and style: MGH. In addition to the references alread given in the Bibliography on VI A (in the section on the Latinity of the Barbarian Cod and related works) and <u>VI D</u> (in the section on <u>Merovingian writers</u>, <u>formulae</u>, etc.,) see: <u>Leges: Sect. II, Capitularia regum Francorum</u> II, edd. A. Boretius et V. Krause, <u>Index rerum et verborum</u> 588-718; <u>Sect. III, Concilia</u>: II, Concilia aevi Karolini, ed. A. Werminghoff, <u>Index auctoritatum</u> 888-907, and <u>Index verborum et rerum</u> 945-1006

<u>Fontes Iuris Germanici</u> antiqui: Hincmarus De ordine palatii, ed. V. Krause, <u>Index</u> 26-31; <u>Leges Saxonum et Lex Thuringorum</u>, ed. C. Von Schwerin, <u>Wort-und Sachverzeichnis</u> 67-75

<u>Diplomata Karolinorum</u>: I, Die Urkunden Pippins, Karlmanns, und Karls d. Grossen, edd. A. Dopsch, J. Lechner, M. Tangl, E. Mühlbacher, <u>Wort-und Sachregister</u> 543-560

<u>Diplomata regnum Germaniae ex stirpe Karolinorum</u>: I, ed. P. Kehr, <u>Namen-Register</u> 377-403, <u>Wort-und Sachregister</u> 404-431; II, ed. P. Kehr, <u>Namen-Register</u> 347-376, and <u>Wort-und Sachregister</u> 377-419

<u>Epistolae</u>: IV: <u>Epistolae Karolini aevi</u> II, ed. E. Duemmler, <u>Index verborum et rerum</u> 629-634 (inadequate); V. <u>Epistolae Karolini aevi</u> III, edd. E. Duemmler et A. de Hirsch-Gereuth, <u>Index verborum et rerum</u> 666-674; VI. <u>Epistolae Karolini aevi</u> IV, ed. E. Perels, <u>Index rerum et verborum</u> 782-798

<u>Antiquitates. Poetae Latini</u>. I, Poetae Latini aevi Carolini, ed. E. Duemmler, <u>Initia carminum</u> 634-639, <u>Index vocum rariorum</u> 648-650, <u>Index rerum memorabilium</u> 650-652; II, ed. <u>id.</u>, <u>Initia carminum</u> 702-704, <u>Index vocum rariorum</u> 715-718; <u>Index rerum memorabilium</u> 718-721; III, ed. L. Traube, <u>Initia carminum</u> 761-764, <u>Index nominum</u> 765-779, <u>Index scriptorum</u> 780-784, <u>Index grammaticus in carmina Hispanorum</u> 790-795 (Orthographica 791-792), <u>Index orthographicus in carmina Scottorum</u> 795-796, <u>Index grammaticus in carmina Italorum</u> 797-798, <u>Index rerum et verborum generalis</u> 798-814, <u>Index metricus et rhythmicus</u> 815-818; IV, edd. P. de Winterfeld et K. Strecker, <u>Index initiorum carminum</u> 1136-1139, <u>Index initiorum carminum in reliquis tomis impressorum</u> 1139-1140, <u>Index nominum</u> 1140-1158, <u>Index scriptorum</u> 1158-1161, <u>Index metricus et rhythmicus</u> 1161-1164, <u>Index grammaticus</u> 1164-1169, <u>Index rerum et verborum generalis</u> 1169-1177.

<u>N.B.</u>: The <u>Indices</u> in the volumes of the <u>MGH</u> published before c. 1880 are unsatisfactory on the linguistic side.

<u>Editions of and studies on some of the more important writers of the Carolingian Age and their Latinity</u>

<u>N.B.</u>: Since the letters and poems of the Carolingian writers are edited in the <u>MGH</u>, <u>Epistolae</u> and <u>Poetae</u>, listed <u>supra</u>, it will not be necessary to advert to this fact in the case of each writer mentioned <u>infra</u>. For linguistic or stylistic studies on the poets of the Carolingian Age, see, especially the systematic bibliography in Raby's <u>Christian Latin Poetry</u> and <u>Secular Latin Poetry</u>.

Paul the Deacon: A. Dall, "Notes on the Vocabulary of the Homiliary of Paul the Deacon," ALMA 6 (1931) 160-175

Alcuin: E. S. Duckett, Alcuin, Friend of Charlemagne: His Life and Work (New York 1951); L. Wallach, Alcuin and Charlemagne: Studies in Carolingian History and Literature (Ithaca 1959); id., "The Unknown Author of the Libri Carolini", in R. Prete ed., Didascaliae. Studies in Honor of Anselm M. Albareda (New York 1961) 471-515; W. Schmitz, Alcuins ars grammatica, die Schulgrammatik der karolingischen Renaissance (Diss. Bonn 1908); W. G. Howell, The Rhetoric of Alcuin and Charlemagne. A Translation, with an Introduction, the Latin Text, and Notes (London 1941); A. Marsili ed., Alcuin. Orthographia (Padua 1952). On the Altercatio Hadriani Augusti et Epicteti and its connections with Alcuin, see the edition of that work by L. W. Daly and W. Suchier (Urbana 1939; Illinois Studies in Language and Literature 24. 1-2) L. Wallach, "Charlemagne's De Litteris colendis and Alcuin," Speculum 26 (1951) 288-305; id., "Charlemagne and Alcuin," Traditio 9 (1953) 127-154; id., "The Epitaph of Alcuin: A Model of Carolingian Epigraphy," Speculum 30 (1955) 367-373; id., "Alcuin on Virtues and Vices," Harvard Theological Review 48 (1955) 176-195 (These studies by Wallach have been reprinted in his Alcuin and Charlemagne listed supra.)

Einhard: O. Holder-Egger, Einhardi Vita Karoli Magni (6th ed. 1911; MGH, SS rer. Germ. in usum schol.); H. Bachmann, Einhardi Vita Karoli Magni für den Schulgebrauch (Münster i. W. 1926); A. Schmidt, Die Sprache Einhards (Diss. Greifswald 1904)

Amalarius of Metz: I. Cecchetti, "Amalario," in Enciclopedia Cattolica 1 (1948) 959-962; A. Cabaniss, Amalarius of Metz (Amsterdam 1954)

Rhabanus Maurus: A. Knöpfler ed., Rabani Mauri De institutione clericorum (Munich 1901)

Lupus of Ferrières: C. H. Beeson, Lupus of Ferrières. Scribe and Text Critic (Cambridge [Mass.] 1930: Mediaeval Acad. of America Publ. No. 4); L. Levillain, Loup de Ferrières: Correspondance (2 vols. Paris 1927; Classiques de l'histoire de France au moyen âge); C. Snijders, Het latijn der briefen van Lupus van Ferrières, middeleeuws humanist (Diss. Amsterdam 1943)

John Scotus Eriugena: P. G. Théry, O. P., "Scot Érigène, traducteur de Denys," ALMA 6 (1931) 185-278; Dom. M. Cappuyns. O. S. B., Jean Scot Érigène. Sa vie, son oeuvre, sa pensée (Louvain 1933. See, especially, ch. I, "En Irlande. L'écolier," ch. II, "En Gaule. Le grammairien," and ch. IV, "Le traducteur"); C. E. Lutz ed., Ioannis Scotti Annotationes in Marcianum (Cambridge [Mass.] 1939; Med. Acad. of Am. Publ. No. 34)

The Annales Fuldenses: C. H. Beeson, "The Vocabulary of the Annales Fuldenses," Speculum 1 (1926) 31-37

The Annales Mettenses priores: Ed. B. von Simson, with notes and index (1905; MGH, SS rer. Germ. in usum schol.).

2. From the End of the Carolingian Renaissance to the Beginning of the Renaissance of the Twelfth Century: From the Death of Charles the Bald to the Death of St. Anselm of Canterbury (877-1109)

N.B.: This survey is based primarily on De Ghellinck, Littérature latine au moyen âge 2.

General characterization of the period: the tenth century, especially, an age of political, social, economic, religious, and intellectual decline; Norman and Saracen invasions and devastations; the disappearance or weakness of central authority; an age not as intellectually dark, even in the tenth century, however, as once thought; the Ottonian Renaissance in Germany and the age of King Alfred in England; the special significance of the schools in this period and the solid preparation that they furnished for the great intellectual activity of the late eleventh and the twelfth centuries; the rise of new monastic centers and the development of libraries; the Cluniac Reform (910) and its great importance in the history of Western Monasticism

A. The Chief Schools and Writers of the Tenth Century

a. The immediate successors of the Carolingians: Notker Balbulus of St. Gall (840-912), teacher and scholar, author of the De gestis Karoli Magni, and first outstanding writer of sequences; Remigius of Auxerre (c. 840-c.908), an influential teacher especially well versed in the trivium and quadrivium and in Patristic works, a commentator on Terence, Juvenal, the Disticha Catonis, the Latin grammarians, etc., in the Irish manner; Hucbald of St. Amand (c.840-930), grammarian and poet – his curious Ecloga de calvis

b. King Alfred (848-930) and his great work as a restorer of learning in England and translator of Latin authors into Old English: the continuation of his work by St. Dunstan (c. 924-988), abbot of Glastonbury (945), bishop of Worcester (958), and archbishop of Canterbury (961), by Ethelwald (c. 908-984), abbot of Abington and bishop of Winchester (963), and by Aelfric (died c. 1030), abbot of Eynsham (1005)

c. German centers and writers: the Ottonian Renaissance

Saxony: the Poeta Saxo and his Vita Karoli Magni; Widukind of Corvey (died after 973) and his Res gestae Saxonicae; Hroswitha of Gandersheim (born c. 935, year of death unknown) and the marked influence of Terence and Vergil on her dramatic and historical works; the apparent neglect of Hroswitha in the Middle Ages

Southern Germany and Lotharingia: the anonymous Gesta Apollonii (written perhaps at Tegernsee): the Waltharius probably composed by Ekkehard I (died 973) and its revision by Ekkehard IV (died 1060) of St. Gall; the Ecbasis Captivi (written at St. Èvre at Toul c. 930); Fromond of Tegernsee (born c. 960) and his carmina figurata; Regino of Prüm (died 915) and his De harmonica institutione, De synodalibus causes et disciplinis ecclesiasticis, and De temporibus dominicae Incarnationis

The region of the Rhine and the Moselle: Heriger of Lobbes (died 1007) and the Classical reminiscences in his Gesta episcoporum Leodiensium; Egbert of Liége (born 972) and his Fecunda ratis; St. Bruno (925-965), brother of Otto I and archbishop of Cologne, lover of books and promoter of learning

    d. French centers and writers: Flodoard of Rheims (894-966) and his Historia ecclesiae Remensis; Gerbert of Aurillac (born between 940-945, died 1003) archbishop of Rheims (991) and pope (Sylvester II, 999-1003), teacher, scholar, bibliophile and humanist, the most learned man of his age; Abbo of Fleury (died 100 magister famosissimus totius Franciae; Abbo of St. Germain and his Bella Parisiac urbis (completed c. 897); the foundation of Cluny (910) and the reform inspired by the work and writings of St. Benedict of Aniane (c. 750-821) in the Carolingian Age; the rapid spread of the reform and its great influence on the religious, political, economic, intellectual, and artistic life of the Middle Ages; Odo of Cluny (died 942) and Odilo of Cluny (944-1049) and their preoccupation with ascetical writing — no really important writer at Cluny, however, before Peter the Venerable (c. 1092-1156

    e. Italian centers and writers: Ratherius of Liége (890-974), bishop of Verona, the best stylist of his age, but a man of unstable temperament and with a propensity for strife — his curious Praeloquia and his Sermons; Atto of Vercelli (885-961) and the glossarial character of his vocabulary, especially in his Polipticum; Liutprand of Cremona (920-972), resembling Ratherius in temperament and character, but one of the most distinguished writers of the tenth century — the stylistic affectation but personal character of his Antapodosis, De rebus gestis Ottonum, and Relatio de legatione Constantinopolitana; Eugenius Vulgarius and Auxilius of Naples and their defense of Pope Formosus (891-896); Vulgarius' carmen figuratum and Pyramida ad Leonem imperatorem, and his familiarity with Seneca's Tragedies; the Chronicon Salernitanum (c. 978); the general dearth, however, of literary productions in central and southern Italy in the tenth century

B.   The Chief Schools and Writers of the Eleventh Century to c. 1075

    General characterization of the period: The majority of writers still closely attached to schools; the continuation of the old Benedictine centers and the rise of new; the growth of important cathedral and capitular schools like those of Eichstätt and Würzburg, and especially Chartres; the decline in fame of Tours, Corbie, Reichenau, and Fulda, and the greater prestige and importance of Monte Cassino, Cluny, Bec, and Fleury-sur-Loire in this period; the more personal character of the writings of this age and the greater flexibility of its Latinity, especially in vocabulary; Latin as the symbol and bond of religious and intellectual unity in an age of weak central authority

    a. The schools and writers of southern Germany: Notker Labeo of St. Gall (c. 950-1022), influential teacher and translator of Latin works into Old High German; Ekkehard IV of St. Gall (c. 980-1060), editor of the Waltharius and author of the poetic miscellany, Liber benedictionum, and of the Casus Sancti Galli with its delightfully told stories; Othlo of St. Emmeran (1010-1070), one of the most attractiv writers of his age, whose works, chiefly theological in character, are very personal and reflect a strong moral and psychological interest and a reaction against Classica education; the anonymous Ruodlieb, a Latin epic full of life and charm based on a German original, written at Tegernsee (c. 1050); Herman the Lame (Hermanus Contractus) of Reichenau (1013-1054), one of the greatest scholars of the Middle Ages, the German Bede – mathematician, writer on musical theory, historian, and poet; Wipo (died c. 1050), a Swabian or Burgundian, historian and poet, author of the Gesta Chuonradi and the Easter sequence, Victimae paschali laudes

      b. The schools and writers of the region of the Rhine, of Lotharingia, and of northern Germany: Burchard of Worms (c. 965-1025) and his important canonical collection, the Decretum or Brocardus, and his Lex familiae; the Sermones of Amarcius (pseudonym), an unidentified monk probably from the Middle Rhine who wrote, in the last years of Henry III (1039-1056), the earliest important mediaeval satirical poem extant; Marianus Scottus (1028-1082 or 1083), monk at Cologne, Fulda, and Mainz, and his curious World Chronicle, one of the last important works by an Irish scholar on the Continent; Thietmar of Merseburg (975-1018), his Chronicle and his method of working; Thangmar of Hildesheim (c. 950-1024) and his Vita Bernwardi; Lampert of Hersfeld (priest in 1058, died 1077) and the distinguished Sallustian style of his Annales Hersfeldenses; Adam of Bremen (head of the school at Bremen 1066, died c. 1076) and his Gesta Hammaburgensis ecclesiae pontificum – in method, content, and style, one of the most significant and influential historical works of the Middle Ages

      c. The schools and writers of southern and northern Italy: Alphanus, monk of Monte Cassino (1055) and archbishop of Salerno (1058-1085), close friend of Desiderius III, abbot of Monte Cassino and, later, pope (Victor III, 1087), student of medicine and collector of a medical library, well versed in Classical literature and metrics, writer of hymns and theological works, translator of Greek (Nemesius of Emesa, De natura hominum); Constantine the African (1015-1087), monk of Monte Cassino, medical writer and translator and adapter of Greek and Arabic treatises on medicine, whose work constituted the foundation of the medical course in mediaeval universities to the end of the fifteenth century; Papias the Lombard's encyclopedic glossary or dictionary, Elementarium doctrinae rudimentum (completed c. 1053), and its great influence (see XI. DICTIONARIES OF MEDIAEVAL LATIN); St. Peter Damiani (born at Ravenna 1007, died at Faenza 1072), zealous reformer and ascetic, theologian and canonist, religious poet, preacher, and letter writer, unusually well versed in Classical and Patristic literature, who through the originality and force of his works, which have a strongly personal character and exhibit a mastery of linguistic expression, exercised great influence not only on his contemporaries but also on later times

      d. French and Norman schools and writers: the continuation of the schools of Tours, Corbie, Ferrières, Saint-Riquier, Auxerre, Rheims, Laon, and Orleans, but without marked distinction in their work in this period; Fulbert of Chartres (c. 960-1029), pupil of Gerbert at Rheims (c. 984), master of the cathedral school of Chartres and then bishop of that city (1007-1029), well versed in the Classics, student of medicine, poet, exegete, hagiographer, preacher and letter writer, but above all, a brilliant teacher and man of high character who attracted students from all France and Lotharingia (Angelram of Saint-Riquier, Olbert of Gembloux, Wazo, Adelman, and Lampert of Liége, Berengarius of Tours) to Chartres and established the fame of that school; Radolphus Glaber (c. 988 - died before 1050), monk of Auxerre, Dijon, etc., and his Historiarum libri quinque; Adhemar of Chabannes (988-1034) monk in St. Cibard's in Angoulême and in St. Martial's at Limoges, poet, scribe, and historian – his Chronicon and Epistola de apostolatu s. Martialis; Fulcoius of Beauvais (fl. c. 1060) and his De nuptiis Christi et Ecclesiae; Lanfranc (1005-1089), born at Pavia, trained in law at Bologna, the first of that great band of Italian scholars to migrate to the north in this period, monk at Bec in Normandy (1042), abbot of Bec (1045-1066), archbishop of Canterbury (1070-1089), influential teacher well versed in law and dialectic (Yves of Chartres, William of Rouen, and especially, the future St. Anselm, among his many pupils and disciples), theologian, exegete, corrector of Biblical and liturgical texts, ecclesiastical reformer

C. The Latin Literature of the Last Quarter of the Eleventh Century and the Beginning of the Renaissance of the Twelfth Century

General characterization: The quickening of intellectual progress occasioned by the Struggle over Investitures and the Berengarian Heresy; the continuation of the school tradition, but greater emphasis on dialectic and greater independence in handling theological questions; the increasing importance of the cathedral schools, the forerunners of the mediaeval universities; the convenience of grouping most writers in this period according to their central interest – the Struggle over Investitures, the Berengarian Heresy, the Crusades; St. Anselm, unique in his great-ness in this age, called the "Father of Scholasticism," but better regarded as the most illustrious representative of the Benedictine school tradition of the eleventh century

a. The polemical literature of the Struggle over Investitures

General characterization: apart from letters and canonical collections, more than 130 polemical works extant; the spread of the controversy throughout Europe and its repercussions in all classes of society; the majority of polemical writers from Germany and Italy, some twenty from France, and a few from England and Spain; the flexibility of eleventh century Latin and the adaptation of this Latin to the needs of political and theological controversy; almost all writers ecclesiastics, the copious collections of papal letters dealing with the controversy (Gregory VII, 1073-1085; Urban II, 1088-1099; Paschal II, 1099-1118; Callixtus II, 1119-1124)

Representative Italian writers: supporters of Gregory, the Cardinals St. Peter Damiani, Humbert of Silva Candida, Odo of Ostia, Hugh of Lyons, Deusdedit, and the monk Alberic of Monte Cassino; supporters of the antipope, Clement III (1080) – the cardinals and bishops Guido of Ferrara, Benzo of Alba, Hugh the Orthodox, the lay jurist Peter Crassus, and the monk Gregory Catina of Farfa

Representative German writers: Popes Leo IX and Stephen IX, Wazo of Liége, Gebhard of Salzburg, Bernard and Bernold of Constance; opponents of the Pope, Hugh Candidus of Lotharingia, Sigebert of Gembloux (died 1112), Walram of Naumburg (extreme in his views); the majority of the monks supporters of the Pope

Representative French writers: <u>Yves of Chartres</u>, moderate and profound, who laid the foundation for a solution of the problem, <u>Geoffrey of Vendôme</u>, <u>Hildebert of Lavardin</u>, and <u>Hugh of Fleury-sur-Loire</u>

Spanish and English writers: <u>Garcia of Toledo</u> and his <u>Tractatus</u>, <u>St. Anselm of Canterbury</u> (see <u>infra</u>), the <u>Tractatus Eboracenses</u> (c. 1104) attributed to <u>Gerard Archbishop of York</u>, and the <u>De Simoniaca haeresi carmen</u> of <u>Gilbert Crispin</u> abbot of Westminster (died 1114)

The numerous anonymous writers in the controversy

The participation of itinerant preachers in the conflict and the appeal to the various classes of the population – the significance of this for literature

Literary types employed in the controversy: histories, chronicles, sermons, Scriptural commentaries, biography, treatises, dialogues, letters, and pamphlets in verse of a satirical and ironic turn; macaronic compositions; the style and tone of this literature of controversy as reflected, e.g., in the <u>Liber ad amicum</u> of <u>Bonizo of Sutri</u> (c. 1045-1090) and the anonymous <u>De ecclesiae unitate</u> (c. 1090)

b. <u>The literature occasioned by the Berengarian Heresy</u>: a controversy confined to the schools and learned ecclesiastical circles; <u>Berengarius of Tours</u> (1010-1088) pupil of <u>Fulbert of Chartres</u>, master at Tours, devoted to dialectic and author of heretical tracts on the Eucharist; the copious literature against him produced by scholars trained at Chartres or Bec, the most important work being Lanfranc's <u>De corpore et sanguine Domini adversum Berengarium Turonensem</u>; the significant role of the Carolingian theologian <u>Paschasius Radbertus</u> as an authority in the controversy; the continuation of the polemic against Berengarius in the twelfth century; the treatise of <u>Alger of Liége</u> (written before 1120), interesting from the viewpoint of both content and style, and that of <u>Gregory of Bergamo</u> (written c. 1130-1140)

c. <u>The literature occasioned by or stimulated by the First Crusade and Norman expansion</u>: the stimulus of great new experiences and vastly widened horizons; the anonymous <u>Gesta Francorum et aliorum Hierosolymitorum</u> (c. 1100) and the biblical simplicity of its style (worked over and embellished by <u>Robert of Rheims</u> [1107] and by <u>Baudry of Bourgueil</u> a little after 1107); <u>Fulcher of Chartres</u> (1059-1127) and his <u>Gesta Francorum Jerusalem expugnantium</u> (1105-1127); <u>Guibert of Nogent</u> (1053-1121), one of the most interesting personalities of this age, an enthusiastic student of Ovid – until turned to Gregory the Great by St. Anselm – author of the following works, among others: <u>Gesta Dei per Francos</u> (1108-1121), <u>De vita sua, sive monodiarum libri tres</u>, <u>De incarnatione contra Judaeos</u>, and <u>De pignoribus sanctorum</u> – surprisingly modern in its critical attitude and observations; the <u>Gesta Normannorum ducum</u> of <u>William Calculus of Jumièges</u>, written in 1070 and appearing in four subsequent editions (two before 1096-1097; a third, much augmented, by <u>Ordericus Vitalis</u> c. 1130, and a fourth, by <u>Robert of Mont-St. Michel</u> c. 1150); the panegyrical <u>Gesta Guillelmi ducis</u> of <u>William of Poitiers</u> (died 1101); the attractive epic, <u>Historicum poema</u> (completed in 1111), of <u>William of Apulia</u> and its utilization of the lost Latin original of the <u>Historia Normannorum</u> of <u>Amatus of Monte Cassino</u>, a contemporary of Robert Guiscard

Universal chronicles and related works: the Chronographia (completed 1111), and, especially, the De viris illustribus (1111-1112) of Sigebert of Gembloux (c.1030-1112), a very important work and the first of its kind since St. Jerome and his Spanish successors of the seventh century; the Chronicon (to 1102) of Hugh of Flavigny (c.1065-died after 1111); Hugh of Fleury-sur-Loire (died c. 1118), author of the famous treatise De regia potestate et sacerdotali dignitate (c.1102), and the historical works, Historia ecclesiastica (1108, and in a much revised form, 1110), a kind of universal history without independent value, and Modernorum regum Francorum liber (1114), which is still useful

The rise in the eleventh century of a copious religious literature assigned either by mistake – or deliberately by its anonymous authors – to St. Augustine: the De vera et falsa paenitentia ad Christi devotam, the De visitatione infirmorum, and similar works, and, especially, series of Meditationes and Preces; the assignment of similar works in the twelfth and thirteenth centuries to St. Augustine, St. Anselm, St. Bernard, St. Bonaventure, etc.

d. Contemporaries of St. Anselm – Desiderius, Leo, and Alberic of Monte Cassino, and Bruno of Segni: Desiderius of Monte Cassino (1058-1086), who became Pope Victor III (1087), champion of the papacy and "fourth founder" of his abbey, greatly enriching its library and promoting the copying of ancient authors; Leo of Monte Cassino, the future Cardinal of Ostia (1101-1115), the great historian of his abbey (his work continued to 1138 by Peter of Monte Cassino); Alberic of Monte Cassino (died c. 1105-1108), hagiographer, master of grammar, and theological polemist whose works, with the possible exception of the Liber dictaminum, are largely lost; Bruno of Segni (c.1045-1049 - 1123), polemist, theologian, hagiographer, exegete – perhaps the best in the Middle Ages, liturgist, letter writer, and the master of an excellent Latin style – his vehement Sermo de Simoniacis (before 1109)

Bernold of Constance, Manegold of Lautenbach, Yves of Chartres, Geoffrey of Vendôme: Bernold of St. Blaise or of Constance (c.1054-1100), polemist, historian, liturgist, and canonist, possessor of a good Latin style, author of the important canonical work, De statutis ecclesiae sobrie legendis, of a Chronicle – of which we have the autograph with all its precious indications of his method of composition, and a valuable liturgical work, Micrologus or De divinis officiis; Manegold of Lautenbach (c. 1030 - died before 1109-1112), author of a number of works on the arts of the trivium and violent polemist in the Investiture Controversy; Yves of Chartres (c.1040-1117), preacher, letter writer, and the greatest canonist of the Middle Ages before Gratian, familiar with the Theodosian and Justinian legislation, as well as with the Fathers and Classical writers, a man of unusually sound judgment and moderation in an age of violent controversy, author of the voluminous Collectio trium partium, Decretum, and Panormia, which had a great influence in the history and literature of canon law; Geoffrey of Vendôme (c.1070, abbot of Vendôme, 1093, died 1132), a publicist of extreme views, author especially of a large collection of letters dealing mainly with the Investiture Controversy

Aimeric of Angoulême and Conrad of Hirschau: the Ars lectoria (written in 1086) of Aimeric of Angoulême, self-styled metricus, and its importance for its numerous citations from ancient pagan and Christian authors, but, especially, for its detailed classification of these authors, thus reflecting mediaeval literary tastes and interests; the somewhat related and equally important Dialogus super auctores of Conrad of Hirschau (born c. 1070)

Baudry of Bourgueil, Marbod of Rennes, Hildebert of Lavardin, and Odo of Cambrai: Baudry (c. 1046-1130), abbot of Bourgueil (1089) and archbishop of Dol (1107), once known chiefly as the author of the Historia hierosolymitana, but now as a man of letters deeply devoted to ancient literature and especially fond of Ovid, a prolific and graceful writer of occasional verse, in constant literary communication with a wide circle of writers, "a mature product of the eleventh century cathedral schools" (Raby); Marbod of Rennes (1035-1123), master of the cathedral school at Angers and then bishop of Rennes (1095), like Baudry, devoted to Classical as well as to Christian literature, a facile writer of metrical and accentual verse rather than a true poet although enjoying a high literary reputation in the Middle Ages, essentially a didactic writer in his maturer years and one who was especially interested in the symbolism he believed to be hidden in nature, author, among other works, of the Passio S. Laurentii, De ornamentis verborum (based on the Ad Herennium), Liber lapidum or Lapidarius (of great influence), Carmina varia (occasional poems of all sorts and in various meters), Liber decem capitulorum (no. 3, De meretrice, no. 4, De matrona); Hildebert of Lavardin (c. 1056-1133), master of the cathedral school of Le Mans, and later bishop of that see (1096), archbishop of Tours (1125), zealous and active churchman, and at the same time a distinguished man of letters, filled with an intense love of Rome and Antiquity, a forerunner of the Christian humanists of the Italian Renaissance; his prose works written in an excellent Latin style and his numerous poems exhibiting not only a mastery of metrical and accentual verse technique, but also the feeling and expression of a truly gifted poet; Odo of Cambrai (died 1113), master at Toul and at Tournai, liturgist, theologian, and polemist

e. St. Anselm of Canterbury, Doctor of the Church

Born at Aosta in North Italy 1033; a monk at Bec in Normandy under Lanfranc 1060; prior of Bec 1063, and abbot 1078; archbishop of Canterbury 1093, died 1109; unique in his greatness in this age, the glory of the Benedictine schools, the most illustrious representative of the school tradition of the ninth, tenth, and eleventh centuries but at the same time the harbinger of a new epoch, the greatest and most original thinker between St. Augustine and St. Thomas Aquinas; the master of a distinguished and attractive Latin prose style; an outstanding administrator and courageous defender of the rights of the Church and of the oppressed; a great saint possessing exceptional personal charm and sweetness of character ("All good men who have known me have loved me, and they have loved me the more the better they have known me," Anselm, Epist. 3. 7); author, among other works, of De libertate arbitrii, De grammatico, Monologion, Proslogion, De veritate (all written at Bec), the De fide Trinitatis or De Incarnatione Verbi, Cur Deus homo, De processione Spiritus Sancti contra Graecos, De concordia (written after 1093), and a voluminous correspondence (447 letters)

D. A Survey of the Mediaeval Latin Literature of the Tenth and Eleventh Centuries According to Types

a. Theology, dialectic, the trivium and quadrivium, law

Theology and dialectic: the slight production of theological works from the end of the Carolingian Age to c. 1050; the great impetus given to theological discussion and literature by the Struggle over Investitures and the Berengarian Controversy; the growth of the study and use of dialectic; the study of Boethius and pseudo-Boethius by Gerbert of Rheims and Abbo of Fleury; the new impulse given by the problem of universals; the entrance of dialectic into all domains of literature from the end of the eleventh century and the importance of this fact; the champions and opponents of dialectic; the polemists in the Struggle over Investitures chiefly adherents of the argument from authority (St. Cyprian and St. Augustine) at least to the end of the eleventh century; the copious theological literature in the field of spirituality ascribed erroneously or by design to St. Augustine

The trivium and quadrivium: the great progress made in the studies of the trivium (grammar, rhetoric, and dialectic) in the eleventh century based in large part on the improved social and economic conditions, the renewal and growth of schools, and the development of urban life; the less spectacular development of the studies of the quadrivium (arithmetic, geometry, astronomy, and music), but the multiplication of treatises and manuals -- the work of Gerbert of Rheims, Fulbert of Chartres, Abbo of Fleury, Herman the Lame, and anonymi; the use of Islamic sources as early as the late tenth century, and not from the end of the eleventh, as was formerly thought; the special interest in music and its importance

Law: law regarded as an extension of rhetoric, and hence as part of the trivium, to the time of Irnerius of Bologna (c. 1050-c. 1130); the discovery of or reawakened interest in the Digests of Justinian in the eleventh century and the rise of a science of law in Italy, particularly at Bologna; the great influence of the study of Roman law on the development of canon law; the special impetus given to legal studies by the Struggle over Investitures; the great canonical collections of the eleventh century and the steady improvement in and elaboration of method -- Burchard of Worms, Fulbert of Chartres, Bernold of Constance, Anselm of Lucca, Deusdedit, Bonizo of Sutri, Yves of Chartres; the elaborate method of interpretation developed by Irnerius of Bologna and its great influence -- explanatory glosses, critical notes, conciliation of "antimonies, " maxims ("brocards"), juridical problems and their solution

b. History and hagiography: the few universal histories in this period almost all written in Germany or Lotharingia -- the Chronographia of Sigebert of Gembloux the most important work; recourse to historical arguments in the Struggle over Investitures and the development of a somewhat more critical historical sense; histories of abbeys, bishoprics, etc., and biographies of great bishops and abbots; the few biographies of laymen, such as Asser's Life of Alfred and Wipo's Life of Conrad II; the annales of the period -- Lampert of Hersfeld the most distinguished writer in this field; the tenth century in particular an age of "typical" hagiography, historical facts being sacrificed in the interests of edification, literary conventions, and local glorification; the composition of legendaries and collections of saints' lives in the order of the calendar and martyrology, frequently emphasizing the saints of a given region or center; Notker Balbulus and the end of the great age of the historical martyrologies; the reworking of earlier vitae in accordance with the hagiographical principles and conventions of the tenth and eleventh centuries; falsifications and apocrypha in hagiography and their purposes; the Latin style employed in saints' lives and its backgrounds; the genuine historical value of certain vitae as biographies -- Ruotger's St. Bruno of Cologne, Gerhard of Augsburg's St. Ulric of Augsburg (his predecessor, died 973), Aelfric of Eynsham's St. Ethelwold of Winchester (died 984, work written 1006), the anonymous Life of Thierry of St. Hubert (died 1087), and Eadmer's (died 1134) St. Anselm of Canterbury, Southern, R. W., St. Anselm and His Biographer (Cambridge [Engl.] 1963)

c. The influence of the Classics on the style of prose and poetry: the influence of Suetonius, and especially of Sallust, on the historians, hagiographers, and other prose writers; Caesar less known and far less used than Sallust; Livy little known or little employed before the fourteenth century; the knowledge and use of Tacitus confined largely to Germany -- Fulda, Corvey, Hersfeld; Cicero known and used, but not as influential as might be expected -- especially studied in the post-Carolingian Age by Gerbert of Rheims and by men like Conrad of Hirschau and Lampert of Hersfeld; the universal influence of Vergil, Horace, and Ovid -- the aetas Vergiliana (eighth and ninth centuries), the aetas Horatiana (tenth and eleventh centuries), the aetas Ovidiana (twelfth and thirteenth centuries); the great popularity of Lucan, Terence, Juvenal, and Persius, and the Christian poets Prudentius and Sedulius; the use of Seneca the Tragedian confined almost entirely to Italy before the twelfth century

d. Characteristic features of Mediaeval Latin prose style and their development in this period: riming prose, the cursus, the ars dictaminis. See XIII. MEDIAEVAL RHETORIC AND POETIC

e. Poetry and versification -- the great development of accentual poetry in form and content: the temporary decline in poetic composition before the middle of the tenth century; the rapid development, especially, of accentual verse from the middle of the tenth century and its full flowering in the eleventh and twelfth centuries; the abbeys and episcopal sees more important in fostering poetry in the tenth and eleventh centuries than the imperial court; the continued wide use of verse, usually metrical hexameters or pentameters, in works on grammar, medicine, and theology, in letters, in lives of saints, etc.; the predominance of accentual verse in the lyrical poetry of this period and the greater personal character and higher poetic worth of this poetry as compared with that of the Carolingians; the development of irony and parody and their reflection of individuality; the great hymns of this period -- the Ave Maris stella, Alma Redemptoris mater, Salve Regina misericordiae, and perhaps the Ave Regina caelorum and the Regina coali; the earlier accentual verse forms based on adaptations of Classical metrical verse

forms, e.g., O Roma nobilis; the development of the sequence and of new accentual
verse forms unfettered by Classical models or rules; the important role of music
in this development; the Cambridge Songs; the development of the trope and the beginnings of liturgical drama; the intimate relations between accentual Latin poetry
and vernacular poetry. For verse technique in detail, see XIII. MEDIAEVAL
RHETORIC AND POETIC.

N.B.: There is an excellent summary of the characteristic literary features and
achievements of the period from the close of the Carolingian Age to the
death of St. Anselm in De Ghellinck, Littérature latine au moyen âge
2: 185-190.

N.B.: On the knowledge of Greek and Arabic, etc., in the tenth and eleventh
centuries, see VIII and IX, infra. On Latin lexicography and Latin grammar in this period, see XI and XII, infra. On the vernacular languages
and literatures in this period, see X, infra.

Bibliography on VII 2. From the End of the Carolingian Renaissance to the
Beginning of the Renaissance of the Twelfth Century

General background (see also the Bibliography on VII supra): C. Dawson, The
Making of Europe 234 to the end; CMH 3 and 5; Shorter Cambridge Mediaeval History 1: 379-506, and 507ff.; I. Hashagen, Europa im Mittelalter (Munich 1951) 111-
202 and 203ff.; A. Fliche, L'Europe occidentale de 888 à 1125 (Paris 1930; Glotz,
Histoire générale: Histoire du Moyen Âge 2); L. Halphen, Les Barbares. Des
grandes invasions aux conquêtes turques du XIe siècle (2nd ed. Paris 1930; Halphen-
Sagnac, Peuples et Civilisations 5); id., L'Essor de l'Europe (XIe - XIIIe siècles)
(2nd ed. Paris 1945; same series 6); E. Amann and A. Dumas, L'Église au pouvoir
des laïques (888-1057) (Paris 1940; Fliche-Martin, Historie générale de l'Église 7);
A. Fliche, Réforme grégorienne et la reconquête chrétienne (1057-1125) (Paris
1944; same series 8); G. Schnürer, Kirche und Kultur im Mittelalter 2 (2nd ed.
1929) 119-284; F. L. Ganshof, Qu'est-ce la féodalité? (Brussels 1957); M. Bloch,
Feudal Society (English trans. by L. A. Manyon, Chicago 1961); E. H. Kantorowicz,
The King's Two Bodies: A Study in Mediaeval Political Theology (Princeton 1957);
M. Pacaut, La théocratie: L'Église et le pouvoir au moyen âge (Paris 1957); Dom
D. Knowles, The Monastic Order in England (2nd ed. revised Cambridge 1963);
G. de Valous, "Cluny (Abbaye et Ordre de)", DHGE 13 (1953) 35-174, especially,
35-39, 162-174 (valuable systematic bibliography)

Histories of Latin literature, philosophy, theology, and canon law: Wright and
Sinclair, History of Later Latin Literature 167-215 (very brief); De Ghellinck,
Littérature latine au moyen âge 2 (excellent); A. Baumgartner, Die lateinische und
griechische Literatur der christlichen Völker 306-378 (still valuable); M. Manitius,
Geschichte der lateinischen Literatur des Mittelalters 1-3 (indispensable for ref-
erence. It is an encyclopaedic work, while De Ghellinck furnishes a synthesis.);
Raby, Christian Latin Poetry 202-298; id., Secular Latin Poetry 1: 252-408; A.
Viscardi, Le origini (2nd ed. revised Milan 1950; Storia letteraria d'Italia 1) 44-127

and 297-354; A. D. von den Brincken, Studien zur lateinischen Weltchronistik bis in das Zeitalter Ottos von Freising (Düsseldorf 1957); G. A. Bezzola, Das ottonische Kaisertum in der französchischen Geschichtsschreibung des 10. und beginnenden 11. Jahrunderts (Köln 1956); De Wulf, History of Mediaeval Philosophy. Engl. trans. 1: 136-170; Gilson, La philosophie au moyen âge 222-258; id., History of Christian Philosophy in the Middle Ages 128-139 and 613-619; Cayré, Précis de Patrologie 2: 381-404; Ueberweg-Geyer, Geschichte der patristischen und scholastischen Philosophie 141-203; Grabmann, Geschichte der scholastischen Methode 1: 215-339; id., Geschichte der katholischen Theologie seit dem Ausgang der Väterzeit 28ff.; De Ghellinck, Le mouvement théologique du XIIe siècle (2nd ed. revised 1948) 37-112 (excellent on development of schools and on canon law as well as on philosophy and theology); H. D. Hazeltine, "Roman and Canon Law in the Middle Ages," CMH 5. 704ff.; Fournier-Le Bras, Histoire des collections canoniques en Occident 1. 20 (to end), and 2. 1-114

Schools, scriptoria, libraries, learning in general (in addition to works listed supra): Bolgar, The Classical Heritage and Its Beneficiaries 127-158; M. Deansley, "Medieval Schools to c. 1300," CMH 5: 765-779, especially 776-779; Lesne, Les écoles de la fin du VIIIe siècle à la fin du XIIe; Sandys, A History of Classical Scholarship 1: 502-523; Hall, Companion to Classical Texts 70-93; R. M. Martin, "Arts libéraux (sept)," DHGE 4 827-843, especially 831-837; J. Koch, ed., Artes Liberales. Von der antiken Bildung zur Wissenschaft des Mittelalters (Leiden and Köln 1959); A. Viscardi, Le origini (2nd ed. Milan 1950; Storia letteraria d'Italia 1) 355-461; J. Leclercq, O.S.B., "L'humanisme bénédictin du VIIIe au XIIe siècle," Studia Anselmiana 20 (1948) 1-20; id., L'amour des lettres et le désir de Dieu. Initiation aux auteurs monastiques du moyen âge (Paris 1957; Engl. trans. New York 1961); J. R. Williams, "The Cathedral School of Rheims in the Eleventh Century," Speculum 29 (1954) 661-667; Thompson, The Mediaeval Library 129ff.; K. Christ and A. Kern, "Das Mittelalter," in Milkau-Leyh, Handbuch der Bibliothekswissenschaft 3 (revised ed. 1955) 245-498; Lesne, Les Livres. Scriptoria et Bibliothèques du VIIIe à la fin du XIe siècle; R. S. Lopez, "Still Another Renaissance?," American Historical Review 57 (1951) 1-21 (on the tenth century); H. Naumann, Karolingische und ottonische Renaissance (Frankfurt 1927); C. Foligno, Latin Thought in the Middle Ages (Oxford 1929) 87-113; E. R. Curtius, European Literature and the Latin Middle Ages (New York 1953 passim. The rich and varied content of this important work can be easily controlled through the Index.); Taylor, The Mediaeval Mind 1: 239-407; Artz, The Mind of the Middle Ages 223ff.; Thorndike, History of Magic and Experimental Science 1: 672-682; Sarton, Introduction to the History of Science 1: 582-783

On the text of the Bible and on Biblical interpretation in this period, see also the references given to Robert-Tricot, Berger, De Lubac, Glunz, McNally, Smalley, etc., in the Bibliography on V C. The Christian Element.

N.B.: On the history of the text and influence of the Rule of St. Benedict in this period, see the references given supra under General background and in the Bibliography on VI A.

Hagiography and liturgy: See the references given in the Bibliography on VI D and F, supra. See also: L. Zöpf, Das Heiligenleben im zehnten Jahrhundert (Leipzig 1908); Aigrain, L'hagiographie, Part 1, ch. III, "Les martyrologies historiques," 53-68, and Part 3, "Histoire de l'hagiographie," especially 305ff.; Eisenhofer, Handbuch der katholischen Liturgik 1: 92-96; H. Leclercq, "Martyrologie," DACL 10.2 (1932) 2523-2619; id., "Reliques et Reliquaires," ibid. 14.2: (1948) 2294-2359. For texts of the vitae sanctorum of the 9th and 10th centuries, see, especially, MGH, Scriptores XV, Vitae aliaeque historiae minores (1887-1888

Editions of and studies on Mediaeval Latin authors and works of this period: MGH (see also Bibliography on VII. 1 supra.)

Leges: Sect. IV, Constitutiones et acta publica imperatorum et regum: I, Inde ab a. DCCCCXI usque ad a. MCXCVII, ed. L. Weiland (1893), Glossarium 731-735

Diplomata regum et imperatorum Germaniae: I, Conradi I Heinrici I et Ottonis I diplomata, ed. Th. Sickel (1879-1884), Wort-und Sachregister 721-736; II, Ottonis II et Ottonis III diplomata, ed. id. (1888-1893), Wort-und Sachregister 980-990; III, Heinrici II et Arduini diplomata, edd. H. Bresslau and H. Bloch (1888-1893), Wort-und Sachregister 834-849; IV, Conradi II diplomata, mit Nachträgen zu den Urkunden Heinrichs II, edd. H. Wibel, A. Hessel, H. Bresslau (1909), Wort-und Sachregister 532-551; V, Heinrici III diplomata, edd. H. Bresslau and P. Kehr (1926-1931), with Wort-und Sachregister; VIII, Lotharii III diplomata nec non et Richenzae imperatricis placita, edd. E. Von Ottenthal and H. Hirsch (1927), Wort-und Sachregister 298-312

Libelli de lite imperatorum et pontificum saeculis XI et XII conscripti: I (1891), Index nominum et rerum memorabilium 633-654, and Index auctoritatum 655-666; II (1892), Index nom. et rer. mem. 704-730, and Index auct. 731-743; III (1897), Index nom. et rer. mem. 743-764, and Index auct. 765-755.

Epistolae Selectae: II, Gregorii VII registrum, ed. E. Caspar (1923), Sachregister 675-707; III, Die Tegernseer Briefsammlung (Froumund), ed. K. Strecker (1925), Wort-und Sachregister 165-170

Antiquitates: Poetae Latini V. 1, Poetarum Latinorum medii aevi: Die Ottonenzeit, ed. K. Strecker (1937; Index grammaticus in preparation)

N.B.:   Special attention is called to the accounts on individual writers and to the systematic bibliographies on individual writers furnished by Manitius and Raby.

Notker Balbulus: W. von den Steinen, Notker der Dichter (2 vols. Bern 1948)

Nithard of St. Riquier: E. Müller ed., Nithardi Historiarum libri III (3rd ed. 1907; MGH, SS rer. Germ. in usum schol., with brief notes); H. Prümm, Sprachliche Untersuchungen über Nithard (Diss. Greifswald 1910)

Ruopert of Mettlach: J. A. Juffermans, "La vie de saint Adalbert par Ruopert, moine de Mettlach," ALMA 5 (1930) 52-68

Widukind: K. A. Kehr ed., Widukindi Corbeiensis Rerum gestarum Saxonicarum libri III (4th ed. 1904; MGH, SS rer. Germ. in usum schol., with notes and Index rerum et verbum 151-161)

Chronicon Salernitanum: U. Westerbergh ed., with Studies on Literary and Historical Sources and on Language (Stockholm 1956)

Hroswitha of Gandersheim: P. von Winterfeld ed., Hroswithae Opera (1902: MGH, SS rer. Germ. in usum schol., with notes, and exhaustive indices: Index verborum 251-512; Index grammaticus 513-542; Index metricus 543-588)

The Ecbasis captivi: K. Strecker ed., Ecbasis cuiusdam captivi (1935; MGH, SS rer. Germ. in usum schol., with notes and indices: Autorenverzeichnis 46-51; Prosodie und Metrik, Grammatisches 52-53; Wort-und Sachregister 54-64)

Regino of Prüm: O. N. Dorman, "A Study of the Latinity of the Chronica of Regino of Prüm," ALMA 8 (1933) 173-216

Gerbert of Aurillac (Pope Sylvester II): N. Bubnow ed., Gerberti postea Silvestri papae Opera mathematica (972-1103) (Berlin 1899, with Index rerum et verborum 579-612); M. Uhlirz, Untersuchungen über Inhalt und Datierung der Briefe Gerberts von Aurillac, Papst Sylvester II (Göttingen 1957)

Liutprand of Cremona: J. Becker ed., Liutprandi episc. Cremonensis opera (3rd ed. 1915; MGH, SS rer. Germ. in usum schol., with notes, and Wort-und Sachregister 233-246)

The Ruodlieb: H. Ottinger, "Zum Latein des Ruodlieb," Historische Vierteljahrschrift 25 (1931) 449-535

Wipo of Liége: H. Bresslau ed., Wiponis opera (3rd ed. 1915; MGH, SS rer. Germ. in usum schol., with notes, and Wort-und Sachregister 117-126)

Othlo of St. Emmeran: W. C. Korfmacher ed., Othloni Libellus Proverbiorum (Chicago 1936)

Adam of Bremen: B. Schmeidler ed., Adam Bremensis Gesta Hammalburgensis ecclesiae pontificum (3rd ed. 1917; MGH, SS rer. Germ. in usum schol., with notes, and Wort-und Sachregister 324-353)

St. Peter Damiani: J. A. Endres, Petrus Damiani und die weltliche Wissen-schaft (Münster i. Westf. 1910; Beitr. z. Gesch. der Phil. des Mittelalters VII [1910] No. 3); O. Blum, O.S.F., St. Peter Damian and His Teaching on the Spirit-ual Life (Washington 1947; CUA Studies in Mediaeval History, N. S. 10)

Fulcoius of Beauvais: Sister M. Isaac Jogues Rousseau ed., Fulcoii Belva-censis Utriusque: De Nuptiis Christi et Ecclesiae libri VII (Washington 1959; CUA Studies in Mediaeval and Renaissance Language and Literature 22)

Yves of Chartres: R. Sprandel, Ivo von Chartres und seine Stellung in der Kirchengeschichte (Stuttgart 1962)

The anonymous Gesta Francorum: J. J. Gavigan, O.S.A., The Syntax of the Gesta Francorum (Diss. University of Pennsylvania 1943, and published in the Supplement to Language, Language Dissertations No. 37)

Ruotger, Vita Brunonis archiepiscopi Coloniensis: P. Geyer, "Literarische Entlehnungen in Ruotgers Lebensbeschreibung des Erzbischofs Bruno von Köln," Neues Archiv 48 (1931) 354-383; I. Schmale-Ott ed., Ruotgeri Vita Brunonis archiep. Coloniensis (1951; MGH, SS rer. Germ. N.S., with notes and indices)

Lampert of Hersfeld: O. Holder-Egger ed., Lamperti monachi Hersfeldensis opera (1894; MGH, SS rer. Germ. in usum schol., with notes, and Index locutionum — a list of borrowings from ancient authors)

The Cambridge Songs: K. Strecker, Die Cambridger Lieder (1926; MGH, SS rer. Germ. in usum schol., with a long introduction, good notes, and a Wort-und Sachregister, 124-135)

N.B.:   There are still far too few critical editions of mediaeval Latin texts with adequate notes and indices.

3.   The Renaissance of the Twelfth Century: From the Last Years of St. Anselm (died 1109) to the Beginning of the Teaching Career of Albert the Great (1225-1230)

General characterization: the new political, social, economic, and intellectual conditions of the age; the growth of towns and the rise of the middle class; the in-tellectual supremacy of France and the rise of Paris as its chief center; the school of Chartres and the schools of Tournai, Laon, Poitiers, Tours, Rheims, and Liége; the rise of vernacular literature and the development of Gothic art and architecture; the apogee of the Norman literary contribution and its cosmopolitan character; the flowering of Latin literature in all fields, the intense study and marked imitation of the Classical writers, the golden age of the Mediaeval Latin lyric; Mediaeval Humanism at its zenith in John of Salisbury and Peter of Blois; the translations from the Arabic and Greek and their great importance; the comprehensiveness and intensity of intellectual interest in the twelfth century and its homogeneous and autonomous character; the increasing interest in logic and the decline in the study of the ancient Classics; the spread of the ars dictaminis; the break with the authority of the authors reflected in the Doctrinale (1199) of Alexander of Villa Dei; Early Scholasticism; the rise of the Mediaeval university

Bibliography

N.B.: An excellent comprehensive treatment is easily available in De Ghellinck, L'Essor de la littérature latine au XIIe siecle and, accordingly, there is no need of furnishing a detailed topical survey here. In addition to the copious bibliography given by De Ghellinck, see the pertinent sections in SELECT BIBLIOGRAPHY, in particular: 2, Encyclopedic Works, Political and Cultural History, Law, and Liturgy; 4, Mediaeval Latin Literature, Philosophy, Theology, and Science; 5, Scripture and Exegesis; 6, Byzantine and Islamic Civilization, the Knowledge of Greek in the West, Translations from Greek and Arabic, the Jews; 9, Education, the Classical and Patristic Tradition, Humanism.

4.   The Thirteenth and Fourteenth Centuries: From c. 1225 to the Renaissance

General characterization: political, social, economic, religious, and intellectual conditions in the thirteenth and fourteenth centuries; the papacy at its zenith of influence, its decline, and the rise of the national monarchies; the decline of the Byzantine Empire; Mongol destruction and conquests in Asia; the rise of the Ottoman Turks and their conquests; the last Crusades and their failure; the growing ascendency of Islam and the threat to Europe; the Avignon Exile and the Great Schism; new religious orders; late mediaeval spirituality and mysticism; the Black Death; the thirteenth and early fourteenth century the great age of the mediaeval university and Scholasticism; the new Latin translations of Aristotle from the Greek and the Latin translations of Aristotle's Greek and Arabic commentators; the neglect of the auctores and the preoccupation of the best minds of the period with theology, philosophy, canon and civil law, science, and medicine; the decline of Latin literature from the early thirteenth century apart from the sacred lyric as represented by the hymns of St. Thomas Aquinas and the Franciscan School; the decline of Scholasticism and its causes; the rapid rise of the vernacular literatures and the appearance of literary masterpieces in the vernacular – Dante; the emergence of an educated laity; the revival of the study of the Classics and the recovery of a knowledge of Greek and of Greek literature in the West; the attempt in Italy and elsewhere to produce a new Latin literature on the Classical model and its ultimate failure; Latin confined more and more to use in the Catholic Church and to employment as a vehicle for learned works in theology, philosophy, law, science, and medicine; the triumph of the vernaculars long before the Protestant Revolt as vehicles for literature in the strict sense

Bibliography

For general political and cultural background, see the Cambridge Medieval History and the other works listed in SELECT BIBLIOGRAPHY 2 and 9. For the Latin literature of the thirteenth and fourteenth centuries we do not have as yet comprehensive, detailed works corresponding to Manitius and De Ghellinck. Raby's Christian Latin Poetry carries us to the end of the thirteenth century but no further. Hence, except for in part antiquated or brief treatments like those of Gröber, Baumgartner, Taylor, Wright and Sinclair, and Artz, we must rely on the catalogs of authors, etc., published in ALMA, on monographs dealing with various literary genres, and especially on the chapters devoted to Mediaeval Latin literature in the comprehensive scholarly histories of the vernacular literatures. For such works, see SELECT BIBLIOGRAPHY: 1, General Introductions, Bibliographical Guides, etc.; 4A, Mediaeval Latin Literature; 7, The Vernacular Languages of the Middle Ages; 11C, Rhetoric and Poetics: Ars dictaminis, Ars versificatoria, Ars praedicandi, Literature in Verse.

For theology (including Scripture and exegesis), philosophy, and science, the situation is much more satisfactory. See the works of Grabmann, Gilson, Ueberweg, Geyer, Haskins, Rashdall-Powicke-Emden, Sarton, Thorndike, Crombie, Histoire de la science (Encyclopédie de la Pléiade), among others, listed in SELECT BIBLIOGRAPHY: 4B, Theology, Philosophy, and Science; 5, Scripture and Exegesis.

VIII. THE KNOWLEDGE OF GREEK IN THE WEST IN LATE ANTIQUITY AND IN THE MIDDLE AGES

Bibliography

See especially the treatments of this subject by Bardy, Marrou, Courcelle, McGuire, Laistner, Bischoff (of primary importance), Siegmund, Haskins, De Ghellinck, Grabmann, Altaner, and Kristeller. See SELECT BIBLIOGRAPHY 6: Byzantine and Islamic Civilization, the Knowledge of Greek in the West, Translations from the Greek and Arabic, the Jews. It should be noted that Haskins has become in part antiquated. A comprehensive monograph by R. Weiss, Greek in Western Europe before the Renaissance, is to appear in the Italian series, Storia e Letteratura, but it is uncertain at this date (June, 1964) when it will be published.

IX. THE KNOWLEDGE OF ORIENTAL LANGUAGES AND LITERATURES IN THE WEST IN THE MIDDLE AGES

Bibliography

See especially the treatments of this subject by Leclercq, Haskins, De Wulf, Ueberweg-Geyer, De Ghellinck, Baron, and Berthier in the works listed in SELECT BIBLIOGRAPHY 6.

X. THE DEVELOPMENT OF THE VERNACULAR LANGUAGES AND LITERATURES IN WESTERN EUROPE IN THE MIDDLE AGES

Bibliography

See the works listed in SELECT BIBLIOGRAPHY: 7A-E, The Vernacular Languages of Western Europe. Under each vernacular the references are ordinarily arranged in this order: bibliography, history of the language, historical grammar, dictionaries, history of literature. For a recent comprehensive, though very brief, survey of Mediaeval vernacular literature, see Artz, Mind of the Middle Ages 320-383 (with valuable bibliography 530-539). See also the small but important work of H. J. Chaytor, From Script to Print. An Introduction to Medieval Vernacular Literature (Cambridge [England] 1945; reprinted 1951).

XI. DICTIONARIES OF MEDIAEVAL LATIN

Bibliography

On dictionaries of Classical and Late Latin, as well as of Mediaeval Latin, see M. R. P. McGuire, Introduction to Classical Scholarship (Washington 1961) 62-72. See also: SELECT BIBLIOGRAPHY 11 B, Glossaries, Dictionaries, Indices, etc.; Strecker-Palmer, 38-46.

XII. THE LATIN GRAMMAR OF THE MIDDLE AGES

Bibliography

On 1, Mediaeval Theories and Textbooks, on 2, The Rise of the Modern Scientific Study of Late and Mediaeval Latin since the Last Quarter of the 19th Century, and on 3, The Present Status of Research in This Field, see especially the works of Robins, Traube (Einleitung 98-103), Baebler, Thurot (still basic), Grabmann, and Roos, listed in SELECT BIBLIOGRAPHY 11 A (near the end), Strecker-Palmer 20-38, SELECT BIBLIOGRAPHY 11 A (from the beginning on), and, especially, the pertinent sections under V, VI, and VII in this SYLLABUS and the copious bibliography following each section.

On 4, Pronunciation and Orthography of Mediaeval Latin, on 5, Declension and Conjugation, on 6, Formation and Signification of Words – Importance of Semantic Change, and on 7, New Formations to Meet Scientific Requirements, see Strecker-Palmer 46-62, and in particular Sturtevant, Blatt ("Sprachwandel..."), Brittain, and the other articles or studies by L. R. Palmer, Battisti, Rohlfs, Jellinek, Beaulieux, Hubert, and Chenu listed in SELECT BIBLIOGRAPHY 11 A. An essay by the writer, "The Pronunciation of Latin: Its History and Practical Problems," is printed in M. R. P. McGuire, ed., Teaching Latin in the Modern World (Washington 1960) 68-83 (with bibliography).

On 8, Characteristic Syntactical Usages, see the pertinent works listed under V, VI, and VII in this SYLLABUS, Strecker-Palmer 63-68, and, especially, the books of the following scholars listed in SELECT BIBLIOGRAPHY 11A: L. R. Palmer, Ernout-Thomas, Leumann-Hofmann, Blaise (Manuel), Löfstedt, Norberg, Skahill, Blatt ("Sprachwandel..."), Garvin, Uddholm, and Most.

N.B.: It is absolutely necessary to have a good knowledge of Late Latin syntax, as almost all the so-called characteristic syntactical usages found in Mediaeval Latin proper already occur occasionally or even frequently in Late Latin.

XIII. MEDIAEVAL RHETORIC AND POETIC

Bibliography

On 1, The Inheritance from Antiquity, and 2, Mediaeval Treatises and Basic Ideas, see especially: Baldwin, Mediaeval Rhetoric and Poetic 1-125, Clarke, Rhetoric at Rome 100-164, Raby, Secular Latin Poetry 1: 1-47, and Curtius, European Literature and the Latin Middle Ages (passim). See also the copious pertinent bibliography listed under V, VI, and VII in this SYLLABUS, and the references given in SELECT BIBLIOGRAPHY 11C, Rhetoric and Poetics: Ars dictaminis, Ars versificatoria, Ars praedicandi, Literature in Verse (see also SELECT BIBLIOGRAPHY 4).

On 3, Metrical Verse, Accentual Verse, the Earlier and Later Accentual Verse Forms, the Development of Rime, and the Artes Versificatoriae, see: Strecker-Palmer 71-84, Browne, British Latin Selections A.D. 500-1400 pp. XXXVII-L, Baldwin, Mediaeval Rhetoric and Poetic, Norberg, Introduction à l'étude de la versification latine médiévale (the most comprehensive and authoritative work on Mediaeval Latin versification, with valuable bibliography), Curtius (passim), De Ghellinck, L'Essor... 2: 199-299 (very important), Faral, Les arts poétiques du XIIᵉ et du XIIIᵉ siècle, Raby, Christian Latin Poetry, and Secular Latin Poetry (both furnished with copious bibliographies). For full bibliographical data on these works, and for further bibliography, see SELECT BIBLIOGRAPHY 11C. For Mediaeval aesthetic theory, etc., see Curtius, op. cit., De Bruyne, and the other works listed in SELECT BIBLIOGRAPHY 12.

On 4, Mediaeval Rhetoric, Prose Style, Prose Rime, Cursus, and Ars Dictaminis, see: Baldwin, Mediaeval Rhetoric and Poetic, Curtius, op. cit., especially "4. Rhetoric", and "8. Poetry and Rhetoric", Browne, British Latin... XXXIV-XXXVII, and L-LIX, De Ghellinck, L'Essor... 1. 54-68 (on the ars dictaminis), Mann, Nicolau, Di Capua, Polheim, and the other pertinent works listed in SELECT BIBLIOGRAPHY 11C.

On 5, the Ars Praedicandi, see: Baldwin, op. cit. 228-257, Charland, Artes praedicandi, Caplan's articles and lists, and the other works listed in SELECT BIBLIOGRAPHY 11C (near end).

XIV. THE KNOWLEDGE AND INFLUENCE OF THE ANCIENT PAGAN AND CHRISTIAN AUTHORS IN THE MIDDLE AGES

Bibliography

See especially Curtius, op. cit. (he overemphasizes the ancient influence), and the books or studies by Highet, Bolgar (important), De Ghellinck 1: 64-68, Fontaine, Liebeschütz, Rand, Ullman, Sanford, Kristeller, Seznec, and others listed in SELECT BIBLIOGRAPHY 9. See also the pertinent references in this SYLLABUS under V 3. For annual bibliography see the section, "Humanisme: histoire et tradition des études classiques," in L'Année Philologique.

XV. THE HISTORY OF MEDIAEVAL LATIN LITERATURE: ITS PRESENT STATUS AND ITS PROBLEMS

Bibliography

On the history of literature and literary studies in the Middle Ages, see: Curtius 446-467, and, especially, P. Lehmann, "Literaturgeschichte im Mittelalter," in his Erforschung des Mittelalters 1 (Leipzig 1941; reprinted Stuttgart 1959) 82-113.

For the standard histories of Late Latin – Christian and profane – and Mediaeval Latin literature, see SELECT BIBLIOGRAPHY 4A and 11C, and Strecker-Palmer 90-116. These references also include special works on historiography, satire, drama, etc.

For the standard histories of the vernacular literatures, which often include special chapters on the Mediaeval Latin literature of the respective peoples, see SELECT BIBLIOGRAPHY 7A-E, and Strecker-Palmer 96-100. Let it suffice to refer, e. g., to the sections on Mediaeval Latin writers and their works in Baugh et al., A Literary History of England, and to K. Hauck's section, "Mittellateinische Literatur," in W. Stammler, ed., Deutsche Philologie im Aufriss 2: 1841-1904.

For translations from Mediaeval Latin and vernacular literature, see Strecker-Palmer 117-118, but, especially, C. Farrar and A. Evans, Bibliography of English Translations from Medieval Sources (New York 1946).

For collections and editions of texts and related works, see SELECT BIBLIOGRAPHY 3, and Strecker-Palmer 105-116.

XVI. THE EDITING OF MEDIAEVAL LATIN TEXTS

Bibliography

See, especially, the articles or books, by Thomson, Bieler, Dearing, Chaytor, Vinaver, and Delatte-Severyns, listed in SELECT BIBLIOGRAPHY 10 E.

SELECT BIBLIOGRAPHY

1. General Introductions, Bibliographical Guides, etc.

Traube, L., Einleitung in die lateinische Philologie des Mittelalters. Edited by P. Lehmann (Munich 1911; Vorlesungen und Abhandlungen 2)

Lehmann, P., Vom Mittelalter und von der lateinischen Philologie des Mittelalters (Munich 1914; Traube-Lehmann, Quellen und Untersuchungen zur lateinischen Philologie des Mittelalters, 5. 1 [Munich 1914] 1-25); id., Aufgaben und Anregungen der lateinischen Philologie des Mittelalters (Sitzungsber. d. Kgl. Bayer. Ak. d. Wiss. Philos.-philol. und hist. Kl. 1918, 8. Abh.; reprinted with revisions in P. Lehmann, Erforschung des Mittelalters 1 [Leipzig 1941; reprinted Stuttgart 1959] 1-46); id., "Mittelalter und Kuchenlatein", Historische Zeitschrift 87 (1928) 197-213 (reprinted with revisions in P. Lehmann, Erforschung des Mittelalters 1: 46-62); id., Erforschung des Mittelalters (5 vols. Stuttgart 1959-1962)

Strecker, K., Introduction to Medieval Latin. English translation and revision by R. B. Palmer (Berlin 1957); cited as Strecker-Palmer

Meyer, O., and R. Klauser, Clavis mediaevalis (Wiesbaden 1962)

K. Langosch, Lateinisches Mittelalter. Einleitung in Sprache und Literatur (Darmstadt 1963)

Lind, L. R., Medieval Studies. Their Nature and Possibilities (University of Kansas Publications, Humanistic Studies No. 261, 1941)

Progress of Medieval and Renaissance Studies in the United States and Canada (Boulder [Col.] 1923 ff.)

Pepe, G., Introduzione allo studio del medio evo latino (2nd ed. Naples 1950)

Répertoire des médiévistes européens (Portiers 1960 ff.)

Gordon, G., Medium Aevum and the Middle Age (Oxford 1925; Society for Pure English, Tract XIX)

Falco, G., "Medioevo", Enciclopedia italiana XXII (1934) 740-744 (with good bibliography)

Faral, E., "L'Orientation actuelle des études relatives au latin médiéval", Revue des Études latines 1 (1923) 26-47

Rumpf, P., "L'étude de la latinité médiévale", Archivum Romanicum 9 (1925) 218-391 (also published separately, Geneva 1925)

Franceschini, E., "Limiti e compiti di una nuova disciplina", Annuario della Università Cattolica del Sacro Cuore 17 (1938-1939) 61-81; "Note di filologia latina medievale", Aevum 12 (1938) 140-163

Hellmann, E., "Das Problem der mittellateinischen Philologie", Historische Vierteljahrschrift 29 (1935) 625-680

De Ghellinck, J., S. J., "Aperçu bibliographique", L'Essor de la littérature latine au XIIe siècle, 1 (Louvain 1946) 19-32

Paetow, L., Guide to the Study of Medieval History (new edition New York 1931; reprinted 1962)

Chevalier, U., Répertoire des sources historiques du moyen âge. Biobibliographie (2 vols. 2nd ed. Paris 1905-1907); Topobibliographie (2 vols. ibid. 1894-1903; both works reprinted, New York 1962)

Fabricius, J. A., Bibliotheca Latina mediae et infimae aetatis (6 vols. Hamburg 1734-1746; revised ed. by J. D. Mansi, Padua 1756; reprinted Florence 1858-1859; reprinted, Graz 1962)

Hain, L., Repertorium bibliographicum. . . (4 vols. Stuttgart 1826-1838; Supplements by K. Burger 1891 and W. A. Copinger 1895)

Gesamtkatalog der Wiegendrucke (Leipzig 1925 ff. ; A-Eig – 1964)

Stillwell, M. B., Incunabula in American Libraries (New York 1940; new edition in preparation)

Potthast, A., Bibliotheca historica medii aevi. Wegweiser durch die Geschichtswerke des europäischen Mittelalters bis 1500 (2 vols. 2nd ed. Berlin 1896; reprinted 1954). Repertorium fontium historiae medii aevi primum ab Augusto Potthast digestum, nunc cura collegii historicorum e pluribus nationibus emendatum et auctum. I, Series Collectionum (Rome 1962; in progress). This is an indispensable guide to the contents of all the significant collections of sources of mediaeval history – MGH, Migne, Mansi, Rolls Series, etc. It will be abbreviated in this bibliography thus: Rep. Font. Hist. MA.

Hurter, H., Nomenclator litterarius theologiae Catholicae, theologos exhibens aetate, natione, disciplinis distinctos (3rd ed. 5 vols. Innsbruck 1903-1913; 4th edition by F. Pangerl, Vienna 1926ff.)

Gross, C., The Sources and Literature of English History from the Earliest Times to about 1485 (2nd ed. New York and London 1915; new edition in preparation)

Bateson, F. W., ed., Cambridge Bibliography of English literature I (600-1600) Cambridge [England] 1940; Supplement (1957), with sections on Latin writings in the Anglo-Saxon and Middle English Periods by F. J. E. Raby)

Baxter, J. H., and Others, "An Index of British and Irish Latin Writers A. D. 400-1520", ALMA 7 (1932) 1-115

Lot, F., and Others, "Index scriptorum operumque Latino-Gallicorum medii aevi", ALMA 14 (1939) 113-230

Hélin, M., "Index scriptorum operumque Latino-Belgicorum medii aevi", ALMA 8 (1933) 77-163

Ussani, V., "Index Latinitatis Italicae medii aevi antiquioris", ALMA 6 (1931) 1-96

N. B. : For continuations of such lists, etc., see later volumes of ALMA.

Russell, J. C., Dictionary of Writers of Thirteenth Century England (Special Supplement 3, Bulletin of the Institute of Historical Research, London 1936)

Diaz y Diaz, M. C., Index scriptorum Latinorum medii aevi Hispanorum (Madrid 1959)

Walther, H., ed., Carmina medii aevi posterioris Latina. 1, Initia carminum ac versuum medii aevi posterioris Latinorum. Alphabetisches Verzeichinis der Versanfänge mittellateinischer Dichtungen (Göttingen 1959); 2. 1, Proverbia sententiaeque medii aevi Latina. Lateinische Sprichwörter und Sentenzen des Mittelalters in alphabetischer Anordnung (A-E, 1963).

Kenney, J. F., The Sources for the Early History of Ireland: An Introduction and Guide. I. Ecclesiastical (New York 1929)

Molinier, A., Les sources de l'histoire de France (6 vols. Paris 1901-1906)

Dahlmann-Waitz, Quellenkunde der deutschen Geschichte (9th ed. Leipzig 1932)

Wattenbach, W., Deutschlands Geschichtsquellen im Mittelalter bis zur Mitte des dreizehnten Jahrhunderts (6th ed. 2 vols. Berlin 1893-1894; 1, 7th ed., by E. Dümmler, 1904). Wattenbach-Holtzmann, Deutschlands Geschichtsquellen im Mittelalter: Deutsche Kaiserzeit. 1. 1-4 (3rd ed. Tübingen 1948). Wattenbach-Levison, Deutschlands Geschichtsquellen im Mittelalter: Vorzeit und Karolinger, Hefte 1-3 (Weimar 1952-1957); with a Beiheft, Die Rechtsquellen (ibid. 1953)

Stammler, W., and K. Langosch, edd., Die deutsche Literatur des Mittelalters: Verfasserlexikon (5 vols. Berlin 1933-1935)

Farrar, C. P., and A. P. Evans, Bibliography of English Translations from Mediaeval Sources (New York 1946; Columbia University Records of Civilization)

Williams, H. F., An Index of Mediaeval Studies Published in Festschriften, 1865-1946, with Special Reference to Romanic Material (Berkeley 1946)

Ladner, G. B., "The History of Ideas in the Christian Middle Ages from the Fathers to Dante in American and Canadian Publications of the Years 1940-1942", Traditio 9 (1953) 439-514; id., The Idea of Reform. Its Impact on Christian Thought and Action in the Age of the Fathers (Cambridge [Mass.] 1959)

N.B.: For current bibliography, see Quarterly Check-List of Medievalia, the International Guide to Medieval Studies, the Quarterly Check-List of Renaissance Studies, the L'Année Philologique, and the journals listed in the last section of this BIBLIOGRAPHY.

2. Encyclopaedic Works, Political and Cultural History, Law, and Liturgy

The Catholic Encyclopedia: An International Work of Reference on the Constitution Doctrine, Discipline, and History of the Catholic Church (16 vols. New York 1908-1914; Supplement, 1922. A New Catholic Encyclopedia in 15 vols. will be published in 1966.)

Cross, F. L., ed., The Oxford Dictionary of the Christian Church (London 1957)

Buchberger, M., ed., Lexikon für Theologie und Kirche (10 vols. Freiburg im Br. 1930-1938; new ed. edited by J. Hofer and K. Rahner, 1957 ff.; A-Rol in March 1964)

Fries, H., ed., Handbuch theologischer Grundbegriffe (2 vols. Munich 1962-1963)

Enciclopedia Cattolica (12 vols. Vatican City 1948-1954)

Vacant-Mangenot-Amann, edd., Dictionnaire de théologie catholique (15 vols. Paris 1909-1950; elaborate Tables générales, which include revisions and additions, in course of publication; A-Juv in June 1964)

Cabrol-Leclercq, Dictionnaire d'archéologie chrétienne et de liturgie (15 fols. Paris 1907-1953)

Baudrillart, A., et al., Dictionnaire d'histoire et de géographie ecclésiastiques Paris 1912 ff.; A-Eus in June 1964)

Viller, M., et al., Dictionnaire de spiritualité Ascétique et Mystique (Paris 1932 ff.; A-Fran, in March 1964)

Davis, H. F., et al., A Catholic Dictionary of Theology (London 1962 ff.; Vol. 1 (A-C) 1962)

Klauser, Th., ed., Reallexikon für Antike und Christentum (Stuttgart 1941 ff.; A-Erf in March 1964)

Galling, K., ed., Religion in Geschichte und Gegenwart (3rd ed., 6 vols. Tübingern, 1957-1962)

La Monte, J. L., The World of the Middle Ages. A Reorientation of Medieval History (New York 1949)

Strayer, J. R., and D. C. Münro, The Middle Ages 395-1500 (New York 1959)

Halecki, O., The Millenium of Europe (Notre Dame, Ind., 1963)

Calmette, J., Le monde féodal (Paris 1934; "Clio": Introduction aux études historiques 4; new ed. 1951); id., L'élaboration du monde moderne (3rd ed. 1949)

Ferguson, W. K., Europe in Transition 1300-1520 (Boston 1963)

Heers, J., L'Occident aux XIVe et XVe siècles; Aspects économiques et sociaux (Paris 1963; "Nouvelle Clio", No. 23)

Quirin, H., Einführung in das Studium der mittelalterlichen Geschichte (Braunschweig 1961)

Von Brandt, A., Werkzeug des Historikers (Stuttgart 1958)

Samaran, C., ed., L'Histoire et ses méthodes (Paris 1961)

Bloch, M., Feudal Society (Chicago 1961)

Blair, P. H., Roman Britain and Early England 55 B.C.-A.D. 871 (London 1963)

Deansley, M., The Preconquest Church in England (London and New York 1961)

Godfrey, C. J., The Church in Anglo-Saxon England (Cambridge [England] 1962)

Jacob, E. F., The Fifteenth Century, 1309-1485 (London and New York 1961; Oxford History of England. See also the volumes covering the preceding period in the same series.)

Richardson, H. G., and G. O. Sayles, The Government of Mediaeval England from the Conquest to Magna Carta (Edinburgh 1963)

Settimane di studio del centro italiano di studi sull'alto medioevo (Spoleto 1954ff. A valuable series of studies on various aspects of Early Mediaeval history and culture.)

Delorme, J., Chronologie des civilisations (new and revised ed. 1956)

Palmer, R. R., ed., Atlas of World History (New York 1957)

Shepherd, W. R., Historical Atlas (8th ed. New York 1956)

Stier, H. E., and Others, Westermanns Atlas zur Weltgeschichte: Vorzeit, Altertum, Mittelalter, Neuzeit (Braunschweig 1956)

Bengtson, H., and Others, Grosser Historischer Weltatlas. 1, Vorgeschichte und Altertum (Munich 1953; 3rd ed. revised 1958); 2, Mittelalter (in preparation); 3, Neuzeit (1957; 2nd ed. revised 1962)

Van der Meer, F., Atlas of Western Civilisation (London 1955); id. and C. Mohrmann, Atlas of the Early Christian World (London and New York 1958)

Kimble, G. H. T., Geography in the Middle Ages (London 1938)

Previté-Orton, C. W., The Shorter Cambridge Medieval History (2 vols. London and New York 1952)

The Cambridge Medieval History (8 vols. London and New York 1911-1936)

Glotz, F., ed., Histoire générale: Histoire de moyen âge (4 vols. Paris 1927-1939)

Halphen-Sagnac, edd., Peuples et civilisations: Histoire générale (Vols. 5 [2nd. ed. Paris 1930], 6 [1932], 7 [1931], and 8 [1929] cover the Middle Ages and the Renaissance.)

Stein, E., Histoire du Bas-Empire. Translated and furnished with additional notes by J. R. Palanque. 1, De l'état romain à l'état byzantin (284-476) Brussels 1959); 2, De la disparition de l'empire d'occident à la mort de Justinien (1949)

Vasiliev, A., A History of the Byzantine Empire (Madison 1952)

Ostrogorsky, G., History of the Byzantine State. Translated by J. Hussey (Oxford 1956; also available in an American edition with illustrations and map edited by P. Charanis [New Brunswick, N. J., 1958])

Ganshof, F. L., Le moyen âge. Histoire des relations internationales. 1 (Pari 1953)

Dvornik, F., The Slavs in European History and Civilization (New Brunswick, N. J., 1962)

Runciman, S., A History of the Crusades (3 vols. Cambridge [England] 1951-1954)

Setton, K. M., ed., A History of the Crusades (Philadelphia 1955 ff.; to be completed in 5 vols.)

Bihlmeyer-Tüchle, Kirchengeschichte. 1, Das christliche Altertum (15th ed. Paderborn 1955; English trans. by V. Mills, O. F. M. [Westminster, Md., 1958]); 2, Das Mittelalter (15th ed. 1955; English trans. 1963)

Fliche-Martin, edd., Histoire de l'Église depuis les origines jusqu'à nos jours (Paris 1934 ff. Vols. 1-14 cover Antiquity, the Middle Ages, and the Renaissance.)

Jedin, H., ed., Handbuch der Kirchengeschichte (Freiburg im Br. 1962 ff.). 1, Die Kirche in der antiken und frühbyzantinischen Welt, by K. Baus. 2, Die Kirche im Kraftfeld des früh-und hochmittelalterlichen Abendlandes, by F. Kempf (in preparation)

Rogier, L., and Others, edd., Nouvelle Histoire de l'Église (Paris 1963 ff.). 1, Des Origines à saint Grégoire le grand, by J. Daniélou and H. Marrou

Grotefend, H., Taschenbuch der Zeitrechnung des deutschen Mittelalters und de Neuzeit (6th ed. Hannover 1928)

Lietzmann, H., Zeitrechnung für die Jahre 1-2000 nach Christus (3rd ed. Berli 1956; Sammlung Göschen)

Poole, R. L., Medieval Reckonings of Time (London 1918; SPCK)

Martin, C. T., The Record Interpreter (2nd ed. London 1910)

N.B.: See also the handbooks of diplomatics listed under 10 B below.

De Mas-Latrie, L., Trésor de chronologie, d'histoire et de géographie pour l'étude et l'emploi des documents du moyen âge (Paris 1889)

Grumel, V., La chronologie. Traité d'Études Byzantines 1 (Paris 1958; in the series Bibliothèque Byzantine)

Eubel, C., Hierarchia catholica medii aevi (3 vols. Münster 1898-1910; 2nd ed. 1913-1923; covers the period 1198-1600)

Gams, P. B., Series episcoporum ecclesiae catholicae (Regensburg 1873; Supplement, 1886; reprinted 1957)

Cottineau, L. H., Répertoire topobibliographique des abbayes et prieurés (Macon 1935-1937)

Graesse, G. E., Orbis Latinus oder Verzeichnis der wichtigsten lateinischen Orts-und Ländernamen (3rd ed. by F. Benedict, Berlin 1922; 4th ed. revised and enlarged by H. Plechl in press, March 1964)

Cochrane, C. N., Christianity and Classical Culture. A Study of Thought and Action from Augustus to Augustine (London and New York 1944)

Dawson, C., The Making of Europe (London 1941)

Crump, F. C., and E. F. Jacob, The Legacy of the Middle Ages (Oxford 1926)

Moss, H. St. L. B., The Birth of the Middle Ages 395-814 (Oxford 1935; reprinted 1963)

Southern, R. W., The Making of the Middle Ages (London 1953)

Salin, E., La civilisation mérovingienne d'après les sépultures, les textes et le laboratoire (4 vols. Paris 1950-1959)

Poole, A. L., ed., Medieval England (2 vols. Oxford 1958)

Evans, J., Life in Medieval France (New York 1957)

Hefele-Leclercq, Histoire des conciles (8 vols. Paris 1907-1921)

Ullmann, W., Principles of Government and Politics in the Middle Ages (New York 1961)

Carlyle, R. W., and A. J. Carlyle, A History of Medieval Political Theory in the West (6 vols. Edinburgh and London 1903-1936)

Ziegler, A. K., "Pope Gelasius I and His Teaching on the Relation of Church and State", Catholic Historical Review 27 (1942) 412-437

Kantorowicz, E. H., The King's Two Bodies: A Study in Mediaeval Political Theory (Princeton 1957)

Wilks, M. J., The Problem of Sovereignity in the Later Middle Ages. The Papal Monarchy with Augustinus Triumphus and the Publicists (Cambridge [England] 1963)

Tierney, B., Foundations of the Conciliar Theory. The Contribution of the Medieval Canonists from Gratian to the Great Schism (Cambridge [Eng.] 1955)

Lot, F., La fin du monde antique et le début du moyen âge (Paris 1927; new ed. 1951. There is an English translation of the first ed.); L'art militaire et les armées au moyen âge en Europe et dans le Proche Orient (2 vols. Paris 1946)

Hashagen, J., Europa im Mittelalter. Alte Tatsachen und neue Gesichtspunkte (Munich 1951)

Heer, F., Aufgang Europas. Eine Studie zu den Zusammenhängen zwischen politischer Religiosität, Frömmigkeitsstil und dem Werden Europas im 12. Jahrhundert (Vienna and Zürich 1949)

Altheim, F., and Others, Frühes Mittelalter (Bern 1956; Historia Mundi, ed. F. Valjavec, 5)

Brunner, O., and Others, Hohes und Spätes Mittelalter (ibid. 1958; same series 6)

Schnürer, G., Kirche und Kultur im Mittelalter (3 vols. 2nd ed. Paderborn 1927-1929; English trans. of Vol. 1 by G. J. Undreiner [Paterson, N. J., 1956])

Von den Steinen, W., Der Kosmos des Mittelalters von Karl dem Grossen zu Bernhard von Clairvaux (Bern and Munich 1959)

Grupp, G., and A. Diamand, Kulturgeschichte des Mittelalters (6 vols. 3rd ed. Paderborn 1921-1925)

Coulton, G. G., Five Centuries of Religion (4 vols. Cambridge [England] 1923-1950; to be used with care)

Gougaud, L., Christianity in Celtic Lands: A History of the Churches of the Celts, Their Origin, Their Development, Influence, and Mutual Relations (London 1932)

Bieler, L., Ireland, Harbinger of the Middle Ages (London 1963)

Knowles, Dom D., The Monastic Order in England to 1216 (Cambridge [England] 1940; 2nd ed. revised 1963); id., The Religious Orders in England (3 vols. ibid. 1948-1959; covers from 1216 to the dissolution of the monasteries unde Henry VIII); id. Great Historical Enterprises and Problems of Monastic History (ibid. 1963)

Baynes, N. H., and H. St. L. B. Moss, edd., Byzantium, An Introduction to East Roman Civilization (Oxford 1948; with good bibliography)

Bréhier, L., Le monde byzantin (3 vols. Paris 1946-1950)

Schulz, F. History of Roman Legal Science (Oxford 1946)

Plöchl, W., Geschichte des Kirchenrechts (Vienna 1953 ff.; Vols 1 and 2 [1953-1955] cover the Middle Ages.)

Hazeltine, H. E., "Roman and Canon Law in the Middle Ages, CMH 5 (1929) 697-764

Fournier, P., and G. Le Bras, Histoire des collections canoniques en Occident depuis les Fausses Décrétales jusqu'au Décret de Gratien (2 vols. Paris 1931-1932)

Maassen, F., Geschichte der Quellen und der Literatur des canonischen Rechts im Abendlande (Graz, 1870; reprinted 1956)

Kuttner, S., Repertorium der Kanonistik (1140-1234) (Vatican City 1937; new edition in preparation)

Van Hove, A., Commentarium Lovaniense in CIC. 1.1, Prolegomena (2nd ed. Malines and Rome 1945)

Naz, R., ed. Dictionnaire du droit canonique (Paris 1935 ff.; A-Tit in March 1964)

Eisenhofer, L., Handbuch der katholischen Liturgik (2 vols. Freiburg im Br. 1932-1933; revised edition 1941)

Lechner, J., and L. Eisenhofer, Grundriss der Liturgik des römischen Ritus 6th ed. ibid. 1953)

Jungmann, J. A., S.J., Missarum Sollemnia. Eine genetische Erklärung der römischen Messe (2 vols. Vienna 1948; 2nd ed. 1949; 3rd ed. 1952. There are English and French translations of the 2nd edition.)

Batiffol, P., Histoire du bréviaire romain (Paris 1911. There is an English translation.)

Andrieu, M., Les Ordines Romani du haut moyen âge (4 vols. Louvain 1931-1956)

Leclercq, Dom. H., "Lexique liturgique (Latin)", DACL 9. 1: 14-30

Righetti, M., Storia liturgica (4 vols. Milan 1945-1953; 2nd ed., 1950-1956)

Miller, J. H., C.S.C., Fundamentals of the Liturgy (Notre Dame 1959)

3. Collections of Sources and Related Works

A. Major Collections, etc.

Migne, J. P., Patrologiae Cursus Completus. Series Latina (221 vols. 1844-1864; now being reprinted by Éditions Brepols, Turnhout, Belgium. For the contents of the PL see Rep. Font. Hist. MA 434-454.)

Hamman, A. O.F.M., ed., Patrologiae Latinae Supplementum (Paris 1959 ff.; to be completed in 4 vols.; Parts 1-8, covering Vols. 1-48, published as of March, 1964)

Glorieux, P., "Pour revaloriser Migne. Tables rectificatives", Mélanges de science religieuse 9 (1952), Cahier supplémentaire

Vattasso, M., Initia Patrum (2 vols. Rome 1906-1908; in Studi e Testi)

Corpus Scriptorum Ecclesiasticorum Latinorum (Vienna 1866 ff.; 77 vols. in 1962. For contents, see Rep. Font. Hist. MA 197-201.)

Dekkers, E., Clavis Patrum Latinorum (Steenbrugge and The Hague 1951; new ed. revised and enlarged 1961)

Corpus Christianorum. Series Latina (Brepols, Turnhout [Belgium] 1953 ff.; to comprise 180 vols. and to include authors and works from Tertullian to Bede). Continuatio Mediaevalis (Brepols, 1962 ff. See the prospectus, Corpus Christianorum, published by Brepols in 1963.)

Sources Chrétiennes. Directed by H. de Lubac, S.J., J. Daniélou, S.J., et al., (Paris 1943 ff.; texts and translations; 97 vols. in June 1964)

Monumenta Germaniae historica (500-1500) (Berlin 1826 ff. For a conspectus of its contents, see Rep. Font. Hist. MA 466-479; Quirin, Einführung 110-114.)

Acta Sanctorum (Antwerp 1643 ff. and Paris 1863 ff.; 65 vols. in 1964. For the complicated history of the series, see H. Delehaye, op. cit. infra 166-173.)

Delehaye, H., S.J., L'oeuvre des Bollandistes à travers trois siècles 1615-1915 (2nd ed. with a "Guide bibliographique mis à jour" [Brussels 1958])

Peeters, P., L'Oeuvre des Bollandistes (new ed. Brussels 1951)

Bibliotheca hagiographica Latina antiquae et mediae aetatis (3 vols. Brussels 1898-1911; new edition of the third volume, Supplementum, in preparation)

Rerum Gallicarum et Francicarum Scriptores. Recueil des historiens des Gaules et de la France. Edited by M. Bouquet and Others (24 vols. Paris 1783-1904. For the contents, see Rep. Font. Hist. MA 7-9.)

Rerum Britannicarum medii aevi scriptores. The "Rolls Series" (99 works
in 244 vols. London 1858-1896. For an analysis of the contents, see
Gross, Sources of English History 704-777); Rep. Font. Hist. MA
612-619.)

Rerum Italicarum scriptores ab anno aerae Christianae 500 ad 1500, ed.
L. A. Muratori (25 vols. in 28 Milan 1723-1751; Indices, Turin, 1885;
new edition in progress, 1900 ff. For the contents of the two editions,
see Rep. Font. Hist. MA 509-522.)

Collection de documents inédits sur l'histoire de France (Paris 1835 ff. For
its contents, see Rep. Font. Hist. MA 156-160.)

Collection de textes pour servir à l'étude et à l'enseignement de l'histoire.
1er série: Des origines au XVIIIe siècle (Paris 1886-1929; 51 vols. For
its contents, see Rep. Font. Hist. MA 161-163.)

Les classiques de l'histoire de France au moyen âge. Publiés sous la di-
rection de L. Halphen (Paris 1923 ff. ; 23 vols. in 1964. For contents of
the series, see Rep. Font. Hist. MA 130-131.)

Histoire littéraire de la France (38 vols. 1733-1941; begun by the Maurists
and continued by the Académie des Inscriptions et Belles-Lettres)

Hauréau, B. , Notices et extraits de quelques manuscripts de la Bibliothèque
Nationale (6 vols. Paris 1890-1892); id. , a whole series of important
studies in Notices et extraits des manuscrits de la Bibliothèque national.
Vols. 20-36 (1885-1896)

Recueil des historiens des croisades (Paris 1841-1906. For contents see
Rep. Font. Hist. MA 5-7.)

Colección de documentos inéditos para la historia de España (112 vols.
Madrid 1842-1895)

Florez, E. , and Others, edd. , España Sagrada (56 vols. Madrid 1747-
1956. For its contents, see Rep. Font. Hist. MA 252-255.)

Thesaurus mundi. Bibliotheca scriptorum Latinorum mediae et recentioris
aetatis (Zürich 1950 ff. For contents of the series, see Rep. Font. Hist.
742-743.)

Nelson's Mediaeval Texts, edd. V. H. Galbraith and R. A. B. Mynors
(Oxford 1949 ff. For contents of the series, see Rep. Font. Hist. MA 4

Scriptores Latini Hiberniae, edd. D. A. Binchy, A. Gwynn, L. Bieler
(Dublin 1957 ff.)

Mansi, J. D. , and Others, edd. , Sacrorum Conciliorum nova et amplissin
collectio 31 vols. Florence and Venice 1759-1798; new edition and continuation, Paris 1900 ff. For the contents, see Rep. Font. Hist.
MA 402-404.)

Gamber, K. , Sakramentartypen. Versuch einer Gruppierung der Hand-
schriften und Fragmente bis zur Jahrtausendwende in beratender
Verbindung mit Alban Dold und Prof. Bernard Bischoff (Beuron 1958;
Texte und Arbeiten 49/50)

Sacramentarium Leonianum, ed. M. Feltoe (Cambridge [England] 1896)

The Gelasian Sacramentary. Liber Sacramentorum Romanae ecclesiae, e
H. A. Wilson (Oxford 1894)

Das Sacramentarium Gregorianum nach dem Aachener Urexemplar, ed.
H. Lietzmann (Münster i. W. 1921)

Liber Mozarabicus Sacramentorum, ed. Dom M. Férotin (Paris 1912; in Cabrol-Leclercq, Monumenta Ecclesiae liturgica 6); id., Le Liber Ordinum en usage dans l'église visigothique et mozarabe d'Espagne du cinquième au onzième siècle (Paris 1904; same series 5, with excellent indices, cols. 551-800)

Liber Pontificalis, ed. L. Duchesne (2 vols. Paris 1886-1892; reprinted 1956; Vol. 3, 1958)

Foerster, H., ed., Liber diurnus Romanorum Pontificum (Munich 1958)

Regesta Pontificum Romanorum ad annum 1198, ed. P. Jaffé et al. (2 vols. 2nd ed. Leipzig 1885-1888; reprinted Graz 1956)

Regesta Pontificum Romanorum ab anno post Christum natum 1198 ad annum 1304, ed. A. Potthast (2 vols. Berlin 1874-1875; reprinted 1958)

Regesta Pontificum Romanorum, ed. P. F. Kehr (7 vols. Berlin 1906-1925)

Theodosiani libri XVI, edd. T. Mommsen et P. M. Meyer (2 vols. in 3 Berlin 1905; English translation by C. Pharr et al. (Princeton 1952)

Corpus iuris civilis, edd. P. Krüger et al. 1 (15th ed. Berlin 1928); 2 (9th ed. 1915); 3 (5th ed. 1928)

Corpus iuris canonici, ed. E. Friedberg (2 vols. Leipzig 1879-1881. Pars prior: Decretum Magistri Gratiani)

Monumenta iuris canonici, ed. S. Kuttner et al. (Washington and New Haven. Vol.. 1 in press in March 1963.)

Analecta hymnica medii aevi, edd. C. Blume and G. M. Dreves (55 volumes Leipzig 1886-1911; reprinted 1963. For a conspectus of the contents, see art. "Hymnes" in DACL 6.2:2917-2920; Rep. Font. Hist. MA 29-30.)

Chevalier, U., Repertorium hymnologicum: Catalogue des chants, hymnes, proses, sequences, tropes, en usage dans l'Église latine depuis les origines jusqu'à nos jours (6 vols. Louvain and Brussels 1892-1921; in Subsidia hagiographica)

Dreves, G. M., Repertorium Repertorii. Kritische Wegweiser durch U. Chevaliers Repertorium hymnologicum (Leipzig 1902)

Julian, J., A Dictionary of Hymnology (revised ed. London 1915; reprinted in 2 vols. New York 1957)

Szövérffy, J., Die Annalen der lateinischen Hymnendichtung. 1 (Berlin 1964)

B. Smaller Collections, School Editions, etc.

N.B.: For a more complete list, see Strecker-Palmer, Introduction to Medieval Latin 15-20, and 105-111.

Beeson, C. H., A Primer of Medieval Latin (Chicago 1925)

Harrington, K. P., Mediaeval Latin (Boston 1925; reprinted Chicago 1962)

Browne, R. A., British Latin Selections A.D. 500-1400 (Oxford 1954)

Watenphul, H., Mittellateinisches Lesebuch (Leipzig 1929)

Schuster, M., Spätlatein, Mittellatein, Neulatein (Leipzig 1929)

Schulz, H., Mittellateinisches Lesebuch (Paderborn 1960)

Raby, F. J. E., ed., The Oxford Book of Medieval Verse (Oxford 1959)

Brittain, F., The Medieval and Romance Lyric to A.D. 1300 (2nd ed. Cambridge [England] 1951)

Vecchi, G., Poesia Latina medievale. Introduzione, testi, traduzioni, note, trascrizione musicale (Parma 1952)

Boutémy, A., Recueil de textes historiques latins du moyen âge écrits en Belgique... (Brussels 1942)

Latouche, R., Textes d'histoire médiévale: V^e-XIe siècle (Paris 1951)

Gessler, J., Stromata mediae et infimae aetatis (Brussels 1944)

Geyer, B., and J. Zellinger, edd., Florilegium Patristicum tam veteri quam medii aevi auctores complectens (44 vols. Bonn 1904-1941. For the contents of the series, see Rep. Font. Hist. MA 261-262.)

Heraeus-Morf, Sammlung vulgärlateinischer Texte (6 fascicles, Heidelberg 1908-1922; available in later reprints)

Hilka, A., Sammlung mittellateinischer Texte (10 vols. Heidelberg 1911-1929)

Messenger, R. E., The Medieval Latin Hymn (Washington 1953; with valuable bibliography)

Connelly, J., Hymns of the Roman Liturgy (Westminster, Md., 1957)

Phillimore, J. S., ed., The Hundred Best Latin Hymns (London 1926)

Dreves, G. M., Ein Jahrtausend lateinischer Hymnendichtung (2 vols. Leipzig 1910)

Walpole, A. S., Early Latin Hymns, with Introduction and Notes (Cambridge [England] 1922)

Bulst, W., Hymni Latini antiquissimi LXXV. Psalmi III (Heidelberg 1956)

Britt, M., O.S.B., The Hymns of the Breviary and Missal (New York 1922; revised ed. 1948)

N.B.: On hymns see also Raby, Christian Latin Poetry, and the copious bibliography listed.

Ross, J. B., and M. M. McLaughlin, The Portable Medieval Reader (New York 1949; English translations only)

Jones, C. W., Medieval Literature in Translation (New York 1950)

Jackson, W. T. H., The Literature of the Middle Ages (New York 1960)

N.B.: See also Farrar-Evans, listed near the end of 1 supra.

4. Mediaeval Latin Literature, Philosophy, Theology, Science

N.B.: For Christian literature to the beginnings of the Middle Ages, see, M. R. P. McGuire, Introduction to Classical Scholarship (Washington 1961), Part IV, Sect. VII, "The Early History and Literature of Christianity", 227-249.

A. Mediaeval Latin Literature (chiefly)

Quasten, J., Patrology. 1, The Beginnings of Patristic Literature (Utrecht-Brussels 1950); 2, The Ante-Nicene Literature after Irenaeus (1953); 3, The Golden Age of Greek Patristic Literature (1960); 4 in preparation (March 1964)

Altaner, B., Patrologie. Leben, Schriften und Lehre der Kirchenväter (2nd ed. Freiburg im Br. 1950; new and revised ed. 1958; English translation 1959)

Cayré, F., Précis de Patrologie. Histoire et doctrine des Pères et Docteurs de l'Église (3rd ed. revised 2 vols. Paris 1945; to St. Francis de Sales. There is an English translation.)

De Labriolle, P., Histoire de la littérature latine chrétienne (3rd ed. revised and enlarged by G. Bardy, 2 vols. Paris 1947)

Norden, E., Die lateinische Literatur mit Anhang: Die lateinische Literatur im Uebergang vom Altertum (5th ed. by H. Fuchs, Leipzig 1954)

Schanz-Hosius-Krüger, Geschichte der römischen Literatur. 1 (4th ed. Munich 1927); 2, (4th ed. 1935); 3 (3rd ed. 1922); 4. 1, Die Literatur des vierten Jahrhunderts (2nd ed. 1914); 4. 2, Die Literatur des 5. und 6. Jahrhunderts (1920)

Bardenhewer, O., Geschichte der altkirchlichen Literatur. 1 (2nd ed. Freiburg im Br. 1913); 2 (2nd ed. 1914); 3, Das vierte Jahrhundert (2nd ed. with Supplement 1923); 4, Das fünfte Jahrhundert mit Einschluss der syrischen Literatur des vierten Jahrhunderts (1st and 2nd ed. 1924); 5, Die letzte Periode der altkirchlichen Literatur (1932. The 5 vols. were reprinted in 1963.)

Moricca, U., Storia della letteratura latina cristiana. 2. 1-2, Il IV secolo: L'età d'oro della letteratura ecclesiastica occidentale (Turin 1928); 3. 1-2, La letteratura dei secoli V e VI da Agostino a Gregorio Magno (1932-1934)

Dekkers, E., O.S.B., Clavis Patrum Latinorum (Bruges and The Hague 1951; new ed. revised and enlarged 1961)

Hélin, M., Histoire des lettres latines du moyen âge (Brussels 1943; Collection Lebègue; English trans. by J. C. Snow [New York 1949]. See also the critical review by A. K. Ziegler, Catholic Historical Review (38 [1952-1953] 346-348.)

Wright, F. A., and T. A. Sinclair, A History of Later Latin Literature from the Middle of the Fourth to the End of the Seventeenth Century (London 1931)

Baumgartner, A., S.J., Geschichte der Weltliteratur. 4, Die lateinische und griechische Literatur der christlichen Völker (3rd ed. Freiburg im Br. 1905)

Ebert, A., Allgemeine Geschichte der Literatur des Mittelalters im Abendlande (3 vols. Leipzig 1874-1887; 1 [2nd ed. 1889]; French trans. by J. Aymeric and J. Condamin [3 vols. Paris 1883-1889])

Manitius, M., Geschichte der lateinischen Literatur des Mittelalters. 1, Von Justinian bis zur Mitte des zehnten Jahrhunderts (Munich 1911); 2, Von der Mitte des zehnten Jahrhunderts bis zum Ausbruch des Kampfes zwischen Kirche und Staat (1923); 3, Vom Ausbruch des Kirchenstreites bis zum Ende des zwölften Jahrhunderts (1931; Handbuch der Altertumswissenschaft 9. 2. 1-3)

Gröber, G., Uebersicht über die lateinische Litteratur von der Mitte des 6. Jahrhunderts bis 1350 (new ed. by W. Bulst, with table of contents and Register, Munich 1963)

DeGhellinck, J., S.J., Patristique et moyen âge. Études d'histoire littéraire et doctrinale. 2, Introduction et compléments à l'étude de la patristique (Brussels and Paris 1947; Part 1, "Progrès et tendances des études patristiques depuis quinze siècles"; Part 2, "Diffusion et transmission des écrits patristiques"); 3, Compléments à l'étude de la patristique (1948; various studies); id., Littérature latine au moyen âge (2 vols. Paris 1939); id., L'Essor de la littérature latine au XIIe siècle (2 vols. Brussels and Paris 1946. This work contains an excellent treatment of literary genres: 1, Ch. III, "Spiritualité et prédication", 173-230; 2, Ch. IV, "L'ars dictaminis", 54-68; Ch. V, "Histoire universelle, régionale, monastique", 89-163; "Hagiographie", 164-198; Ch. VI, "Poésie profane et poésie religieuse", 199-299. There is copious bibliography in each chapter or section.)

Curtius, E. R., Europäische Literatur und lateinisches Mittelalter (Bern 1948); English trans. by W. R. Trask (New York 1953 [Bollingen Series 36])

Foligno, C., Latin Thought during the Middle Ages (Oxford 1929)

Taylor, H. O., The Mediaeval Mind (2 vols. New York 1911; 4th ed. 1925)

Artz, F. B., The Mind of the Middle Ages (3rd ed. revised 1958)

Dawson, C., Medieval Essays (New York 1954)

Lagarde, G. de, La naissance de l'esprit laïque au declin du moyen âge (5 vols. revised ed. Paris and Louvain 1956 ff.). 1, Bilan du XIIIe siècle (1956)

Rand, E. K., Founders of the Middle Ages (Cambridge [Mass.] 1928)

Leyser, P., Historia poetarum et poematum medii aevi (Halle 1721)

Raby, F. J. E., A History of Christian Latin Poetry from the Beginnings to the Close of the Middle Ages (Oxford 1927; new and revised ed. 1953); id., A History of Secular Latin Poetry in the Middle Ages (2 vols. ibid. 1930; new and revised ed. 1957. Both works have excellent bibliographies

Kusch, H., Einführung in das lateinische Mittelalter. 1, Dichtung (Berlin 1957)

Laistner, M. L. W., Thought and Letters in Western Europe A. D. 500-900 (New York 1931; new and revised ed. Ithaca 1957); id., The Intellectual Heritage of the Early Middle Ages. Edited by C. G. Starr (Ithaca 1957)

Duckett, E. S., Gateway to the Middle Ages (New York 1938); id., Anglo-Saxon Saints and Scholars (ibid. 1947); id., Alcuin, Friend of Charlemagne: His World and His Work (ibid. 1951)

Levison, W., England and the Continent in the Eighth Century (Oxford 1946)

Waddell, H., The Wandering Scholars (Boston 1927)

Delehaye, H. A., Les passions des martyrs et les genres littéraires (Brussels 1921); id., Les légendes hagiographiques (3rd ed. revised ibid. 1927; English trans. by D. Attwater, New York 1962); id., Cinq leçons sur la méthode hagiographique (Brussels 1934)

Lanzoni, F., Genesi, svolgimento, e tramento delle leggende storiche. Studio critico (Rome 1925; Studi e Testi 43)

Loomis, C. G., White Magic. An Introduction to the Folklore of Christian Legend (Cambridge [Mass.] 1948; Mediaeval Academy of America Publication 52. See also the review by M. R. P. McGuire in Catholic Historical Review 37 [1951-1952] 179-180.)

Thompson, S., Motif Index of Folk Literature (6 vols. Bloomington [Md.] 1932-1936; new ed. revised and enlarged, 1955-1958)

Welter, J. T., L'exemplum dans la littérature religieuse et didactique du moyen âge (Paris 1927)

Owst, G. R., Literature and Pulpit in Medieval England. A Neglected Chapter in the History of English Letters and of the English People (Cambridge [England] 1933)

Frenken, G., Die Exempla des Jacob von Vitry. Ein Beitrag zur Geschichte der Erzählungsliteratur des Mittelalters (Munich 1941; Traube-Lehmann, Quellen und Untersuchungen zur lateinischen Philologie des Mittelalters 5. 1.)

Chambers, E. K., The Medieval Stage (2 vols. Oxford 1903)

Young, K., The Drama of the Mediaeval Church (2 vols. Oxford 1933)

Donovan, R. B., C.B.C., The Liturgical Drama in Medieval Spain (Toronto 1958)

Craig, H., The English Religious Drama of the Middle Ages (Oxford 1955)

Stratman, C. J., Bibliography of Medieval Drama (Berkeley 1954)

Sticca, S., "The Priority of the Montecassino Passion Play", Latomus 20 (1961) 827-839

Dunn, E. C., "Lyrical Form and the Prophetic Principle in the Towneley Plays", Mediaeval Studies 23 (1961) 80-90

Cohen, G., ed., La "comédie" latine en France au XIIe siècle (2 vols. Paris 1931)

Walther, H., Das Streitgedicht in der lateinischen Literatur des Mittelalters (Munich 1920; Traube-Lehmann, Quellen und Untersuchungen 5. 2)

Lehmann, P., Die Parodie im Mittelalter (Munich 1922)

Haskins, C. H., The Renaissance of the Twelfth Century (Cambridge [Mass.] 1927; Ch. VIII, "Historical Writing", 224-277)

Thompson, J. W., History of Historical Writing (2 vols. New York 1942). 1, From the Earliest Times to the End of the Seventeenth Century: Bk. II, "Western Europe in the Middle Ages to the End of the Thirteenth Century", 143-294; Bk. III, "Eastern Europe and the Orient to the End of the Crusades", 295-362; Bk. IV, "The Close of the Middle Ages", 363-472.

Schulz, M., Die Lehre von der historischen Methode bei den Geschichtsschreibern des Mittelalters, VI-XIII. Jahrhundert (Berlin 1909)

Spörl, J., Grundformen der hochmittelalterlichen Geschichtsanschauung. Studien zum Weltbild der Geschichtsschreiber des XII. Jahrhunderts (Munich 1935)

Wolter, H., S.J., Ordericus Vitalis. Ein Beitrag zur Kluniazensischen Geschichtsschreibung (Wiesbaden 1957); id., "Geschichtliche Bildung im Rahmen der Artes liberales", in J. Koch, ed., Artes Liberales. Von der antiken Bildung zur Wissenschaft des Mittelalters (Leiden-Köln 1959) 50-83

Bezzola, G. A., Das ottonische Kaisertum in der französchischen Geschichtschreibung des 10. und beginnenden 11. Jahrhunderts (Köln 1956; Veröffentlichungen des Inst. für österreichische Geschichtsforschung Bd. 18)

Zimmermann, H., Ecclesia als Objekt der Historiographie. Studien zur Kirchengeschichtsschreibung im Mittelalter und in der frühen Neuzeit (Vienna 1960)

Uhlirz, M., Untersuchungen über Inhalt und Datierung der Briefe Gerberts von Aurillac, Papst Sylvesters II (Göttingen 1957)

Von den Brincken, A. D., Studien zur lateinischen Weltchronistik bis in das Zeitalter Ottos von Freising (Düsseldorf 1957)

Misch, G., Geschichte der Autobiographie (3 vols. in 6, Leipzig, Berlin, and Frankfurt 1931-1962)

Singer, S., Sprichwörter des Mittelalters (3 vols. Bern 1944-1947)

Korfmacher, W. C., ed., Othloni Libellus proverbiorum (Chicago 1936)

Arbusow, L., Liturgie und Geschichtsschreibung im Mittelalter. In ihrer Beziehung erläutert an den Schriften Ottos von Freising (Bonn 1951)

Poole, R. L., Chronicles and Annals: A Brief Outline of Their Origin and Growth (Oxford 1926)

Galbraith, V. H., Historical Research in Medieval England (London 1951)

Lehmann, P., "Literaturgeschichte im Mittelalter", in his Erforchung des Mittelalters 1 [Leipzig 1959] 82-113)

Werner, J., Beiträge zur Kunde der lateinischen Literatur des Mittelalters (2nd ed. Aarau 1905)

Bezzola, R. R., Les origines et la formation de la littérature courtoise en Occident (500-1200) (3 vols. Paris 1944-1963)

Paré, G., Le Roman de la Rose et la scolastique courtoise (Paris 1941)

Denomy, A. J., "Courtly Love and Courtliness", Speculum 28 (1953) 44-63

Lewis, C. S., The Allegory of Love. A Study of Mediaeval Tradition (Oxford 1936)

Paetow, J. L., Two Medieval Satires on the University of Paris. La Bataille des VII ars of Henri d'Andeli, and the Morale scolarium of John of Garland. Edited with Renderings into English (Berkeley 1927)

De Valous, G., "La poésie amoureuse en langue latine au moyen âge", Classica et Mediaevalia 13 (1952) 285-345; 14 (1953) 156-204; 15 (1954) 146-197; 16 (1955) 195-266

B. Theology, Philosophy, and Science (chiefly)

Grabmann, M., Geschichte der katholischen Theologie (Freiburg im Br. 1933, with copious bibliography 283-346); id., Geschichte der scholastischen Methode (2 vols. ibid. 1909-1911; reprinted 1957); id., Mittelalterliches Geistesleben. 1-2 (Munich 1926-1936); 3 (1956)

Denzinger-Schönmetzer, Enchiridion symbolorum (32nd ed. Freiburg im Br. 1963)

De Ghellinck, J., S.J., Le Mouvement théologique du XIIe siècle: La préparation lointaine avant et autour de Pierre Lombard, ses rapports avec les initiatives des canonistes. Études, recherches et documents (2nd ed. revised and enlarged Brussels and Paris 1948)

Forest, A., and M. de Gandilhac, Le Mouvement doctrinale du XIe au XIVe siècle (Paris 1951; Fliche et Martin, Histoire de l'Église 13)

Ueberweg-Geyer, Die patristische und scholastische Philosophie (11th ed. Berlin 1928; available in a recent reprint)

DeWulf, M., Histoire de la philosophie médiévale (6th ed. 3 vols. Paris 1934-1947. There is an English translation by E. C. Messenger.)

Gilson, E., L'Esprit de la philosophie médiévale (2nd ed. revised Paris 1944. There is an English translation of the first edition by A. H. C. Downes: The Spirit of Mediaeval Philosophy [New York 1936]; id., History of Christian Philosophy in the Middle Ages (New York 1955); id., Introduction à l'étude de saint Augustin (2nd ed. revised and enlarged Paris 1943); id., Le Thomisme. Introduction à la philosophie de saint Thomas d'Aquin (5th ed. revised and enlarged Paris 1948); id., La philosophie de saint Bonaventure (2nd ed. revised and corrected Paris 1943)

Maurer, A. A., Medieval Philosophy (New York 1962)

Copleston, F., S. J., A History of Philosophy. 2, Mediaeval Philosophy: Augustine to Scotus (Westminster, Md., 1950); 3, Ockham to Suarez (1953)

Knowles, D., Evolution of Medieval Thought (Baltimore 1962)

Chenu, M. D., Introduction à l'étude de saint Thomas d'Aquin (Paris 1950)

Baron, R., Science et Sagesse chez Hugues de Saint-Victor (Paris 1957)

Landgraf, A., Einführung in die Geschichte der theologischen Literatur der Frühscholastik (Regensburg 1948); id., Dogmengeschichte der Frühscholastik (4 vols. in 8, Regensburg 1952-1956)

Viller, M., S. J., and K. Rahner, S. J., Aszese und Mystik im der Väterzeit: Ein Abriss (Freiburg im Br. 1939; with valuable bibliography)

Butler, Dom Cuthbert, Western Mysticism (2nd ed. London 1922)

Pourrat, P., La Spiritualité chrétien (4 vols. Paris 1921-1928). 1, Des origines de l'église au moyen âge [6th ed. 1921]; 2, Le moyen âge [3rd ed. 1921])

Wilmart, Dom A., O.S.B., Auteurs spirituels et textes dévots du moyen âge Paris 1932)

Chadwick, O., Western Asceticism (Philadelphia 1958; Library of Christian Classics)

Leclercq, J. et al., La spiritualité du moyen âge (Paris 1961)

Knowles, Dom David, The English Mystical Tradition (London 1961)

Dickinson, J. C., Monastic Life in Medieval England (New York 1962)

Mullins, Sister Patrick Jerome, O. P., The Spiritual Life according to St. Isidore of Seville (Washington 1940; Catholic University Studies in Mediaeval History N.S. 3)

Carroll, Sister M. Thomas Aquinas, R.S.M., The Venerable Bede: His Spiritual Teachings (ibid. 1946; same series 9)

Blum, Owen J., O.F.M., St. Peter Damian: His Teaching on the Spiritual Life (ibid. 1947; same series 10)

Bloomfield, M., The Seven Deadly Sins: An Introduction to the History of a Religious Concept with Special Reference to Medieval English Literature (East Lansing [Mich.] 1952); id., "A Preliminary List of Incipits of Latin Works on the Virtues and Vices, Mainly in the Thirteenth, Fourteenth, and Fifteenth Centuries," Traditio 9 (1955) 259-279

White, H., The Tudor Books of Private Devotion (Madison 1951)

Delehaye, H., S.J., Les origines du culte des martyrs (2nd ed. revised Brussels 1933)

Haskins, C. H., Studies in the History of Mediaeval Science (2nd ed. Cambridge [Mass.] 1927)

Crombie, A. C., Medieval and Early Modern Science (2 vols. New York 1959; an Anchor Book)

Clagett, M., Science of Mechanics in the Middle Ages (Madison, Wisc., 195

Daumas, M., ed., Histoire de la science des origines au XXe siècle (Paris 1957; Encyclopédie de la Pléiade)

Sarton, G., Introduction to the History of Science (Washington 1927 ff.). 1, From Homer to Omar Khayam (1927); 2, Part 1, From Rabbi Ezra to Gerard of Cremona, and Part 2, From Robert Grosseteste to Roger Bacon (1931); 3, Parts 1 and 2: The Fourteenth Century (1948)

Thorndike, L., A History of Magic and Experimental Science, 1-2, The First Thirteen Centuries of Our Era (New York 1923); 2-4, Fourteenth and Fifteenth Centuries (1934)

Singer, C., E. J. Holmyard, et al., edd., A History of Technology. 2, Th Mediterranean Civilizations and the Middle Ages (Oxford 1956)

White, L., Medieval Technology and Social Change (New York 1961)

Boll, F., and C. Bezold, Sternglaube und Sterndeutung: Die Geschichte und das Wesen des Astrologie (4th ed. Berlin 1931)

Storms, G., Anglo-Saxon Magic (The Hague 1949)

5. Scripture and Exegesis

Robert, A., and A. Tricot, edd., Initiation Biblique. Introduction à l'étude des saintes écritures (3rd ed. revised and enlarged Paris, Tournai, Rome; English translation: Guide to the Bible: An Introduction to the Study of Holy Scripture. By E. P. Arbez and M. R. P. McGuire. 1 [2nd ed. Paris, Tournai, and New York 1960]. See especially, Ch. VIII, "The Versions: III: The Latin Versions. The Vulgate", 637-677; Ch. IX, "Interpretation: I, History of Exegesis, and II, Catholic Exegesis", 678-713; Ch. II, "Appendix: The Apocrypha of the Old and New Testaments", 103-128.)

Stummer, F., Einführung in die lateinische Bibel (Paderborn 1928)

Bischoff, B., "Neue Materialien zum Bestand und zur Geschichte der altlateinischen Bibelübersetzungen", Miscellanea G. Mercati. 1:407-436 (Studi e Testi 121 [1946])

Bonsirven, J., S.J., G. Bardy, and Others, "Interprétation (Histoire de l')", Dictionnaire de la Bible. Supplément, edd. Pirot-Robert-Cazelles, 4 (Paris 1949) 561-646, especially 569-627

Pontet, M., L'Exégèse de s. Augustin prédicateur (Paris 1946)

De Lubac, H., S.J., Exégèse Médiévale. Les quartre sens de l'Écriture (4 vols. Paris 1959-1963; in progress)

Daniélou, J., G. Devoto et al. La Bibbia nell'alto Medioevo (Settimana di studio, Spoleto 1962)

Pépin, J., Mythe et allégorie (Paris 1958)

Spicq, C., O.P., Esquisse d'une histoire de l'exégèse latine au moyen âge (Paris 1944; from the 8th to the end of the 14th century)

Vosté, J. M., "Medieval Exegesis", Catholic Biblical Quarterly 10 (1948) 229-246

Glunz, H. H., History of the Vulgate in England from Alcuin to Roger Bacon Cambridge [England] 1933)

Smalley, B., The Study of the Bible in the Middle Ages (Oxford 1941; new ed. 1951)

Rost, H., Die Bibel im Mittelalter (Augsburg 1939)

Laistner, M. L. W., "Antiochene Exegesis in Western Europe," Harvard Theological Review 40 (1947) 19-32

Cordoliani, A., "Le texte de la Bible en Irlande du Ve au IXe siècle", Revue Biblique 57 (1950) 5-41

Bischoff, B., "Wendepunkte in der Geschichte der lateinischen Exegese im Frühmittelalter", Sacris Erudiri 6 (1954) 189-281

McNally, R. E., S.J., The Bible in the Early Middle Ages (Westminster, Md., 1959; Woodstock Papers 4); id., "Notes. The 'Tres Linguae Sacrae' in Early Irish Bible Exegesis", Theological Studies 19 (1958) 395-403; id., "Medieval Exegesis", ibid. 22 (1961) 445-454

Chenu, M. D., O.P., "Les deux âges de l'allégorisme scripturaire au moyen âge", Recherches de Théologie ancienne et médiévale 18 (1951) 19-28

N.B.: The copious commentaries of Cornelius a Lapide (1587-1637) will often be found very useful because they continue the mediaeval tradition to such a large degree and, with their emphasis on allegorical interpretation, furnish a wealth of material from the Fathers of the Church. Editions: 12 vols. (Turin 1838 ff.); 20 vols. (Lyons 1865 ff.); 22 vols. (Paris 1859 ff.)

Frey, J. B., "Apocryphes de l'Ancien Testament", and E. Amann, "Apocryphes du Nouveau Testament", Dictionnaire de la Bible. Supplément 1 (1926) 354-533

Charles, R. H., The Apocrypha and Pseudepigrapha of the Old Testament in English (Oxford 1913)

James, M. R., The Apocryphal New Testament (Oxford 1924; new ed. 1953)

Wordsworth-White-Sparks-Jenkins, Novum Testamentum latine secundum editionem sancti Hieronymi (3 vols. Oxford 1889-1954)

Sabatier, P., Bibliorum sacrorum latinae versiones antiquae seu vetus Italica (3 vols. Reims 1743-1749; 3 vols. [bound in 6] Paris 1749-1751)

Fischer, B., O.S.B., Vetus Latina. Die Reste der altlateinischen Bibel, nach Petrus Sabatier neu gesammelt und herausgegeben von der Erzabtei Beuron (Freiburg im Br. 1949 ff.). 1, Verzeichnis der Sigel für Handschriften und Kirchenschriftsteller (2nd ed. 1962); 2, Genesis (1951-1954); 26, Epistolae Catholicae et Apocalypsis (1956 ff.); 24, Epistolae ad Ephesios, Philippenses, Colossenses (1962 ff.); On the "Old" and the "New" Sabatier see the important review-article by B. M. Peebles in CBQ 16 [1954] 210-225.)

Stegmüller, F., Repertorium Biblicum medii aevi (5 vols. Madrid 1950-1955)

Dutripon, F., Concordantiae Bibliorum Sacrorum vulgatae editionis (Paris 1838; and later reprints)

Peultier-Etienne-Gantois, Concordantiarum universae Scripturae Sacrae Thesaurus (Paris 1899; Cursus Scripturae Sacrae)

6. Byzantine and Islamic Civilization, the Knowledge of Greek in the West, Translations from Greek and Arabic, the Jews

Bardy, G., La question des langues dans l'Énglise ancienne (Paris 1948)

Marrou, H. I., Saint Augustin et la fin de la culture antique (Paris 1938), Ch. II, "Le grec", 27-46, and "Retractatio" (1949) 631-638

Courcelle, P., Les Lettres grecques en Occident de Macrobe à Cassiodore (new ed. revised and enlarged Paris 1948)

Altaner, B., "Der Einfluss und das Fortleben der griechischen Literatur im Abendland vom Ende des 4. bis in die zweite Hälfte des 6. Jahrhunderts", Theologische Revue 48 (1952) 41-50 (a review-article on Courcelle)

Laistner, M. L. W., Thought and Letters in Western Europe: A.D. 500 to 900 (new and revised ed. Ithaca 1958), Ch. X, "The Study of Greek", 238-250

Bischoff, B., "Das griechische Element in der abendländischen Bildung des Mittelalters", Byzantinische Zeitschrift 44 (1951) 27-55 (with valuable bibliography)

Delaruelle, E., "La connaissance du grec en Occident du Ve au IXe siècle", Mélanges de la Société Toulousaine d'Études classiques. 1 (1946) 209-226

Weiss, R., "Lo studio del greco all'abbazia di San Dionizi durante il medio evo", Rivista di storia della chiesa in Italia 6 (1952) 426-438; id., Greek in Western Europe Before the Renaissance (in preparation in the series, Storia e Letteratura, Rome, in March 1964)

Siegmund, A., O.S.B., Die Ueberlieferung der griechischen christlichen Literatur in der lateinischen Kirche bis zum zwölften Jahrhundert (Munich 1949)

Blatt, F., "Remarques sur l'histoire des traductions latines", Classica et Mediaevalia 1 (1938) 217-242

Muckle, J. T., C.S.B., "Greek Works Translated Directly into Latin before 1350", Mediaeval Studies 4 (1942) 33-42, and 5 (1943) 102-114

Altaner, B., "Die Kenntnis des Griechischen in den Missionsorden während des 13. and 14. Jahrhunderts. Ein Beitrag zur Vorgeschichte des Humanismus", Zeitschrift für Kirchengeschichte 53 (1934) 436-493

Grabmann, M., "Methoden und Hilfsmittel des Aristotelesstudiums im Mittelalter", Sitzungsb. d. bayer. Ak. d. Wiss. Philos.-hist. Kl. 5 (1939. See also the long review by E. Franceschini in Bolletino di Filologia classica 46 [1939-1940] 101-121); id., Guglielmo de Moerboeke, O. P., il traduttore delle opere di Aristolele (Rome 1946; Miscellanea Hist. Pont. 11)

Minio-Paluello, L., The Methods of the Medieval Translators of Greek Philosophical Works into Latin (Ph.D. diss. Oxford 1949)

Mansion, A., "Disparition graduelle des mots grecs dans les traductions médiévales d'Aristote", Mélanges Joseph de Ghellinck, 2 (Brussels 1951) 631-645

Leclercq, H., "Colonies d'Orientaux en Occident", Cabrol-Leclercq, DACL 3.2:2266-2277

Théry, P. G., "Scot Érigène, traducteur de Denys", ALMA 6 (1931) 185-278

Cappuyns, Dom M., Jean Scot Érigène, sa vie, son oeuvre, sa pensée (Louvain 1933), especially, Ch. I, "En Irlande, l'écolier", Ch. II, "En Gaule, le grammairien", and Ch. IV, "Le traducteur"

Haskins, C. H., Studies in the History of Mediaeval Science (2nd ed. Cambridge [Mass.] 1927); id., The Renaissance of the Twelfth Century (ibid. 1927), Ch. IX, "The Translations from Greek and Arabic", 278-302

Rashdall-Powicke-Emden, The Universities of Europe in the Middle Ages. 1 (Oxford 1936) 360-362

De Wulf, M., Histoire de la philosophie médiévale (6th ed. Paris 1934-1936). 1:64-80, and 2:25-58 (with bibliography revised by A. Pelzer)

Ueberweg-Geyer, Die patristische und scholastische Philosophie (Berlin 1928; reprinted Basel 1951) 342-351

Sarton, G., Introduction to the History of Science (see 4, near end, above), Chs. III, XIV, XXVIII, XXX, and XLIV (especially important for thirteenth and fourteenth centuries)

De Ghellinck, J., S.J., L'Essor de la littérature latine au XIIᵉ siècle. 2 (Brussels 1946), Ch. IV, "Le groupe strictement didactique et ses instruments de travail; II, Les traducteurs et les agents de liaison avec l'Orient grec ou arabe", 15-42 (excellent)

Dix années d'études byzantines. Bibliographie internationale (1939-1948). (Published by the Association des Études Byzantines [Paris 1950]

Dölger, F., and A. M. Schneider, Byzanz in der historischen und philologischen Forschung, 1938-1950 (Bern 1952)

Krumbacher, K., Geschichte der byzantinischen Litteratur (2nd ed. Munich 1897)

Beck, H. G., Kirche, Theologie und geistliche Literatur des byzantinischen Reiches (Munich 1959; Handbuch der Altertumswissenschaft 11. 2. 1)

Baynes, N., and H. St. L. S. Moss, edd. Byzantium. An Introduction to Byzantine Civilization (Oxford 1948)

Bréhier, L., Le monde byzantin (3 vols. Paris 1948-1950), especially 3, La civilisation byzantine

Setton, K. M., "The Byzantine Background to the Italian Renaissance", Trans. Am. Phil. Soc. 100. 1 (1956) 1-76

Aristoteles Latinus, Pars prior. Codices descripsit G. Lacombe, in societatem operis adsumptis A. Birkenmajer, M. Dulong, Aet. Franceschini (Rome 1939; Corpus Philosophorum Medii Aevi sponsored by the Union Académique Internationale); Aristoteles Latinus, Pars Posterior, ed. L. Minio-Paluello (Cambridge [England] 1954); Supplementum, ed. L. Minio-Paluello (Bruges and Paris 1961)

Franceschini, E., Aristotele nel medio evo latino (Padua 1935)

Corpus Philosophorum Medii Aevi. Aristoteles Latinus. 4.2, Analytica posteriora, translatio anonyma, ed. L. Minio-Paluello (Bruges-Paris 1955); 4.3, Analytica posteriora, Gerardo Cremonensi interprete, ed. id. (1954); 7.2, Physica, translatio Vaticana, ed. A. Mansion (1957); 11. 1-2, De Mundo, translatio anonyma et translatio Nicolai, ed. W. L. Lorimer (Rome 1951); 33, De arte poetica, Guillelmo de Moerbeke interprete, edd. E. Valmaggi et al. (Bruges-Paris 1953). A number of new volumes are in course of publication.

Klibansky, R., The Continuity of the Platonic Tradition during the Middle Ages: Outlines of a Corpus Platonicum medii aevi (London 1939; The Warburg Institute)

Corpus Platonicum medii aevi. Plato Latinus 1, Meno interprete Henrico Aristippo, edd. V. Kordeuter and C. Labowsky (London 1940); 2, Phaedo interprete Henrico Aristippo, ed. L. Minio-Paluello (1950); 4, Timaeus a Calcidio translatus, ed. J. H. Waszink (1962)

Catologus Translationum et Commentariorum. Mediaeval and Renaissance Latin Translations and Commentaries: Annotated Lists and Guides, ed. P. O. Kristeller, et al. 1 (Washington 1960; sponsored by the Union Académique Internationale and published by The Catholic University of America Press. In progress.)

Berthier, A., "Les écoles de langues orientales fondées au XIIIe siècle par les Dominicains en Espagne et en Afrique", Revue africaine 63 (1932) 84-103

Hitti, P., History of the Arabs from the Earliest Times to the Present (5th edition revised London and New York 1953)

Arnold, T. W., and A. Guillaume, The Legacy of Islam (Oxford 1931)

Pareja, F. M., A. Bausani, and L. Hertling, Islamologia (Rome 1951)

Gibb, H. A. R., and J. H. Kramers, Shorter Encyclopedia of Islam (Leiden and Ithaca [N.Y.] 1953)

Houtsma, M. T., et al., edd., The Encyclopedia of Islam (4 vols. Leiden 1913-1938; new edition in progress 1953 ff.)

Bell, R., Introduction to the Qur'an (Edinburgh 1953)

Lammens, H., S.J., L'Islam (Beyrouth 1926; 2nd edition 1944. English translation of the first edition by D. Ross, London 1928)

Von Grunebaum, G. E., Medieval Islam. A Study in Cultural Orientation (Chicago 1946)

Southern, R. W., Western Views of Islam in the Middle Ages (Cambridge [Mass. 1962)

Kritzeck, J., Anthology of Islamic Literature from the Rise of Islam to Modern Times (New York 1963)

Gibb, H. A. R., Arabic Literature (London 1926)

Nicholson, R. A., A Literary History of the Arabs (2nd edition Cambridge [England] 1930)

Graff, G., Geschichte der christlichen arabischen Literatur (5 vols. Rome 1944-1953; Studi e Testi 118, 133, 146, 147, 172 [Register])

De Ghellinck, J., S. J., L'Essor de la littérature latine au XIIe siècle. 2 (Brussels 1946) 15-42 (with excellent bibliography)

Corpus Commentariorum Averrois in Aristotelem, ed. H. A. Wolfson (Cambridge [Mass.] 1949 ff.; published by the Mediaeval Academy of America)

Bevan, E. R., and C. Singer, edd., The Legacy of Israel (Oxford 1927)

Roth, C., "The Jews in the Middle Ages", CMH 7 (1932) 632-664, with bibliography 937-847

Baron, S., A Social and Religious History of the Jews (8 vols. 2nd ed. New York 1952-1958); Index to vols. 1-8 (1960. The long notes in each volume contain a copious and very valuable bibliography.)

Bonsirven, J., S. J., "Judaism in the Christian Era", in Robert-Tricot, Guide to the Bible. 2 (Tournai and New York 1955) 469-484 (with additional bibliography furnished by E. P. Arbez)

7. The Vernacular Languages and Literatures of Western Europe

Chaytor, H. J., From Script to Print. An Introduction to Medieval Vernacular Literature (Cambridge [England] 1945; reprinted 1951)

Artz, F., The Mind of the Middle Ages (3rd ed. revised New York 1958) 320-383 (with bibliography 530-539)

Queneau, R., ed., Histoire des littératures. 1, Littératures anciennes, orientales et orales (Paris 1956; Encyclopédie de la Pléiade); 2, Littératures occidentales (1956); 3, Littératures françaises, connexes et marginales (1958)

A. Old and Middle English Language and Literature

Bateson, F. W., Cambridge Bibliography of English Literature. 1 (600-1600). See 1 above.

Watson, G., ed., The Concise Bibliography of English Literature 600-1950 (London 1958)

Annual Bibliography of English Language and Literature (Cambridge [Engl.] 1921 ff.)

Bonser, W., An Anglo-Saxon and Celtic Bibliography (450-1087) (2 vols. Berkeley 1957)

Wells, J. E., A Manual of Writings on Middle English, 1050-1400 (New Haven 1916; with a series of later Supplements)

Baugh, A. C., History of the English Language (New York 1935)

Blair, P. H., An Introduction to Anglo-Saxon England (Cambridge [England] 1956)

Bosworth, J., and T. N. Toller, An Anglo-Saxon Dictionary (Oxford 1899); Supplement, by T. N. Toller (ibid. 1921)

Hall, J. R. C., A Concise Anglo-Saxon Dictionary (4th ed. by H. D. Merritt, Cambridge [Engl.] 1961)

Mossé, F., A Handbook of Middle English. Translated by J. A. Walker (Baltimore 1952)

Legge, M. D., Anglo-Norman Literature and Its Background (London 1963)

Mustanoja, T. F., A Middle English Syntax. Part 1, Parts of Speech (Helsinki 1960)

Stratmann, F. H., and H. Bradley, A Middle English Dictionary (Oxford 1891)

Kurath, H., et al., edd., Middle English Dictionary (Ann Arbor [Mich.] 1952 ff.; A-Gos at end of 1963)

New English Dictionary on Historical Principles (Oxford English Dictionary), ed. by J. A. H. Murray (Oxford 1884-1928)

The Shorter Oxford Dictionary on Historical Principles. Revised and edited by C. T. Onions (2 vols. Oxford 1933)

Baugh, A. C., ed., A Literary History of England (New York and London 1948. "The Old English Period (to 1100)", by Kemp Malone; "The Middle English Period (1100-1500)", by A. C. Baugh. Anglo-Latin and Anglo-Norman writers are included and the bibliographies are short but excellent.)

Chambers, E. K., English Literature at the Close of the Middle Ages (Oxford 1945; Oxford History of English Literature)

Wilson, R. M., The Lost Literature of Medieval England (London 1952)

B. Romance Languages and Literatures: Old French, Old Provençal, Old Italian, Old Spanish, and Old Portuguese

Palfrey-Fucilla-Holbrook, A Bibliographical Guide to the Romance Languages and Literatures (5th ed. Evanston, Ill., 1963)

Elcock, W. D., The Romance Languages (London 1960)

Rohlfs, G., Romanische Philologie (2 vols. Heidelberg 1950-52; Winters Studienführer)

Lausberg, H., Romanische Sprachwissenschaft (2 vols. Leipzig-Berlin 1956; Sammlung Göschen)

Wartburg, W. von, Die Entstehung der romanischen Völker (2nd ed. Tübingen 1951); id., Französisches etymologisches Wörterbuch (Bonn, Leipzig, Bâle, 1922 ff.)

Meier, H., "Ueber das Verhältnis der romanischen Sprachen zum Lateinischen", Romanische Forschungen 54 (1940) 165-201

Kuhn, A., Romanische Philologie. 1, Die romanischen Sprachen (Bern 1951)

Bourciez, E., Éléments de linguistique romane (4th ed. revised Paris 1946)

Meyer-Lübke, W., Introducción a la lingüística románica. Translated into Spanish from the 3rd German edition by Americo Castro (Madrid 1926); id., Romanisches etymologisches Wörterbuch (3rd ed. Heidelberg 1935)

Holmes, U. T., A Critical Bibliography of French Literature: The Medieval Period (revised ed. Syracuse 1952)

Bossuat, R., Manuel bibliographique de la littérature française du moyen âge (Melun 1951)

Holmes, U. T., and Schutz, A. H., A History of the French Language (2nd ed. New York 1948; revised ed. 1962)

Zumthor, P., Histoire de la littérature de la France médiévale (Paris 1954)

Bruneau, Ch., Petite histoire de la langue française. 1, Des origines à la Révolution (Paris 1955)

Gamillscheg, E., Historische französische Syntax (Tübingen 1957 ff.)

Anglade, J., Grammaire élémentaire de l'Ancien Français (9th ed. Paris 1952)

Voretzsch, K., Einführung in das Studium der altfranzöschischen Sprache (8th ed. by G. Rohlfs, Halle 1955)

Bartsch, K., Chrestomathie de l'Ancien Français (12th ed. Leipzig 1927)

Pope, M. K., From Latin to Modern French: With Special Consideration of Anglo-Norman (new ed. Manchester 1952)

Bloch, O., and von Wartburg, W., Dictionnaire étymologique de la langue française (2 vols. 2nd ed. Paris 1950)

Grandsaignes d'Hauterive, R., Dictionnaire d'ancien français. Moyen âge et Renaissance (Paris 1947)

Godefroy, G., Dictionnaire de l'ancienne langue française de tous ses dialectes du XIe au XVIe siècle (10 vols. Paris 1881-1902)

Tobler-Lommatzsch, Altfranzöschisches Wörterbuch (Berlin 1925 ff.; A-Mout at end of 1963)

Holmes, U. T., A History of Old French Literature from the Origins to 1300 (New York 1937)

Bédier, J., and P. Hazard, Histoire de la littérature française illustrée (2 vols. new ed. Paris 1948-1949. See, especially, the section by J. Bédier and E. Faral in Vol. 1.)

Bossuat, R., Le moyen âge (Paris 1955; in Histoire de la littérature française edited by J. Calvet)

Cohen, G., La vie littéraire au moyen âge (Paris 1954)

Frank, G., The Medieval French Drama (Oxford 1954)

Jeanroy, A., La poésie lyrique des troubadours (2 vols. Paris 1934)

Anglade, J., Grammaire de l'ancien-provençale (Paris 1921)

Aebischer, P., Chrestomathie franco-provençal. Recueil de textes francoprovençaux antérieurs à 1630 (Bern 1950)

Lommatzsch, E., Leben und Lieder der provenzalischen Troubadours. 1, Minnelieder (Berlin 1957)

Grandgent, C. H., From Latin to Italian: An Historical Outline of the Phonology and Morphology of the Italian Language (Cambridge [Mass.] 1927)

Rohlfs, G., Historische Grammatik der italienischen Sprache. 1, Lautlehre (Bern 1949); 2, Erster Teil: Formenlehre und Syntax (1949); 3, Zweiter Teil: Wortbildungslehre und Syntax (1954)

Monaci, E., Crestomazia italiana dei primi secoli (2nd ed. Città di Castello 1912)

Viscardi, A., et al., Le origini. Testi latini, italiani, provenzali e franco-italiani (Milan and Naples 1956)

Tommaseo-Bellini, Dizionario della lingua italiana (7 vols. Turin 1861-1879; reprinted 1939)

Reynolds, B., ed., The Cambridge Italian Dictionary. 1, Italian-English
(Cambridge [Engl.] 1962)

Battisti, C., and G. Alessio, Dizionario etimologico italiano (Florence
1950 ff.; to Te- at end of 1963)

Fay, E. E., Concordance of the Divina Commedia (Cambridge [Mass.] 1888

Edler, F., A Glossary of Mediaeval Terms of Business: Italian Series
(Cambridge [Mass.] 1934; Mediaeval Academy of America Publication 18)

Wilkins, E. R., A History of Italian Literature (Cambridge [Mass.] 1954)

Tiraboschi, R., Storia della letteratura italiana (new ed. 9 vols. Florence
1785-1792; especially, 3-5 [476-1400])

Storia letteraria d'Italia scritta da una società di professori (12 vols. Milan
1895-1926). 1, Le origini, by F. Novati and A. Monteverdi (1900-1926).
Nuova serie (1928 ff.); 1, Le origini, by A. Viscardi (1939; 2nd ed. re-
vised 1950); 2, Il duecento, by G. Bertoni (1930); 3, Dante, by M.
Zingarelli (2 vols. 1947-1948); 4, Il trecento, by N. Sapegno (1948); 5,
Il quattrocento, by V. Rossi (1932; new ed. 1949)

Entwistle, W. J., The Spanish Language, Together with Portuguese,
Catalan, and Basque (London 1936; new and revised ed. 1962)

Alvar, M., A. Badía, et al., edd., Enciclopedia Lingüística Hispánica
(Madrid 1960 ff.; to be completed in 6 vols.)

Menéndez Pidal, R., Orígenes del español: estudio lingüístico de la
península ibérica hasta el siglo XI (3rd ed. Madrid 1950); id., Manual de
gramática histórica española (ibid. 1949)

Hanssen, F., Gramática histórica de la lengua castellana (Halle 1945)

Real Academía española, Diccionario de la lengua española (16th ed.
(Madrid 1936)

Cejador y Frauca, J., Vocabulario medieval castellano (Madrid 1929)

Corominas, J., Diccionario crítico etimológico de la lengua castellana (4
vols. Madrid 1955-1957)

Brenan, G., The Literature of the Spanish People (London and New York
1951)

Fitzmaurice-Kelly, J., Historia de la literatura española (Buenos Aires
1942)

Diaz-Plaja, G., ed., Historia general de las literaturas hispánicas (Barcelona 1949 ff.). 1, Desde los origines al 1400 (1949); 2, Pre-
Renacimiento y Renacimiento (1951); 3, Renacimiento y Barroco (1953)

Williams, E. B., From Latin to Portuguese. Historical Phonology and
Morphology of the Portuguese Language (Philadelphia and Oxford 1938;
new ed. 1962)

Taylor, J. L., A Portuguese-English Dictionary (Stanford, Cal., 1958)

Bell, A. F. G., Portuguese Literature (Oxford 1922)

C. Old High German and Middle High German Language and Literature

Raabe, P., Einführung in die Bücherkunde zur deutschen Literaturwissenschaft (2nd ed. Stuttgart 1961; Sammlung Metzler)

Schwarz, E., Deutsche und germanische Philologie (Heidelberg 1951; Winters Studienführer)

Stroh, F., Handbuch der germanischen Philologie (Berlin 1952)

Stammler, W., ed., Deutsche Philologie im Aufriss (3 vols. Berlin-Bielefeld 1952-1957); Register zu Band I bis III der ersten Auflage (1959). The work began appearing in a revised second ed. in 1955 (Vol. 1, 1957; Vol. 2, 1960; Vol. 3, 1963)

Priebsch, R., and W. E. Collinson, The German Language (New York 1938)

Curme, G. O., A Grammar of the German Language (new ed. New York 1952)

Hempel, H., Gotisches Elementarbuch. Grammatik, Texte mit Uebersetzung und Erläuterungen (Berlin 1962; Sammlung Göschen)

Mossé, F., Manuel de l'Allemand du moyen âge (revised ed. Paris 1947)

Braune, W., et al., Abriss der althochdeutschen Grammatik (11th ed. Tübingen, 1959); id., Althochdeutsches Lesebuch (14th ed. by E. A. Ebbinghaus, Tübingen 1962)

Barber, C. C., An Old High German Reader (Oxford 1951)

Senn, A., An Introduction to Middle High German. A Reader and Grammar (5th ed. New York 1937)

Paul, H., and W. Mitzka, Mittelhochdeutsche Grammatik (Tübingen 1960)

Joos, M., and F. Whitesell, Middle High German Courtly Reader (Madison 1951)

Behagel, O., Deutsche Syntax (4 vols. Heidelberg 1923-1936)

Kluge, F., and W. Mitzka, Etymologisches Wörterbuch der deutschen Sprache (18th ed. Berlin 1960)

Karg-Gasterstadt, E., and T. Frings, Althochdeutsches Wörterbuch (Leipzig 1952 ff.)

Lexer, M., Mittelhochdeutsches Taschenwörterbuch (26th ed. Zürich 1951)

Trübners deutsches Wörterbuch, ed. A. Götze (8 vols. Berlin 1936-1957)

Ehrismann, G., Geschichte der deutschen Literatur bis zum Ausgang des Mittelalters (2 vols. in 4 Munich 1918-1935; reprinted 1954)

De Boor, H., and R. Newald, Geschichte der deutschen Literatur 1: 770-1170 (Munich 1951)

Walshe, M. O'C., Medieval German Literature (Cambridge [Mass.] 1962)

Stammler, W., and K. Langosch, Die deutsche Literatur des Mittelalters. Verfasserlexikon (5 vols. Berlin 1933-1955)

Stammler, W., Die deutsche Dictung, von der Mystik zum Barock, 1400-1600 (Stuttgart 1951)

Nagel, B., Die deutsche Meistergesang. Poetische Technik, musikalische Form und Sprachgestaltung der Meistersinger (Heidelbert 1952)

D. Celtic Languages and Literatures

Best, R. I., Bibliography of Irish Philology and of Printed Irish Literature (Dublin 1913); Bibliography of Irish Philology and Ms. Literature, 1913-1941 (Dublin, Institute of Advanced Studies, 1942)

Bonser, W., An Anglo-Saxon and Celtic Bibliography (450-1087) (2 vols. Berkeley 1957)

Lewis, H., and H. Pedersen, A Concise Comparative Celtic Grammar (Göttingen 1937)

Thurneysen, R., A Grammar of Old Irish. Revised and enlarged edition translated from the German by D. A. Binchy and O. Bergin (Dublin 1940); Old Irish Reader, with a Supplement to the Grammar of Old Irish. Translated from the German by Binchy and Bergin (Dublin 1949)

Dottin, G., Manuel d'irlandais moyen (2 vols. Paris 1913)

Meyer, K., Contribution to Irish Lexicography. 1.1 (Halle 1906; A-DNO)

Dictionary of the Irish Language Based Mainly on Old and Middle Irish Materials, published by the Royal Irish Academy (Dublin 1913-1960); E (1932); F (1950); Contributions to a Dictionary of the Irish Language (ibid. 1939 ff.): M-U (1939-1950); G (1955); I (1952)

Flower, R., The Irish Tradition (Oxford 1947)

Stokes, W., and J. Strachan, Thesaurus Palaeohibernicus (2 vols. Cambridge [England] 1901-1903; a corpus of Old Irish Literature); Supplement by Stokes (Halle 1910)

Thurneysen, R., Irische Königs-und Heldensage bis zum siebzehnten Jahrhundert (Halle 1921)

Dillon, M., The Cycles of the Kings (Oxford 1946); id., Early Irish Literature (Chicago 1948)

Murphy, G. E., ed., Early Irish Lyrics (Oxford 1956)

Dottin, G., L'épopée irlandais (Paris 1926)

Jackson, K. H., A Celtic Miscellany (Cambridge [Mass.] 1951)

Cross, T. P., Motif-Index of Early Irish Literature (Bloomington [Indiana] 1952; Indiana University Publications, Folklore Series No. 7)

Jackson, K., Language and History in Early Britain (Edinburgh 1953), especially Ch. III, "Britons and Romans under the Empire," 76-121; IV, "The British Loanwords in Irish," 122-148; V, "The Early Christian Inscriptions," 149-193; "The Vulgar Latin Accent," 267-271

Jones, J. M., A Welsh Grammar, Historical and Comparative (Oxford 1913)

Strachan, J., An Introduction to Early Welsh (Manchester 1909)

Gruffydd, W. F., "Welsh Language and Literature", Encyclopedia Britannica (14th ed.) 23:504-510

Williams, G., An Introduction to Welsh Poetry. From the Beginnings to the Sixteenth Century (London 1953)

E.   Old Norse Language and Literature

S. Einarsson, History of Icelandic Literature (Baltimore 1957)

R. Cleasby et al., An Icelandic-English Dictionary (2nd ed. Oxford 1957)

J. De Vries, Altnordisches etymologisches Wörterbuch (2nd ed. Leiden 1962

F. Old Saxon, Middle Low German, Old Frisian, and Old and Middle Dutch
See, e.g., Paetow, Guide to the Study of Medieval History 503-505, but
especially the pertinent sections in Stroh, Handbuch der germanischen
philologie (see C above).

N.B.: There is much valuable bibliography on the history of the vernacular
literatures in Strecker-Palmer 90 ff., but it might be better arranged.

8. Art, Architecture, and Music

Janson, H. W., A History of Art (London and New York 1962)
Aubert, M., Nouvelle histoire universelle de l'art. 1 (Paris 1932)
Mâle, E., et al., Histoire générale de l'art (2 vols. Paris 1951; Flammarion).
See especially, "L'art chrétien primitif et l'art byzantin", "L'art roman",
and "L'art gothique", by E. Mâle, 2:253-372 (with bibliography)
Lavedan, H., Histoire de l'art. 2, Moyen âge et Temps modernes (Paris 1944;
"Clio" Series)
Encyclopedia of World Art. McGraw Hill Book Co. (New York 1959 ff.; Vols.
8 [A-Land-] in June 1964)
Thieme-Becker, Allgemeines Lexikon der bildenden Künstler von der Antike bis
zur Gegenwart (37 vols. Leipzig 1907-1950)
Focillon, H., Art d'Occident. Le Moyen Âge roman et gothique (Paris 1938)
Réau, L., and G. Cohen, L'art du moyen âge et la civilisation française (Paris
1951; L'Évolution de l'humanité)
Cabrol-Leclercq, DACL (see 2, above)
Morey, C. R., Early Christian Art. An Outline of the Evolution of Style and
Iconography in Sculpture and Painting from Antiquity to the Eighth Century
(2nd ed. Princeton 1953); id., Medieval Art (New York 1942)
Rice, D. T., The Beginnings of Christian Art (London 1957)
Diehl, C., "Byzantine Art", in Baynes and Moss, Byzantium (Oxford 1948) 166-
199 (with excellent classified select bibliography 403-409)
Rice, D. T., The Great Palace of the Emperor at Byzantium (London 1958)
Bloch, H., "Monte Cassino, Byzantium, and the West in the Earlier Middle
Ages", Dumbarton Oaks Papers, No. 3 (1946) 163-224
Grabar, A., Byzantine Painting (Geneva 1953; Skira Series)
Nordenfalk, K., and A. Grabar, High Middle Ages (ibid. 1957)
Crump and Jacob, Legacy of the Middle Ages (Oxford 1926), "Medieval Archi-
tecture", by W. R. Lethaby; "Medieval Sculpture", by P. Vitry; "Decorative
and Industrial Arts", by M. Aubert, 39-146
Bréhier, L., L'art chrétien: son développement iconographique du moyen âge
(2nd ed. Paris 1928)
Mâle, E., L'Art religieux du XIIe siècle en France: étude sur les origines de
l'iconographie du moyen âge (Paris 1922); id., L'Art religieux du XIIIe
siècle en France: étude sur l'iconographie du moyen âge et sur ses sources
d'inspiration (7th ed. Paris 1931; English trans. of the 3rd French edition by
D. Nussey, Religious Art in France [London and New York 1913]); id., Religious Art from the Twelfth to the Eighteenth Century (New York 1949;
Pantheon Books)

Evans, J., Art in Mediaeval France, 987-1498 (Oxford 1948)

Réau, L., Iconographie de l'art chrétien (Paris 1955-1959). I, Introduction générale (1955); II, Iconographie de la Bible: 1, Ancien Testament (1956); 2, Nouveau Testament (1957); III, Iconographie des saints: 1, A-F (1958); 2, G-O (1958); 3, P-Z, Répertoires (1959)

Vloberg, M., "The Bible in Art", in Robert-Tricot, Guide to the Bible. 2 (Tournai and New York 1955) 547-574 (with valuable bibliography)

Porcher, J., French Miniatures from Illuminated Manuscripts (London 1960)

White, L., "Natural Science and Naturalistic Art in the Middle Ages", American Historical Review 52 (1947) 421-435

Gardner, A., English Medieval Sculpture (revised and enlarged London and New York 1951)

Fisher, E. A., The Greater Anglo-Saxon Churches: An Architectural-Historica Study (London 1962)

Von Simson, O., The Gothic Cathedral. Origins of Gothic Architecture and the Medieval Concept of Order (New York 1956; Bollingen Series 48)

Fitchen, J. F., The Construction of Gothic Cathedrals (Oxford 1961)

Frankl, P., The Gothic: Literary Sources and Interpretations through Eight Centuries (Princeton 1960)

Anderson, M. D., Drama and Imagery in English Medieval Churches (London 1964)

Salzmann, L. F., Building in England down to 1540: A Documentary History (London 1952)

Clasen, K. H., Die Baukunst des Mittelalters (Wildpark-Potsdam 1930)

Leclercq, H., "Lexique archéologique", DACL 8.2: 2996-3048

Gay, V., Glossaire archéologique du moyen âge et de la renaissance (2 vols. Paris 1887-1928)

Réau, L., Dictionnaire polyglotte des termes d'art et d'archéologie (Paris 1953)

The New Oxford History of Music. 2, ed. Dom Anselm Hughes, Early Medieval Music up to 1300 (Oxford 1954); 3, edd. id. and G. Abraham, Ars Nova and the Renaissance (1960)

Apel, W., Gregorian Chant (Bloomington [Indiana] 1958)

Leclercq, H., "Chant romain et grégorien", DACL 3.1: (1913) 256-311

Sessini, U., and G. Vecchi, Poesia e musica nella latinità cristiana dal III al X secolo (Turin 1949)

Apel, W., R. W. Linker, and U. T. Holmes, French Secular Music of the Late Fourteenth Century (Cambridge [Mass.] 1950; Mediaeval Academy of American Publication No. 55)

9. Education, The Classical and Patristic Tradition, Humanism

Marrou, H. I., Histoire de l'éducation dans l'antiquité (3rd ed. Paris 1955; English trans., A History of Education in Antiquity by G. Lamb [New York 1956]. See review by M. R. P. McGuire in Catholic Historical Review 44 [1957-1958] 209-213. See also the review by G. Downey in Classical Journal 52 [1957] 337-345.); id., Saint Augustin et la fin de la culture antique (Paris 1938; Supplément, "Retractatio" 1949)

Gwynn, A., Roman Education from Cicero to Quintilian (Oxford 1926)

Ellspermann, G. L., O.S.B., The Attitude of the Early Christian Latin Writers Toward Pagan Literature and Learning (Washington 1949; Catholic University of America Patristic Studies 82)

Laistner, M. L. W., Christianity and Pagan Culture in the Later Roman Empire (Ithaca 1951); id., Thought and Letters in Western Europe (ibid., 1957; especially Chs. II, VIII, XI); id., "Bede as a Classical and Patristic Scholar", Trans. R. Hist. Soc. 16 (1933) 69-94

Leclercq, H., "École", DACL 4.2: 1730-1883; id., "Lettres classiques", ibid. 8.2: 2886-2942

Roger, M., L'enseignement des Lettres classiques d'Ausone à Alcuin (Paris 1905)

Riché, P., Éducation et culture dans l'Occident barbare VIe-VIIIe siècle (Paris 1932); id., "Recherches sur l'instruction des laïcs du IXe au XIIe siècle", Cahiers de Civ. Méd. 5 (1962) 175-182

Cassiodorus, Institutiones, ed. R. A. B. Mynors (Oxford 1937; English trans., An Introduction to Divine and Human Readings, with an Introduction and Notes, by L. W. Jones [New York 1946]; in Records of Civilization)

Fontaine, J., Isidore de Séville et la culture classique dans l'Epagne wisigothique (2 vols. Paris 1949)

Pirenne, H., "De l'État de l'instruction des laïques à l'époque mérovingienne", Revue Bénédictine 46 (1934) 165-177

Lesne, E., Les écoles de la fin du VIIIe siècle à la fin du XIIe (Lille 1940)

Duckett, E. S., Alcuin, Friend of Charlemagne: His Life and Work (New York 1951)

Ellard, G., S.J., Master Alcuin, Liturgist (Chicago 1956)

Wallach, L., Alcuin and Charlemagne: Studies in Carolingian History and Literature (Ithaca 1959; Cornell St. in Class. Phil. 32)

Martin, R. M., "Arts libéraux (sept)", Baudrillart et al., Dict. d'hist. et géo. eccl. 4 (1930) 827-843

Koch, J., ed., Artes liberales. Von der antiken Bildung zur Wissenschaft des Mittelalters (Leiden and Köln 1959)

Cambridge Medieval History, 5 (New York 1929), Ch. 22, "Medieval Schools to 1300" (M. Deansley), 765-779, and 934-936; 6 (1929), Ch. 17, "The Medieval Universities" (by H. Rashdall), 559-601, and 941-943; 7 (1932), Ch. 25, "The Early Renaissance" (A. A. Tilley), 751-776, and 966-968; 8 (1936), Ch. 23, "Education in the Fourteenth and Fifteenth Centuries" (G. R. Potter), 688-717, and 982-987

De Ghellinck, J., S.J., Le Mouvement théologique du XIIe siècle (2nd ed. Brussels 1948), Ch. 1, especially sections I, "La renaissance carolingienne", and Ch. 2, "Le siècle de fer (Xe siècle)", 9-52; id., L'Essor de la littérature latine au XIIe siècle (2 vols. Brussels 1946). 1, Ch. 1, "Le groupe scolaire", 33-108; 2, Ch. 2, "Le groupe strictement didactique", 1-88, especially section V, "Les catalogues de bibliothèques et les classiques", 68-88 (with full bibliography)

Manacorda, G., Storia della scuola in Italia. 1, 1-2 (Milan 1915)

Haskins, C. H., The Renaissance of the Twelfth Century (Cambridge [Mass.] 1927); id., The Rise of the Universities (New York 1923)

Paré, G., A. Brunet, P. Tremblay, La Renaissance du XIIe siècle. Les écoles et l'enseignement (Paris 1933)

Sanford, E. M., "The Twelfth Century -- Renaissance or Proto-Renaissance?", Speculum 26 (1951) 635-642

Holmes, U. T., Daily Living in the Twelfth Century (Madison [Wis.] 1952); id., "The Idea of the Twelfth Century Renaissance", Speculum 26 (1951) 643-651

Lehmann, P., "Die Vielgestalt des zwölften Jahrhunderts", in his Erforschung des Mittelalters 3 (Stuttgart 1960) 224-246

Rashdall-Powicke-Emden, The Universities of Europe in the Middle Ages (3 vols. Oxford 1936)

D'Irsay, S., Histoire des universités françaises et étrangères des origines à nos jours (2 vols. Paris 1933). 1, Moyen âge et Renaissance

Daly, L. J., S. J., The Medieval University 1200-1400 (New York 1961)

Glorieux, P., Répertoire des maîtres en théologie de Paris au XIIIe siècle (2 vols. Paris 1933)

Emden, A. B., A Biographical Register of the University of Oxford to A. D. 1500 (3 vols. Oxford 1957-1959); id., A Biographical Register of the University of Cambridge to 1500 (Cambridge 1963)

Gabriel, A. L., "The Preparatory Teaching in the Parisian Colleges during the Fourteenth Century", Revue de l'Université d'Ottawa 21 (1951) 449-483; id., Student Life in Ave Maria College, Mediaeval Paris (Notre Dame [Ind.] 1955); id., "Robert de Sorbonne", Revue de l'Université d'Ottawa 13 (1953) 473-514; id., Skara House at the Mediaeval University of Paris: History, Topography, and Chartulary (Notre Dame [Ind.] 1961)

Thorndike, L., University Records and Life in the Middle Ages (New York 1944; Records of Civilization)

Kibre, P., The Nations in the Mediaeval Universities (Cambridge [Mass.] 1948; Mediaeval Academy of America Publication No. 49); id., Scholarly Privileges in the Middle Ages (Cambridge [Mass.] 1962; Mediaeval Academy of America Publ. No. 72)

Sandys, J. E., History of Classical Scholarship. 1 (3rd ed. Cambridge [Eng.] 1921 [reprinted New York 1958])

Norvin, W., "Classica et Mediaevalia", Classica et Mediaevalia 1 (1938) 1-39

Menendez Pelayo, M., Bibliografia hispano-latina clasica (10 vols. Madrid 1950-1953)

Mackinney, L. C., Bishop Fulbert and Education at the School of Chartres (Notre Dame [Ind.] 1958; Texts and Studies in the History of Mediaeval Education, Ed. A. L. Gabriel and J. N. Garvin, C. S. C. See also the other numbers in this series.)

Hugh of St. Victor, Didascalicon: De studio legendi, ed. C. H. Buttimer, F. S. (Washington 1939; Catholic University of America Studies in Medieval and Renaissance Latin 10)

Taylor, J., The Didascalicon of Hugh of St. Victor. A Medieval Guide to the Arts. Translated from the Latin with an Introduction and Notes (New York 1961; Records of Civilization)

Baron, R., Science et sagesse chez Hugues de Saint-Victor (Paris 1957)

McGarry, D. D., "Educational Theory in the Metalogicon of John of Salisbury", Speculum 23 (1948) 659-675; id., The Metalogicon of John of Salisbury, Translated with an Introduction and Notes (Berkeley 1955)

Delhaye, P., "L'organisation scolaire au XIIᵉ siècle", Traditio 5 (1947) 211-268

Oediger, F. W., Ueber die Bildung der Geistlichen im späten Mittelalter (Leiden and Köln 1953)

Walsh, G. G., S.J., Medieval Humanism (New York 1942)

Leclercq, J., O.S.B., "L'Humanisme bénédictin du VIIIᵉ siècle", Studia Anselmiana 20 (1948) 1-20; id., L'Amour des lettres et le désir de Dieu (Paris 1957; English trans., The Love of Learning and the Desire for God [New York 1961])

Curtius, E. R., European Literature and the Latin Middle Ages. Translated from the German by W. R. Trask (New York 1953; Bollingen Series 36), especially Ch. 3, "Literature and Education", and Ch. 14 "Classicism"

Bolgar, R. R., The Classical Heritage and Its Beneficiaries (Cambridge [Eng.] 1954)

Highet, G., The Classical Tradition (New York 1950; very sketchy on the Middle Ages)

Campbell, J. M., "Patristic Studies and the Literature of Mediaeval England", Speculum 8 (1933) 465-478

Lehmann, P., Pseudo-antike Literatur des Mittelalters (Leipzig 1927)

Liebeschütz, H., Medieval Humanism in the Life and Writings of John of Salisbury (London 1950; Warburg Institute)

Gilson, E., "Humanisme médiéval", in Les idées et les lettres (Paris 1932) 171-196

Jaeger, W., Humanism and Theology (Milwaukee 1943; The Aquinas Lecture, Marquette University)

Renucci, P., L'Aventure de l'humanisme européen au moyen âge (IVᵉ-XIVᵉ siècle) (Paris 1953)

Rand, E. K., "The Classics in the Thirteenth Century", Speculum 4 (1929) 249-269; Cicero in the Courtroom of St. Thomas (Milwaukee 1945; The Aquinas Lecture, Marquette University)

Ullman, B. L., "Classical Authors in Mediaeval Florilegia", Classical Philology 23 (1928) 128-174; 24 (1929) 109-132; 25 (1930) 11-21, and 128-154; 26 (1931) 21-30; 27 (1932) 1-42

Gagnér, A., Florilegium Gallicum. Untersuchungen und Texte zur Geschichte der mittellateinischen Florilegienliteratur (Lund 1936)

Beddie, J. S., "The Ancient Classics in Mediaeval Libraries", Speculum 5 (1930) 3-20

Sanford, E. M., "The Use of Classical Latin Authors in the Libri Manuales", Transactions of the Am. Phil. Assoc. 55 (1924) 190-248

Colson, F. H., Quintilian, Institutionis oratoriae Liber I (Cambridge [Eng.] 1924; with excellent Introduction)

Lehmann, P., "Institutio oratoria des Quintilianus im Mittelalter" in his Erforschung des Mittelalters 2 (Stuttgart 1959) 1-28

Boskoff, P. S., "Quintilian in the Late Middle Ages", Speculum 27 (1952) 71-7̶

Marti, B. M., Arnulfi Aurelianensis glosule super Lucanum (Rome 1958; Papers and Monogr. Am. Acad. in Rome 18)

Aubenas, R., and R. Richard, L'Église et la Renaissance (1449-1517) (Paris 1951; Fliche et Martin, Histoire de l'Église 15)

Artz, F. B., The Mind of the Middle Ages (3rd ed. revised New York 1958), especially, Ch. 6, "The Latin West, 5th-10th centuries", and Chs. 7-8, "Learning (1100-1500)"

Brinton, C., Ideas and Men. The Story of Western Thought (2nd ed. New York 1963; especially the sections on the Middle Ages and Renaissance)

Ferguson, W. K., The Renaissance in Historical Thought (Boston 1948; with valuable bibliography); id., "The Interpretation of the Renaissance: Suggestions for a Synthesis", Journal of the History of Ideas 12 (1951) 483-495

The New Cambridge Modern History. 1, The Renaissance 1493-1520 (Cambridge [Eng.] 1957), Ch. 1, "Introduction" (D. Hay), 1-19; Ch. 5, "Learning and Education in Western Europe from 1470 to 1520" (R. Weiss) 95-126

Kristeller, P. O., "Humanism and Scholasticism in the Italian Renaissance", Byzantion 17 (1944-1945) 346-374. Republished with revisions under the title, "Umanesimo e scolastica nel Rinascimento italiano", Humanitas 5 (1950); id., Studies in Renaissance Thought and Letters (Rome 1956); id., Renaissance Thought: The Classic, Scholastic, and Humanistic Strains (New York 1961; a Harper Torchbook)

Helton, T., ed., The Renaissance. A Reconstruction of the Theories and Interpretations of the Age (Madison [Wis.] 1961)

Hay, D., The Italian Renaissance and Its Historical Background (New York 1961)

Ullman, B. L., Studies in the Italian Renaissance (Rome 1955)

Cosenza, M. E., Biographical and Bibliographical Dictionary of the Italian Humanists and of the World of Classical Scholarship in Italy, 1300-1800 (5 vols. Boston 1961)

Nelson, J. S., F.S.C., Aeneae Silvii de liberorum educatione. A Translation with an Introduction (Washington 1940; Catholic University of America Studies in Medieval and Renaissance Latin Language and Literature 12)

Lebègue, R., "L'humanisme latin de la Renaissance", Mémorial Marouzeau (Paris 1943) 271-284

Seznec, J., The Survival of the Pagan Gods. The Mythological Tradition and Its Place in Renaissance Humanism and Art. Translated from the French by B. F. Sessions (New York 1953; Bollingen Series 38; reprinted as a Harper Torchbook, 1961)

10. Palaeography, Diplomatics, the Ancient and Mediaeval Book and the Diffusion and Transmission of Texts, Mediaeval Libraries, Catalogs of Mss., Incipits, Textual Criticism and Editing of Texts

A. Palaeography

Strecker-Palmer, Introduction to Medieval Latin (Berlin 1957) 131-136

Lowe, E. A., "Handwriting", in Crump and Jacob, Legacy of the Middle Ages (Oxford 1926) 197-226; id., The Beneventan Script: A History of the South Italian Minuscule (ibid. 1914); id., English Uncial (Oxford 1960)

Thompson, E. M., Introduction to Greek and Latin Palaeography (Oxford 1912)

Battelli, G., Lezioni de paleografia (3rd ed. Vatican City 1949)

Bischoff, B., "Paläographie, mit besonderer Berücksichtigung des deutschen Kulturgebiete", in W. Stammler, ed., Deutsche Philologie im Aufriss. 1 (Berlin 1952) 379-452; 2nd revised ed. also printed separately (1956)

Leclercq, H., "Paléographie", DACL 13.1 (1937) 610-736

Bretholz, B., Lateinische Paläographie (3rd ed. Leipzig and Berlin 1926)

Prou, M., Manuel de paléographie latine et française (4th ed. with an album of 24 plates, Paris 1914)

Mallon, J., R. Marichal, Ch. Perrat, L'Écriture latine de la capitale romaine à la minuscule (Paris 1939)

Marichal, R., "L'Écriture latine et l'écriture grecque du Ier au VIe siècle", L'Antiquité classique 19 (1950) 113-144

Mallon, J., Paléographie romaine (Madrid 1952)

Natale, A. R., "Il Codice e la Scrittura. Avviamento allo studio della paleografia latina", in Introduzione alla filologia classica, ed. E. Bignone (Milan 1951)

Masai, F., "Paléographie et codicologie", Scriptorium 4 (1950) 279-293 (a critical survey of new views in the field of palaeography)

Wattenbach, W., Das Schriftwesen im Mittelalter (3rd ed. Leipzig 1896; reprinted 1958)

Traube, L., "Geschichte der Paläographie", in his Vorlesungen und Abhandlungen. 1 (Munich 1909) 1-80; 2 (1911) 5-31

Lindsay, W. M., ed., Paleographica Latina (5 vols. London 1922-1929)

Bischoff, B., G. I. Lieftinck, G. Battelli, Nomenclature des écritures livresques du IXe au XVIe siècle. Publication of the Centre National de la Recherche Scientifique (Science humaines 4, Paris 1954)

Ullman, B. L., The Origin and Development of Humanistic Script (Rome 1960)

Wardrop, J., The Script of Humanism. Some Aspects of Humanistic Script 1460-1560 (Oxford 1963)

N.B.: For current bibliography in the field of Latin palaeography see especially the journal Scriptorium and L'Année philologique.

On abbreviations in Latin Mss, see, in addition to Prou, Thompson, etc., the following:

Enciclopedia Cattolica, art. "Abbreviazioni", 1:41-53

Cappelli, A., Dizionario di abbreviature latine ed italiane (3rd ed. Milan 1929; reprinted 1954)

Laurent, M. H., O. P., De abbreviationibus et signis scripturae Gothica (Rome 1939)

Schiaparelli, L., Avviamento allo studio delle abbreviature latine nel medioevo (Florence 1926)

Traube, L., Nomina Sacra. Versuch einer Geschichte der christlichen Kürzung (Munich 1907)

Lindsay, W. M., Notae Latinae: An Account of Abbreviations in Latin Mss of the Early Minuscule Period (c. 700-850) (Cambridge [Eng.] 1951); Supplement (Abbreviations in Latin Mss of 850 to 1050 A.D.), by D. Bains (1936)

Lehmann, P., "Sammlungen und Erörterungen lateinischer Abkürzungen im Altertum und Mittelalter", Abh. d. bayer. Akad. d. Wissensch. Philos.-hist. Abt. 3 (Munich 1929)

Martin, C. T., The Record Interpreter. A Collection of Abbreviations, Latin Words, and Names Used in English Historical Manuscripts and Records (2nd ed. London 1910, and later reprints)

Walther, J. L., Lexicon diplomaticum: abbreviationes vocum in diplomatibus exponens (3rd ed. Ulm 1756)

For facsimiles, and for outstanding examples of modern palaeographical investigation, see:

Ehrle, F., and P. Liebaert, Specimina codicum Latinorum (2nd ed. Bonn 1927)

Kirchner, J., Scriptura latina libraria a saeculo primo usque ad finem medii aevi LXXVII imaginibus illustrata (Munich 1955)

Steffens, F., Paléographie latine. Translated from the 2nd German edition by R. Coulon (Trier 1910)

Lowe, E. A., Scriptura Beneventana (2 vols. Oxford 1929); id., Codices Latini antiquiores. A Palaeographical Guide to Latin Manuscripts Prior to the Ninth Century (ibid. 1934-1964 in 11 parts)

Chatelain, E., Paléographie des classiques latins (2 vols. Paris 1884-1900)

Chroust, A., Monumenta Palaeographica. 3 series. 1 (Munich 1894-1906); 2 (1907-1917); 3 (1918-1935)

Rand, E. K., Studies in the Script of Tours, I and II (Cambridge [Mass.] 1929-1934; Publications of the Mediaeval Academy of America 3)

Beeson, C. H., Lupus of Ferrières as Scribe and Text Critic (ibid. 1930 same series 4)

Jones, L. W., The Script of Cologne from Hildebald to Hermann (ibid. 1932; same series 10)

Umbrae codicum occidentalium, edd. G. Battelli, B. Bischoff, et. al., (Amsterdam 1960 ff.)

For further collections of facsimiles, see Thompson, op. cit. 577-583; Battelli, op. cit. 18-21; Paetow, Guide to the Study of Medieval History 35-38, and 528-529; Leclercq, art. cit. 732-736; Strecker-Palmer, op. cit. 132-136.

B. Diplomatics

Giry, A., Manuel de diplomatique (Paris 1894; reprinted 1925)

Bresslau, H., Handbuch der Urkundenlehre für Deutschland und Italien. 1 (Leipzig 1889; 2nd ed. 1912); 2.1 (1912); 2.2 (1931)

Poole, R. L., Lectures on the History of the Papal Chancery down to the Time of Innocent III (Cambridge [Eng.] 1915)

De Boüard, A., Manuel de diplomatique française et pontificale. 1, Diplomatique générale, avec un album de 54 planches en phototypie (Paris 1929); 2, L'acte privé (1948), with an Album of plates (i-xvii [1949]; xviii-xxxiv [1954])

Johnson, C., and H. Jenkinson, English Court Hand, A.D. 1066-1500 (2 vols. Oxford 1915)

Hector, L. C., The Handwriting of English Documents (London 1958)

Bishop, T. A. M., Scriptores Regis. Facsimiles to Identify and Illustrate the Hands of Royal Scribes in Original Charters of Henry I, Stephen and Henry II (Oxford 1961)

Fridh, Å. J: son, Terminologie et formules dans les Variae de Cassiodore (Stockholm 1956; with valuable bibliography)

Fichtenau, H., Arenga. Spätantike und Mittelalter im Spiegel von Urkundenformeln (Graz 1957)

Wallach, L., "Charlemagne's De litteris colendis and Alcuin -- A Diplomatic Historical Study", Speculum 26 (1951) 288-305; id., "Charlemagne and Alcuin: Diplomatic Studies in Carolingian Epistolography", Traditio 9 (1953) 127-154; id., Alcuin and Charlemagne: Studies in Carolingian History and Literature (Ithaca 1959; Cornell Studies in Classical Philology 32)

C. The Ancient and Mediaeval Book and the Diffusion and Transmission of Texts

Kenyon, Sir F. G., Books and Readers in Ancient Greece and Rome (Oxford 1932; new ed. 1951)

Febvre, L., and H. J. Martin, L'apparition du livre (Paris 1958; L'Évolution de l'humanité)

Hall, F. W., Companion to Classical Texts (Oxford 1913), especially Ch. IX, "The Nomenclature of Mss., with the Names of Former Possessors", 286-357

McCowan, C. C., "Codex and Roll", Harvard Theological Review 34 (1941) 219-250

James, M. R., The Wanderings and Homes of Manuscripts (London 1919; SPCK, Helps No. 17)

Thompson, op. cit. (under A), 8-74

Wattenbach, op. cit. (under A)

Diringer, D., The Hand-Produced Book (New York 1953); id., The Illuminated Book (London and New York 1957)

Birt, Th., Das antike Buchwesen (Berlin 1882); Kritik und Hermeneutik nebst Abriss des antiken Buchwesens (Munich 1913)

Destrez, J., La Pecia dans les manuscrits universitaires du XIIIe et du XIVe siècle (Paris 1935)

Van Hoesen, H., and F. K. Walter, Ch. 14, "Book-Decoration, Book-Selling and Publishing", in their Bibliography: Practical, Enumerative, Historical (New York 1928) 373-405

Wroth, L. C., A History of the Printed Book (New York 1938)

Milkau-Leyh, Handbuch der Bibliothekswissenschaft. 1, Schrift und Buch (2nd ed. Wiesbaden 1952): Ch. 2, "Allgemeine Handschriftkunde" (K. Löffler and P. Ruf), 106-162; Ch. 4, "Die Buchmalerei" (A. Boeckler and A. A. Schmid), 249-287; Ch. 5, "Buckdruck und Buchillustration bis zum Jahre 1600" (E. von Rath and R. Juchhoff), 388-533; Ch. 9, "Geschichte des Bucheinbandes" (M. J. Husing and F. A. Schmidt-Kunsemüller), 782-848; Ch. 10, "Geschichte des Buchhandels" (E. Kuhnert and H. Widmann), 849-1004; Ch. 12, "Geschichte des Papiers" (A. Renker), 1047-1068

Weitzmann, K., Illustration in Roll and Codex. A Study of the Origin and Method of Text Illumination (Princeton 1947)

De Ghellinck, J., S.J., Patristique et Moyen âge. 2 (Brussels 1947), "Étude II: Diffusion et transmission des écrits patristiques", 181-377

Bardy, G., "Copies et éditions du Ve siècle", Revue des Sciences Religieuses 23 (1949) 38-52

Marrou, H. I., "La Technique de l'édition à l'époque patristique", Vigiliae Christianae 3 (1949) 208-224

Heiberg, J. L., "Wie die Schriften des Altertums an uns gelangt sind. I, Das Altertum", Scientia 39 (1926) 81-88; "II, Das Mittelalter", ibid. 153-162

Norden, E., Römische Literatur . . . (See 4 above) 146-154

Maas, P., "Die Schicksale der antiken Literatur in Byzanz", in Gercke-Norden, Einleitung 1 (Leipzig 1927), "Nachträge", 2-5

Traube, L., "Die römische Literatur im Mittelalter (Ueberlieferungsgeschichte)", in his Einleitung in die lateinische Philologie des Mittelalters (Munich 1911; Vorles. und Abh. 2) 121-137; "Textgeschichte der Regula S. Benedicti", Abh. d. k. bayer. Ak. d. Wiss. Philos.-phil. und hist. Kl. 25. Bd. 2 (Munich 1898; 2nd ed. by H. Plenkers, Munich 1910

Hunger, H., O. Stegmüller et al., Geschichte der Textüberlieferung der antiken und mittelalterlichen Literatur. 1, Antikes und mittelalterliches Buch-und Schriftwesen. Ueberlieferungsgeschichte der antiken Literatur (Zürich 1961); 2, Mittelalterliche Ueberlieferungsgeschichte (1963)

Wilmart, A., O.S.B., "La tradition des grands ouvrages de saint Augustin", in Miscellanea Agostiniana 2: Studi Agostiniani (Rome 1931) 257-315

Lehmann, P., "Autographe und Originale namhafter lateinischer Schriftsteller des Mittelalters", in his Erforschung des Mittelalters 1 (Stuttgart 1959) 359-381

McDonald, Sister M. Francis, Saint Augustine's de fide rerum non videntur (Washington 1950; Catholic University of America Patristic Studies 84. See especially the Introduction and Bibliography.)

On the question of interpolations or suppressions in Christian and pagan works see:

Traube, L., Einleitung (listed above) 67-70

Hall, F. W., Companion to Classical Texts (listed above) 182-183, and 188-189.

D. Mediaeval Libraries, Mediaeval and Modern Catalogs of Mss., Incipits, Photostats and Microfilms

Leclercq, H., "Bibliothèques", DACL 2. 1: (1910) 842-904 (in part antiquated)

Traube, L., "Die mittelalterlichen und die modernen Bibliotheken", Vorlesungen und Abhandlungen 1 (Munich 1909) 103-127 (with valuable additional notes by the editor, P. Lehmann)

Laistner, M. L. W., Thought and Letters in Western Europe A.D. 500 to 900 (new ed. revised Ithaca 1957), especially Ch. 9, "Libraries and Scriptoria", 225-237

Thompson, J. W., The Medieval Library (Chicago 1939; reprinted [New York 1957] with valuable Supplement by B. B. Boyer)

Milkau-Leyh, Handbuch der Bibliothekswissenschaft. 3, 1, Geschichte der Bibliotheken (new ed. Wiesbaden 1955): Ch. 2, "Das griechisch-römische Altertum" (C. Wendel and W. Göber), 51-145; Ch. 3, "Der byzantinische Kulturkreis" (V. Burr), 146-187; Ch. 4, "Der Islam" (K. Holter), 188-242; Ch. 5, "Das Mittelalter" (K. Christ and A. Kern), 243-498; Ch. 9, "Von der Renaissance bis zum Beginn der Aufklärung" (A. Börner and H. Widmann), 499-681

De Ghellinck, J., S.J., Patristique et moyen âge 2 (see C above): "Bibliothèques chrétiennes d'Orient", and "Bibliothèques chrétiennes d'Occident", 259-289

Lesne, E., Les livres, Scriptoria, et Bibliothèques du commencement du VIIIe siècle à la fin du XIe siècle (Lille 1938; Histoire de la propriété ecclésiastique en France 4)

Lehmann, P., "Quellen zur Feststellung und Geschichte mittelalterlicher Bibliotheken", in his Erforschung des Mittelalters 1 (Stuttgart 1959) 306-358

Bischoff, B., Die südostdeutschen Schreibschulen und Bibliotheken in der Karolingerzeit 1 (Leipzig 1940); id. and J. Hofmann, Libri sancti Kyliani: Die Würzburger Schreibschule und die Dombibliothek im VIII. und IX. Jahrhundert (Würzburg 1952)

Wormald, F., and C. E. Wright, edd., The English Library. Studies in Its History before 1700 (London 1959)

Vernet, A., "Études et travaux sur les bibliothèques médiévales", Revue de l'histoire de l'Église de France 34 (1948) 63-94

Wilson, W. J., "Manuscript Cataloging", Traditio 12 (1956) 457-555 (with valuable bibliography)

Paetow, L., Guide to the Study of Medieval History (revised ed. New York 1931) 531-532

Kristeller, P. O., Latin Manuscript Books before 1600. A Bibliography of the Printed Catalogues and Unpublished Inventories of Extant Collections (new and revised ed. New York 1960)

Richard, M., Répertoire des bibliothèques et des catalogues des manuscrits grecs (new ed. revised and enlarged Paris 1958)

Manitius, M., Handschriften antiker Autoren in mittelalterlichen Bibliothekskatalogen (Leipzig 1925; Zentralblatt für Bibliothekswesen, Beiheft 67). See also the data furnished on each classical writer in Manitius, Geschichte der lateinischen Literatur des Mittelalters 3 (Munich 1931. Check through the index, 1083 ff.)

Weinberger, W., Catalogus Catalogorum, Verzeichnis der Bibliotheken, die ältere Handschriften der lateinischen Kirchenschriftsteller enthalten (Vienna 1902); id., "Beiträge zur Handschriftenkunde", Sitzungsber. d. kais. Ak. d. Wiss. Wien. Philos.-hist. Kl. 159. 6, and 161. 4 (1908-1909); id., "Wegweiser durch die Sammlungen altphilologischer Handschriften", Sitzungsber. Wien, Philos.-hist. Kl. 209. 4 (1930)

Vielliard, J., and M. Th. Boucrel, "La Recherche des manuscrits latins", in Mémorial Marouzeau (Paris 1943) 442-457

Seymour de Ricci and W. J. Wilson, Census of Medieval and Renaissance Mss in the United States and Canada 1 (New York 1935; 2 (1937); Supplement, by W. H. Bond and C. U. Faye (New York 1963)

Aristoteles Latinus 1 (Rome 1939); 2 (Cambridge [England] 1944). See 6 above.

De Ghellinck, J., S.J., L'Essor de la littérature latine au moyen âge 2 (Brussels 1946), Ch. IV, sect. V, "Les catalogues de bibliothèques et les classiques", 68-88 (with excellent bibliography); "Progrès récents et tendances actuelles en histoire des bibliothèques", Revue d'Histoire ecclésiastique 38 (1942) 156-168

Sabbadini, R., Le scoperte dei codici latini e greci ne'secoli XIV e XV (Florence 1905); 2 (1914)

Becker, G., Catalogi bibliothecarum antiqui (Bonn 1885)

Gottlieb, T., Ueber mittelalterliche Bibliotheken (Leipzig 1890; reprinted 1955)

Vattasso, M., Initia patrum aliorumque scriptorum ecclesiasticorum Latinorum ex Mignei Patrologia et ex compluribus aliis libris collecta (Rome 1906-1908; Studi e Testi)

Little, A. G., Initia operum Latinorum quae saeculis XIII, XIV, XV attribuuntur (Manchester 1904; reprinted New York 1958)

Dekkers, E., O.S.B., "Initia" in Clavis Patrum Latinorum (new ed. revised and enlarged Bruges 1961) 557-584

Morin, G., "Initia et censura sermonum singulorum [S. Augustino adscriptorum] qui post Maurinos editi sunt", Miscellanea Agostiniana 1 (Rome 1930) 721-769; "Initia et censura sermonum [S. Caesario adscriptorum]", S. Caesarii opera omnia. 1. 2 (Maredsous 1937) 907-938

Chevalier, U., Repertorium hymnologicum (see 3 B above)

Thorndike, L., and P. Kibre, A Catalogue of Incipits of Mediaeval Scientific Writings in Latin (revised and augmented ed. Cambridge [Mass.] 1963; Publications of the Mediaeval Academy of America 29)

Pelzer, A., "Répertoires d'incipit pour la littérature latine, philosophique et théologique du moyen âge", Revue d'Histoire ecclésiastique 43 (1948) 495-512. Reprinted with additions in Sussidi eruditi 2 (Rome 1951)

For photostats and microfilms see the excellent section on this subject in Strecker-Palmer, Introduction to Medieval Latin (Berlin 1957) 136-139. On the microfilm reproductions of Vatican Mss. and catalogues at St. Louis University, see Manuscripta (St. Louis 1957 ff.)

For further bibliography on books, libraries, etc., see: Strecker-Palmer op. cit. 131-136, and 118-125, and the pertinent sections in L'Année philologique. The most important journals are Scriptorium, and Zentralblatt für Bibliothekswesen.

E. Textual Criticism and the Editing of Texts

Thomson, S. H., "Editing of Medieval Latin Texts in America", Progress of Medieval and Renaissance Studies in the United States and Canada. Bulletin 16 (1941) 37-49

Bieler, L., "The Grammarian's Craft", Folia 10. No. 2 (1958) 1-42; (an excellent introduction to textual criticism and its methods)

Dearing, V. A., A Manual of Textual Analysis (Berkeley [Cal.] 1959)

Collomp, P., La Critique des textes (Paris 1931; also well adapted for beginners in the field)

Dain, A., Les Manuscrits (Paris 1949; with valuable bibliography. See also the review-article on this work by G. Pasquali, Gnomon 23 [1951] 233-242.)

Maas, P., Textual Criticism. Translated from the German by B. Flower (Oxford 1958)

Hall, F. W., A Companion to Classical Texts (Oxford 1913), especially Ch. VI, "Recension", 108-149; Ch. VII, "Emendation", 150-198; Ch. IX, "The Nomenclature of Greek and Latin Mss with the Names of Former Possessors", 286-357

Birt, T., Kritik und Hermeneutik nebst Abriss des antiken Buchwesens (Munich 1913)

Havet, L., Manuel de critique verbale appliquée aux textes latins (Paris 1911; an indispensable reference work)

Clark, A. C., The Descent of Manuscripts (Oxford 1918)

Kantorowicz, H., Einführung in die Textkritik. Systematische Darstellung der textkritischen Grundsätze für Philologen and Juristen (Leipzig 1921. The emphasis is on juristic texts of the later Middle Ages.)

Pasquali, G., Storia della tradizione e critica del testo (Florence 1934)

Quentin, H., Essais de critique textuelle (Paris 1926. For criticism of the method described, see Collomp, op. cit. 72 ff., and Dain, op. cit. 162-164.)

Andrieu, J., "Principes et recherches de critique textuelle", Mémorial Marouzeau (Paris 1943) 458-474; id., "Problèmes d'histoire des textes", Revue des études latines 24 (1946) 271-314; id., "Pour l'explication psychologique de fautes de copiste", ibid. 28 (1950) 279-292

Bédier, J., "La tradition du Lai de l'Ombre. Réflexions sur l'art d'éditer les anciens textes", Romania 54 (1928) 161-196, and 321-356

Castellani, A., Bédier avait-il raison?: La méthode de Lachmann dans les éditions de texte du Moyen Âge (Fribourg [Switzerland] 1957)

Chaytor, H. J., "The Medieval Reader and Textual Criticism", Bulletin of the John Rylands Library 26 (1941-1942) 49-56; id., From Script to Print (Cambridge [England] 1951)

Vinaver, E., "Principles of Textual Emendation", in Studies in French Language and Medieval Literature Presented to Professor M. K. Pope (Manchester University Press 1939) 351-370

Delatte, A., and A. Severyns, Emploi des signes critiques. Disposition de l'apparat dans les éditions savantes de textes grecs et latins. Conseils et recommandations (Brussels and Paris 1938; Union Académique Internationale. See also the long, constructive review by U. Knoche, Göttinger Gelehrte Anzeiger 202 [1940] 515-531.)

Dondaine, A., O.P., "Abbréviations latines et signes recommandés pour l'apparat critique des éditions de textes médiévaux", Bulletin de la Société Internationale pour l'Étude de la Philosophie Médiévale 2 (1960) 142-149

Stählin, O., Editionstechnik (2nd ed. Leipzig 1914)

11. Mediaeval Latin Language and Style

A. Grammar and Grammatical and Linguistic Theory

N.B.: For comprehensive, systematic control of bibliography in the field of Latin language and style to Pope Gregory the Great, see J. Cousin, Bibliographie de la langue latine (1880-1948) (Paris 1951)

Duff, J. W., A Literary History of Rome from the Origins to the Close of the Golden Age (3rd ed. London 1953), Ch. III, "The Latin Language -- Its History and Qualities", 18-38

Devoto, G., Storia della lingua di Roma (2nd ed. Bologna 1944), especially 275 to the end

Palmer, L. R., The Latin Language (London 1954; a basic work)

Kent, R. G., The Sounds of Latin: A Descriptive and Historical Phonology (2nd ed. revised Philadelphia 1940; especially good on ancient pronunciation of Latin, accent, etc.)

Sturtevant, E. H., The Pronunciation of Greek and Latin (2nd ed. Philadelphia 1940)

Neue-Wagener, Formenlehre der lateinischen Sprache (4 vols. 3rd ed. Leipzig 1902-1905)

Lindsay, W. M., The Latin Language (Oxford 1894; reprinted 1963. It is antiquated in part, but still useful for its copious documentation on pronunciation, etc., from the ancient grammarians.)

Woodcock, E. C., A New Latin Syntax (London and Cambridge [Mass.] 1959)

Kühner-Stegmann, Ausführliche lateinische Grammatik. Zweiter Teil: Satzlehre. Part 1 (Hannover 1912); Part 2 (1914; most complete descriptive grammar of Latin from Plautus to Apuleius)

Leumann-Hofmann, Lateinische Grammatik (Munich 1928; Handbuch der Altertumswissenschaft. It replaces Stolz-Schmalz, Lateinische Grammatik (4th ed., Munich 1910), and is the basic scholarly historical grammar of the Latin language, with excellent systematic bibliography (347-362), and at the end of each section. Part II, Syntax and Stilistik, of the revised edition by A. Szantyr was published early in 1964.)

Löfstedt, E., Syntactica: Studien und Beiträge zur historischen Syntax des Lateins. 1, Ueber einige Grundfragen der lateinischen Nominalsyntax (2nd ed. Lund 1942); 2, Syntaktischstilistische Gesichtspunkte und Probleme (1933; with excellent bibliography; both volumes reprinted [1957]. See especially, 2, Ch. XIII, "Spätlateinische und romanische Sprachentwicklung", Ch. XIV, "Zur Frage der Gräzismen", and Ch. XV, "Zur Entstehung der christlichen Latinität", 373-473.); id., Philologischer Kommentar zur Peregrinatio Aetheriae (Uppsala 1911; reprinted Leipzig 1936); id., Collectanea: Untersuchungen auf dem Gebiete der antiken und mittelalterlichen Latinität 1 (Uppsala 1951); id., Late Latin (Oslo 1959), especially Ch. IV, "Medieval Latin", 59-67

Norberg, D., Syntaktische Forschungen auf dem Gebiete des Spätlateins und des frühen Mittellateins (Uppsala 1943); id., Beiträge zur spätlateinischen Syntax (ibid. 1944); id., "Érudition et spéculation dans la langue latine médiévale", ALMA 22 (1952) 5-16

Svennung, J., Untersuchungen zur Palladius und zur lateinischen Fach-und Volkssprache (Uppsala 1935); id., Compositiones Lucenses. Studien zum Inhalt, zur Textkritik und Sprache (ibid. 1941)

Rohlfs, G., Sermo Vulgaris Latinus. Vulgärlateinisches Lesebuch (Heidelberg 1951)

Vossler, K., Einführung ins Vulgärlatein. Edited by H. Schmeck (Munich 1954)

Battisti, C., Avviamento allo studio del latino vulgare (Bari 1949; with valuable bibliography)

Väänänen, V., Introduction au latin vulgaire (Paris 1964)

Sofer, J., "Reichssprache und Volkssprache im römischen Imperium", Wiener Studien 65 (1950-1951) 138-155

Rosenfeld, H., "Buch, Schrift, und lateinische Sprachkenntnis bei den Germanen vor der christlichen Mission", Rheinisches Museum für Philologie N. F. 95 (1952) 193-209

Bardy, G., La question des langues dans l'Église ancienne. 1 (Paris 1948), especially, Ch. II, "La latinisation de l'Église d'Occident", 81-121; Ch. III, "La culture latine dans l'Orient chrétien", 122-154; Ch. V, "Traducteurs et adapteurs au IVe siècle", 231-289

Schrijnen, J., Charakteristik des altchristlichen Latein (Nijmegen 1932; Latinitas Christianorum Primaeva. Studia ad sermonem Latinum Christianum pertinentia 1); "Le latin chrétien devenu langue commun", Revue des études latines 12 (1934) 96-116; primarily a reply to the criticism of J. Marouzeau in a review of the preceding work, ibid. 10 [1932] 241-242

De Ghellinck, J., S.J., "Latin chrétien ou langue des chrétiens", Les Études Classiques 8 (1939) 449-478

Mohrmann, C., Études sur le latin des chrétiens 1 (Rome 1958. See especially: 1, "Altchristliches Latein. Entstehung und Entwicklung der Theorie der altchristlichen Sondersprache", 3-19; 2, "Quelques traits caractéristiques du latin des chrétiens", 21-50; 3, "Le latin langue de la chrétienté occidentale", 51-81; 9, "La langue et le style de la poésie latine chrétienne", 151-168.); 2, Latin chrétien et médiéval (Rome 1961. See especially: "Die Rolle des Lateins in der Kirche des Westens", 35-62; "Les formes du latin dit vulgaire", 135-155; "Medieval Latin and Western Civilization", 155-179; "Le Latin médiéval", 181-232 [reprinted from Cahiers de Civilisation Médiévale 1 (1958) 265-294]; "La langue de saint Benoît", 325-345; "La style de saint Bernard", 347-367); id., "How Latin Became the Language of Early Christendom", Studies 40 (1951) 277-288; id., Latin vulgaire. Latin des chrétiens. Latin médiéval (Paris 1955); id., "Le dualisme de la latinité médiévale", Revue des Études latines 29 (1951) 330-348; id., Liturgical Latin: Its Origins and Character (Washington 1957)

Blaise, A., Manuel du latin chrétien (Strasbourg 1955)

Robert-Tricot, Guide to the Bible. Translated by E. P. Arbez and M. R. P. McGuire. 1 (2nd ed. Tournai and New York 1960), especiall[y] Ch. VIII, "The Versions. III, The Latin Versions", 637-664, and 674-676

Rönsch, H., Itala und Vulgata. Das Sprachidiom der urchristlichen Itala und der katholischen Vulgata... erläutert (2nd ed. Marburg 1875; old, but still useful)

Plater, W. E., and H. J. White, A Grammar of the Vulgate (Oxford 1926; rather superficial)

Hoogterp, P. W., Étude sur le latin de Codex Bobiensis (k) des Évangiles (Wageningen 1930); id., "Les vies des Pères du Jura. Études sur la langue", ALMA 9 (1934) 129-251

Catholic University of America Patristic Studies, edd. R. J. Deferrari, J. M. Campbell, M. R. P. McGuire, and B. M. Peebles (Washington 1922 ff.; 97 vols. in 1964)

Catholic University of America Studies in Medieval and Renaissance Latin Language and Literature, edd. R. J. Deferrari, M. R. P. McGuire, A. K. Ziegler, and B. M. Peebles (Washington 1933 ff.; 24 vols. in 1964)

N. B.: The majority of the volumes in these two series are devoted to the language and style of Patristic and Mediaeval writers, and each volume is furnished with a select bibliography.

Blatt, F., Die lateinischen Bearbeitungen der Acta Andreae et Matthiae apud anthropagos. Mit sprachlichen Kommentar (Giessen 1930; Beiheft zur ZNTW 12)

Tidner, E., Sprachlicher Kommentar zur lateinischen Didascalia Apostolorum (Stockholm 1938)

Linderbauer, B., O.S.B., S. Benedicti Regula monachorum herausgegeben und philologisch erklärt (Metten 1922)

Bieler, L., "Libri Epistolarum Sancti Patricii Episcopi. Introduction, Texts and Commentaries", Classica et Mediaevalia 11 (1950) 1-150; 12 (1951) 79-214 (reprinted in book form in two parts, Dublin 1952)

Salonius, A. H., Vitae Patrum. Kritische Untersuchungen über Text, Syntax und Wortschatz der spätlateinischen Vitae Patrum (Lund 1920)

Skahill, B. H., The Syntax of the Variae of Cassiodorus (Washington 1934; CUA Studies in Medieval and Renaissance Language and Literature 3)

Fridh, Å. J:son, Études critiques et syntaxiques sur les Variae de Cassiodore (Göteborg 1950)

Bonnet, M., Le Latin de Grégoire de Tours (Paris 1890)

Engels, L. J., Observations sur le vocabulaire de Paul Diaconus (Nijmegen 1962; Latinitas Christianorum Primaeva 17)

Lot, F., "A quelle epoque a-t-on cessé de parler latin?", ALMA 6 (1931) 97-159

N. B.: For further bibliography on Vulgar Latin and its relation to the Romance languages and on Mediaeval Latin in general, see 1, and 7 B above.

Strecker-Palmer, Introduction to Medieval Latin (Berlin 1957); especially 20-38

Blatt, F., "Sprachwandel im Latein des Mittelalters", Historische Vierteljahrschrift 28 (1933) 22-52 (of basic importance)

Garvin, J. N., C.S.C., The Vitas Sanctorum Patrum Emeritensium: Text and Translation, with an Introduction and Commentary (Washington 1946: CUA Studies in Mediaeval History, N.S. 8)

Vielliard, J., Le Latin des diplômes royaux et chartes privées à l'époque mérovingienne (Paris 1927; with valuable bibliography)

Uddholm, A., Formulae Marculfi. Études sur la langue et le style (Uppsala 1953; with copious bibliography)

Löfstedt, B., Studien übur die Sprache der langobardischen Gesetze. Beiträge zur frühmittelalterlichen Latinität (Uppsala 1961)

Most, W. G., The Syntax of the Vitae Sanctorum Hiberniae (Washington 1946; CUA Studies in Mediaeval and Renaissance Latin Language and Literature 20)

Leclercq, J., Études sur le vocabulaire monastique du moyen âge (Rome 1961; in Studia Anselmiana)

Hubert, M., O.P., "Quelques aspects du latin philosophique aux XIIe et XIIIe siècles", Revue des études latines 27 (1949) 211-233; id., "Notes de lexicographie thomiste. I", ALMA 27 (1957) 5-26; "II", ibid. 27 (1957) 167-188; "III", ibid. 287-292

Chenu, M. D., O.P., Introduction à l'étude de saint Thomas d'Aquin (Paris 1950, especially, Ch. III, "La langue. Le vocabulaire", 85-105)

On the pronunciation and orthography of Latin in the Middle Ages see:

McGuire, M.R.P., "The Pronunciation of Latin: Its History and Practical Problems", in M. R. P. McGuire, ed., Teaching Latin in the Modern World (Washington 1960) 69-83

Strecker-Palmer, op. cit. 58-60

Lot, F., "A quelle époque a-t-on cessé de parler latin?" (cited above) passim

Blatt, F., "Sprachwandel im Latein des Mittelalters" (cited above) passim

Traube, Einleitung (see 1 above) 93-94

Jellinek, M. H., "Zur Aussprache des Latein im Mittelalter", Festschrift für W. Braune (Dortmund 1920) 11-26

Beaulieux, C., "Essai sur l'histoire de la pronunciation du latin en France", Revue des études latines 5 (1927) 68-82. See also the section immediately following, "La reforme de la pronunciation du latin" by E. Faral and M. Marouzeau, 82-90)

Ernout, A., review-article on M. Roques, Recueil général des lexique français du moyen âge. I, Lexiques alphabétiques. 1 (Paris 1936), Revue de philologie 11 (1937) 133-145

Brittain, F., Latin in Church. Episodes in the History of Its Pronunciation, Particularly in England (London 1934; new ed. revised and enlarged 1955).

N.B.: See also the works devoted to Vulgar Latin listed above, those devoted to the vernacular languages in the Middle Ages listed under 7, the works of the ancient and mediaeval grammarians listed below, and the glossaries and indices accompanying editions of authors or documents in the MGH.

Grammatici Latini, ed. H. Keil (7 vols. Leipzig 1857-1880; Vols. 5 and 6 republished by offset 1923. For a full indication of the contents of Keil, see, e.g., Introduzione alla filologia classica (cited under 10 A above) 421-422; Supplementum continens Anecdota Helvetica, ed. H. Hagen (Leipzig 1870)

Baehrens, W. A., Sprachlicher Kommentar zur vulgärlateinischen Appendix Probi (Halle 1922)

Hunt, R., "Studies on Priscian in the 11th and 12th Centuries", Mediaeval and Renaissance Studies, edd. R. Hunt and R. Klibansky. 1 (1941-1943) 194-231; 2 (1950) 1-56

Chase, W. J., The Ars minor of Donatus for 1000 Years the Leading Textbook of Grammar (Madison, [Wis.]; University of Wisconsin Studies in Social Sciences and History No. 11); id., The Distichs of Cato. Translated from the Latin with an Introductory Sketch (ibid. 1922; same series No. 7)

Nonius Marcellus, ed. L. Müller, with Latin Commentary (2 vols. Leipzig 1888; edited also by W. M. Lindsay [3 vols. ibid 1903])

Martianus Capella, De nuptiis Philologiae et Mercurii, ed. A. Dick (Leipzig 1925)

Lutz, C. E., Remigii Autissiodorensis Comm. in Mart. Capellam (Leiden 1962)

Disticha Catonis, edd. M. Boas and J. Botschuyver (Amsterdam 1952)

Isidore of Seville, Etymologiae, ed. W. M. Lindsay (2 vols. Oxford 1910)

Eckstein, F. A., Lateinischer und griechischer Unterricht im Mittelalter (Leipzig 1887)

Schmitz, W., Alcuins ars grammatica, die lateinische Schulgrammatik der karolingischen Renaissance (Diss. Greifswald 1908)

Alcuin, Orthographia, ed. A. Marsili (Pisa 1952)

Alexander of Villa Dei, Doctrinale, ed. D. Reichling (Berlin 1893; Monumenta Germaniae Paedagogica 12); id., Ecclesiale, ed. L. R. Lind, with Introduction, Notes, and English Translation (Lawrence [Kans.] 1958)

Eberhard of Bethune, Graecismus, ed. J. Wrobel (Breslau 1887)

Paetow, L., The Arts Course at Mediaeval Universities, with Special Reference to Grammar and Rhetoric (Urbana 1910; University of Illinois Studies III, No. 7)

Sabbadini, R., Il metodo degli Umanisti (Florence 1927)

Robins, R. H., Ancient and Mediaeval Grammatical Theory in Europe with Particular Reference to Modern Linguistic Doctrines (London 1951)

Baebler, J. J., Beiträge zu einer Geschichte der lateinischen Grammatik im Mittelalter (Halle 1885)

Thurot, Ch., "Notices et extraits de divers manuscrits latins pour servir à l'histoire des doctrines grammaticales au moyen âge", Notices et extraits des manuscrits de la Bibliothèque impériale 22. 2 (1868) 1-592 (still of basic importance)

Rotta, P., La filosofia del linguaggio nella Patristica e nella Scolastica (Turin 1909)

Grabmann, M., "Die Entwicklung der mittelalterlichen Sprachlogik (Tractatus de modis significandi)", in his Mittelalterliches Geistesleben

1 (Munich 1926) 104-146 (with copious bibliography); id., "Die geschichtliche Entwicklung der mittelalterlichen Sprachphilosophie und Sprachlogik. Ein Ueberblick", Mélanges Joseph de Ghellinck 2 (Brussels 1951) 421-433

Roos, H., "Martinus de Dacia und seine Schrift De modis significandi", Classica et Mediaevalia 8 (1946) 87-115; id., "Sprachdenken im Mittelalter", ibid. 9 (1946) 200-215; id., "Die Modi significandi des Martinus de Dacia, Forschungen zur Geschichte der Sprachlogik im Mittelalter", Beiträge zur Geschichte der Philosophie und Theologie des Mittelalters 37.2 (1952) 72-120; id., "Die Stellung der Grammatik im Lehrbetrieb des 13. Jahrhunderts", in J. Koch, ed., Artes liberales . . . (Leiden-Köln 1959) 94-106

Nehring, A., "A Note on Functional Linguistics in the Middle Ages", Traditio 9 (1953) 430-434

Kukenheim, L., Contributions à l'histoire de la grammaire grecque, latine et hébraïque à l'époque de la Renaissance (Leiden 1951)

N.B.: On Latin grammar and linguistic theory in the Middle Ages, see also the works of De Ghellinck, Haskins, Manacorda, Paré-Brunet Tremblay, etc., listed under 9 above.

B. Glossaries, Dictionaries, Indices, etc.

Heerdegen, F., "Lateinische Lexicographie", in Stolz-Schmalz, Lateinisch Grammatik (4th ed. Munich 1910) 690-718

Bolognesi, G., "Profilo storico-critico degli studi linguistici greci e latini", in E. Bignone, ed., Introduzione alla filologia classica (Milan 1951), especially 436-447

Sandys, J. E., History of Classical Scholarship. 1 (3rd ed. Cambridge [Eng.] 1921); 2 and 3 (1908. Information must be gathered through the i dices of each volume.)

N.B.: An adequate history of Medieval lexicography remains to be written.

Festus, ed. W. M. Lindsay (Leipzig 1913)

Nonius Marcellus (see A above.)

Isidore of Seville (see A above.)

Corpus Glossariorum Latinorum, ed. G. Goetz (7 vols. Leipzig 1888-1923. 1, De Glossariorum Latinorum origine et fatis, published in 1923, presents Goetz's theory of origins, and also reproduces the prefaces of the works of Papias, Osbern of Gloucester, Huguccio, Joannes of Genoa, etc.)

Glossaria Latina, iussu Acad. Brittannica edita. Edd. W. M. Lindsay and Others (5 vols. Paris 1926-1931 [Les Belles Lettres]. For Lindsay's theory of origins, see Glossaria Latina 1. 1-12, and his reviews of Glossaria Latina in ALMA 3 [1927] 95-110; 8 [1933] 221-229.)

Mountford, J. F., Quotations from Classical Authors in Medieval Latin Glossaries (Ithaca 1925; Cornell Studies in Classical Philology 21)

N.B.: On Papias, etc., see the works of Heerdegen, Bolognesi, Sandys, and Goetz, listed above, and also De Ghellinck, L'Essor de la littérature latine 2. 49-52.

Forcellini-Corradini-Perin, Lexicon totius Latinitatis (4 vols. Padua 1865-1887), with Onomasticon by G. Perin (2 vols. 1913-1924)

Harper's Latin Dictionary (New York 1879; reprinted in 1889, 1907, etc., but never revised. It is now republished in England by the Oxford University Press under the name Lewis and Short.)

Georges, K. E., Ausführliches lateinisch-deutsches Handwörterbuch (8th ed. 2 vols. Hannover 1913-1918; reprinted Tübingen 1952, and Darmstadt 1956)

Benoist-Goelzer, Nouveau Dictionnaire latin-français (9th ed. Paris 1922)

Gaffiot, F., Dictionnaire illustré latin-français (Paris 1934; new edition 1957)

Thesaurus Linguae Latinae, edd. auctoritate et consilio acadd. V. Germanicarum: Berolinensis Gotting. Lips. Monac. Vindobon. (Leipzig 1900 ff.). In March 1964, the status of the work was as follows: Vol. I, II, III, IV, V^1, V^2, VI^1, VI^2, VI^3 (A-H), and Onomasticon, Vols. II-III (C-D), were published in full (The proper names in A and B are incorporated into the general vocabulary of Vols. I-II.); Vol. VII^1 (I) was published as far as integer; Vol. VII^2 was published as far as the demonstrative is; Vol. VIII^1 (M) was published as far as monstro. An indispensable Index librorum scriptorum inscriptionum ex quibus exempla adferuntur was published in 1904. The supplements published in Vols. III, pp. iii-vii (1908), and V, pp. iii-vii (1910), along with further supplementary material, are now available in a single Supplementum (1-958). For a history of the project, see especially G. Meyer, in Eduard Wölfflin: Ausgewählte Schriften (Leipzig 1933) 336-344.

Heumann-Seckel, Handlexikon zu den Quellen des römischen Rechts (9th ed. Jena 1907; and later reprints)

Berger, A., Encyclopedic Dictionary of Roman Law (Trans. Am. Phil. Soc., New Series 43.2, Philadelphia 1953; with a valuable, systematic bibliography)

Meillet-Ernout, Dictionnaire étymologique de la langue latine. Histoire des mots (4th ed. revised and enlarged, 2 vols. Paris 1959-1960)

Walde-Hofmann, Lateinisches etymologisches Wörterbuch (3rd ed. revised 3 vols. Heidelberg 1938-1956)

Souter, A., A Glossary of the Later Latin to 600 A.D. (Oxford 1949. See also J. H. Baxter, "Notes on Souter's Glossary", ALMA 23 [1953] 7-12; ibid. 25 [1955] 102-141.)

Blaise, A., Dictionnaire latin-français des auteurs chrétiens (Strasbourg 1954)

Du Cange, Ch. du Fresne sieur de, Glossarium ad scriptores mediae et infimae Latinitatis (3 vols. folio, Paris 1678. Of the later editions, cf. especially that of G. A. L. Henschel [7 vols. Paris 1840-1850], and that of L. Favre (10 vols. Niort 1883-1887; reproduced by a photographic process at Breslau [1891], Paris [1943], and Graz [1954]. For a full account of Du Cange's lexicographical work and for the later history of his Glossaria, see H. Leclercq, "Latin", DACL 8.2 [1928] 1422-1452.)

For the history and present status of the "New Du Cange", Dictionnaire du latin médiéval, see ALMA 1 (1924), 5-15; ibid. 8 (1933) 169-172; ibid. 15 (1939) 83-93; F. Blatt, "Le Nouveau dictionnaire du latin médiéval", ibid. 24 (1954) 43-83. For the indices of Latin writers and texts compiled for excerpting in each country, see the references given in 1, above.

Du Cange, Glossarium ad scriptores mediae et infimae Graecitatis (2 vols folio Paris 1688; reproduced by a photographic process at Breslau [1891], at Paris [1943], and Graz [1957])

Dieffenbach, L., Glossarium Latino-Germanicum mediae et infimae aetatis (Frankfurt 1857); id., Novum glossarium. . . (ibid. 1867)

Roques, M., "Additions et corrections d'Antoine Thomas au Glossaire de du Cange", ALMA 22 (1952) 89-156

Sophocles, E. A., Greek Lexicon of the Roman and Byzantine Periods (145 B.C. to A.D. 1100) (2nd ed. New York 1888; reprinted ibid. 1957)

Strecker-Palmer, Introduction to Medieval Latin 46-58 ("Word Formation and Meaning")

Maigne d'Arnis, W. H., Lexicon manuale ad scriptores mediae et infimae Latinitatis (Paris 1858; reprinted 1890)

Baxter, J. H., and C. Johnson, Medieval Latin Word List from British and Irish Sources (Oxford 1934)

Latham, R. E., "Suggestions for a British-Latin Dictionary", ALMA 27 (1957) 189-229

Arnaldi, F., M. Turriani, and P. Smiraglia, Latinitatis italicae mediae aevi. . . lexicon imperfectum. Published in parts in ALMA 10 (1936) ff. A - Trans at end of 1963. When completed in ALMA, it will be published separately and with its own pagination

Habel, E., Mittellateinisches Glossar (Paderborn 1931; revised ed. by F. Gröbel 1960)

Langosch, K., Mittellateinisch-deutsches Handwörterbuch (in press, 1964)

Novum Glossarium Mediae Latinitatis ab anno DCCC usque ad annum MCC, ed. cur. F. Blatt. Index Scriptorum, and L (Hafniae [Copenhagen] 1957); M-Moz (1959-1963)

Niermeyer, J. F., Mediae Latinitatis lexicon minus (Leiden 1954 ff.; to Sequipeda in March 1964)

Sleumer, A., Kirchenlateinisches Wörterbuch. Ausführliches Wortverzeichnis zum römischen Missale, Breviarium, Rituale, etc. (Limburg 1926)

Lexicon Mediae et infimae Latinitatis Polonorum, ed. M. Plezia. 1 (War-
saw 1953-1958; A-B); 2 (to Confr in March 1964). Definitions are
given in Polish and Latin.

Mittellateinisches Wörterbuch bis zum ausgehenden 13. Jahrhundert, ed.
O. Prinz (Munich 1959 ff.; to be completed in 4 vols.; Abkürzungs -
und Quellenverzeichnisse, and fasc. 1-4 [to Arm] in March 1964)

Hubschmid, J., "Zur Erforschung des mittellateinischen Wortschatzes",
ALMA 20 (1947-1949) 255-272

Köstler, R., Wörterbuch zum Codex iuris canonici (Munich 1927-1929)

Palazzini, P., Dictionarium morale et canonicum (Rome 1962 ff.)

Haberkern, E., and F. Wallach, Hilfswörterbuch für Historiker:
Mittelalter und Neuzeit (Berlin 1935)

Deferrari, R. J., Sister M. Inviolata Barry, C.D.P., and J. I. McGuiness,
O.P., A Lexicon of St. Thomas (Washington 1949-1953. See also the
review-article by M. Hubert, O.P., Revue des études latines 34 [1956]
254-267.); R. J. Deferrari, A Latin-English Dictionary of St. Thomas
Aquinas (Boston 1960; a glossarial abridgment of the Lexicon of St.
Thomas)

Sancti Thomae Acquinatis Doctoris Angelici Opera omnia iussu edita
Leonis XIII P.M. Vol. XVI, Indices auctoritatum et rerum occurrentium
in Summa Theologiae et Summa contra Gentiles -- id est indices in
integros tomos IV-XV. Cura et studio Fratrum Praedicatorum (Rome
1948)

Fernandez Garcia, M., O.F.M., Lexicon scholasticum philosophico-
theologicum in quo termini, definitiones, distinctiones et effata seu
axiomaticae propositiones philosophiam ac theologiam spectantes a B.
Ioanne Duns Scoto, doctore subtili, exponuntur declarantur (Quaracchi
1910)

Sella, P., Glossario latino italiano. Stato della Chiesa. Veneto-Abruzzi
(Rome 1944; Studi e Testi 109); id., Glossario latino emiliano (Rome
1937; Studi e Testi 74)

Joannes de Tinctoris, Terminorum musicae diffinitorium (c. 1475), ed.
A. Machabey (Paris 1952)

Thomas, A., "Notes lexicographiques sur les recettes médicales du haut
moyen âge publiées par le Dr. H. E. Sigerist", ALMA 5 (1930) 97-166

Castro, A., Glosarios latino-españoles de la edad media (Madrid 1936)

Starnes, De W. T., Renaissance Dictionaries (London 1954)

N.B.: For information on mediaeval vernacular glossaries and for modern dictionaries covering English, French, etc., in the mediaeval
period, see 7 above.

For practically complete control of special lexica, concordances, and
copious indices verborum, etc., of Latin writers to the sixth century A.D.,
see especially:
Faider, P., Répertoire des index et lexiques d'auteurs latins (Paris
1926); id., Répertoire des éditions des scolies et commentaires
d'auteurs latins (ibid. 1931)

Cousin, J., "Lexiques d'auteurs", in his Bibliographie de la langue latine 1880-1948 (Paris 1951) 279-287 (especially valuable as a suplement to Faider for the period 1925-1948)

Bolognesi, G., "Indici e lessici speciali", in E. Bignone ed., Introduzione alla filologia classica (Milan 1951) 442-447 (select list only)

For concordances to the Bible see 5 above. The following related work should be mentioned here:

Bartholomaeus of Urbino (died 1350), Milleloquium Sancti Augustini (printed at Lyons 1555, and at Paris 1645); id., Milleloquium Sancti Ambrosii (printed at Lyons 1556. See the important master's dissertation of V. A. Fitzpatrick, M.S.SS.T., "Bartholomaeus of Urbino: The Sermons Embraced in His Milleloquium S. Augustini" [Catholic University 1954].)

Lenfant, D., O.P., Concordantiae Augustinianae sive Collectio omnium sententiarum quae sparsim reperiuntur in omnibus S. Augustini operibus ad instar Concordantiarum Sacrae Scripturae (2 vols. Paris 1656-1665; reprinted Frankfurt 1963). See also the copious Indices generales in the Benedictine edition of St. Augustine's works (in the Gaume reprint, Vol. XI 2, cols. 929-2196; Migne, PL 46)

N.B.: For indices verborum, grammatical usages, etc., covering authors or collections from the end of the fifth century to the late Middle Ages, see the pertinent sections of this SYLLABUS. Unfortunately, we do not yet have a systematic work like Faider or Cousin covering Mediaeval Latin authors or works.

See also the indices in the following:

Hagenmeyer, H., Anonymi Gesta Francorum et aliorum Hierosolymitanorum (Heidelberg 1890)

Voigt, E., Ysengrimus (written by Nivard of Ghent c. 1146) (Halle 1884) 412-470

Bäumker, Cl., Avencebrolis Fons vitae ex arabico in latinum translatus ab Johanne Hispano et Dominico Gundissalino (Münster 1895; Beiträge zur Geschichte der Philosophie des Mittelalters 1. 2-4: 394-553)

N.B.: On poetic vocabulary, see also the works on ars versificatoria listed under C below.

C.   Rhetoric and Poetics: Ars Dictaminis, Ars Versificatoria, Ars Praedicandi, Cursus, Literature in Verse (See also 4 above.)

Baldwin, C.S., Ancient Rhetoric and Poetic (New York 1924); Medieval Rhetoric and Poetic (New York 1928. Both are available in recent reprints.)

Clarke, M. L., Rhetoric at Rome (London 1953)

Balogh, J., "Voces paginarum. Beiträge zur Geschichte des lauten Lesens und Schreibens," Philologus 82 (1927) 84-109, 202-240

Caplan, H., Ad C. Herennium libri IV (Cambridge [Mass.] 1954; Loeb Classical Library)

Lausberg, H., Elemente der literarischen Rhetorik für Studierende der romanischen und klassischen Philologie (Munich 1949); id., Handbuch der literarischen Rhetorik. Eine Grundlegung der Literaturwissenschaft (2 vols. Munich 1960)

Norden, E., Die antike Kunstprosa vom VI. Jahrhundert v. Chr. bis in die Zeit der Renaissance (2 vols. 4th reprint Leipzig 1923)

Borinski, J., Die Antike in Poetik und Kunsttheorie von Ausgang des klassischen Altertums bis auf Goethe und Wilhelm von Humboldt (2 vols. Leipzig 1914-1924; reprinted 1964)

Curtius, E. R., European Literature and the Latin Middle Ages. English trans. by W. R. Trask (New York 1953; Bollingen Series 36. This is a work of basic importance.)

Auerbach, E., Literatursprache und Publikum in der lateinischen Spätantike und im Mittelalter (Bern 1958); id., Mimesis. The Representation of Reality in Western Literature (New York 1957; an Anchor Book)

Kroll, W., "Rhetorik", in Pauly-Wissowa, RE, Supplementband 7 (1940) 1039-1138

Sykutris, J., "Epistolographie", Pauly-Wissowa, RE, Supplementband 5 (1931) 185-220

Riposati, B., "Problemi di retorica antica", in E. Bignone ed., Introduzione alla filologia classica (Milan 1951) 657-787 (with valuable bibliography)

Volkmann, R., Die Rhetorik der Griechen und Römer in systematischer Uebersicht dargestellt (2nd ed. Leipzig 1885; reprinted 1962)

D'Alton, J. F., Roman Literary Theory and Criticism. A Study in Tendencies (London and New York 1931; reprinted 1963)

Marouzeau, J., Traité de stylistique appliquée au latin (revised ed. Paris 1946)

Hofmann, J. B., and A. Szantyr, "Stilistik", in Leumann-Hofmann-Szantyr, Lateinische Grammatik. Part II (new ed. Munich 1963 ff.) 685-842

On "higher" and "lower" imitatio in Ancient and Mediaeval literature, see, e.g.:

D'Alton, op. cit., 426-434, and 558-559

Stemplinger, E., Das Plagiat in der griechischen Literatur (Leipzig 1912) passim

Traube, L., Einleitung (see 1 above) 70-73

Mahoney, Brother Albertus, C.F.X., Vergil in the Works of Prudentius (Washington 1934; CUA Patristic Studies 29)

Curtius, E. R., op. cit., passim

Laistner, M. L. W., Thought and Letters (see 4 above) 273-275 and 301 ff. (on Einhard and Rhabanus Maurus respectively)

Buttimer, Bro. C. H., F.S.C., Hugonis de Sancto Victore Didascalicon: De studio legendi (Washington 1939; CUA Studies in Mediaeval and Renaissance Latin 10. For identification of further sources, see J. Taylor, The Didascalicon of Hugh of St. Victor (New York 1961)

On the allegorical method of interpretation and on the allegorical treatment of literary themes in Antiquity and in the Middle Ages, see, for Scripture, the works listed under 5 above, and for application outside of Scripture:

Joosen, J. C., and J. H. Waszink, "Allegorese", in T. Klauser, ed., Reallexikon für Antike und Christentum 1 (Stuttgart 1950) 283-293 (with good bibliography)

Pépin, J., Mythe et Allégorie (Paris 1958)

Raby, F. J. E., History of Christian Latin Poetry (see 4 above) 61-63 (on the Psychomachia of Prudentius)

Rand, E. K., Ovid and his Influence (New York 1926), especially, 108-167

Curtius, E. R., op. cit., passim

Works on language and style (continued)

Colson, F. H., M. Fabii Quintiliani Institutionis Liber I. Edited with Introduction and Commentary (Cambridge [England] 1924)

Bernhard, M., Der Stil des Apuleius von Madaura. Ein Beitrag zur Stilistik des Spätlateins (Stuttgart 1927)

Marrou, H. I., Saint Augustin et la fin de la culture antique (Paris 1938); "Retractatio" (1949). This is a basic work, with valuable bibliography.

Barry, Sister Inviolata, St. Augustine the Orator. A Study of the Rhetorical Qualities of St. Augustine's Sermones ad Populum (Washington 1924; CUA Patristic Studies 6)

Sullivan, Sister Thérèse of the Blessed Sacrament, S. Augustini de doctrina Christiana liber IV. A Commentary with a Revised Text, Introduction and Translation (Washington 1930; same series 23)

Finaert, J., L'Évolution littéraire de saint Augustin (Paris 1939); id., Saint Augustin rhéteur (ibid. 1939)

Loyen, A., Sidoine Apollinaire et l'esprit précieux en Gaule aux derniers jours de l'empire (Paris 1943)

Muldowney, Sister M. Sarah, Word-Order in the Works of St. Augustine (Washington 1937; CUA Patristic Series 53)

N.B.: For the works of the ancient grammarians and rhetoricians, see B above.

Sturtevant, E. H., The Pronunciation of Greek and Latin (see A above)

Hardie, R. W., Res metrica: An Introduction to the Study of Greek and Roman Versification (Oxford 1920)

Raby, F. J. E., A History of Secular Latin Poetry in the Middle Ages (2nd ed. Oxford 1957), Ch. I, "The Inheritance of the Middle Ages"; Ch. II, "Poetry of the Rhetorical Tradition from the Fourth to the End of the Fifth Century"; Ch. III, "The Sixth Century"; Ch. IV, "The Age of Transition", 1-177; id., A History of Christian Latin Poetry from the Beginnings to the Close of the Middle Ages (2nd ed. 1953), especially, Chs. I-V: 1-153

De Groot, A. W., La prose métrique des anciens (Paris 1926)

Laurand, L., Études sur le style des discours de Cicéron, avec une esquisse de l'histoire du cursus (2nd and 3rd ed. Paris 1926-1928), especially, 117-230, and 353-361

Mann, Sister M. Emmanuel, The Clausulae of St. Hilary of Poitiers (Washington 1936; CUA Patristic Series 48. It has a good sketch of the history of clausulae and cursus, 1-12. See also the other studies in the CUA Patristic Studies and CUA Studies in Renaissance and Mediaeval Latin Language and Literature devoted to the investigation of prose rhythm.)

Nicolau, M. G., L'Origine du cursus rhythmique et les débuts de l'accent d'intensité en latin (Paris 1930); id., "Les deux sources de la versification latine accentuelle", ALMA 9 (1934) 55-87

Hagendahl, H., "La prose métrique d'Arnobe", Göteborgs Högskolas Årskrift 42 (1936) 1-265

Browne, R. A., British Latin Selections A.D. 500-1400 (Oxford 1954), esp. xxxiv-lxi (on prose rhythm, etc.)

Di Capua, F., Fonti ed esempi per lo studio dello "Stilus Curiae Romanae" medioevale (Rome 1941; with a chronological list of the numerous publications of the author on prose rhythm); id., Il ritmo prosaico nelle lettere dei Papi nei documenti della cancellaria romana dal IV al XIV secolo (3 vols. Rome 1937-1946)

Lundholm, G., Studien zum mittellateinischen Prosarhythmus (Stockholm 1963)

Denholm-Young, N., "The Cursus in England", in Oxford Essays in Medieval History Presented to H. E. Salter (Oxford 1934) 68-103

Polheim, K., Die lateinische Reimprosa (Berlin 1925; reprinted 1963)

Schiaffini, A., "La tecnica della prosa rimata nel medio evo latino", Studi romanzi 21 (1931) 7-115; studies on Guido Faba, Guittone, and Dante)

Strecker-Palmer, op. cit., "Prosody and Accentuation", 58-59, "Style", 68-71, "Poetry and Literary Prose", 71-90 (In many respects, these are the most valuable sections in the book.)

Beare, W., Latin Verse and European Song. A Study in Accent and Rhythm (London 1957; to be used with care)

Norberg, D., La Poésie latine rythmique du haut moyen âge (Stockholm 1954); id., Introduction à l'étude de la versification latine médiévale (ibid. 1958)

Burger, M., Recherches sur la structure et l'origine des vers romans (Geneva and Paris 1957)

N.B.: These studies by Norberg and Burger are of basic importance.

Meyer, W., Gesammelte Abhandlungen zur mittellateinischen Rhythmik. 1-2 (Berlin 1905); 3 (1936)

Taylor, H. O., The Mediaeval Mind. 2 (3rd ed. New York 1919), Ch. XXXII, "Evolution of Mediaeval Latin Prose", 176-214, and Ch. XXXIII, "Evolution of Mediaeval Latin Verse", 215-259

Artz, F. B., op. cit., Chs. IX-X, "Literature"

McKeon, R., "Rhetoric in the Middle Ages", Speculum 18 (1942) 1-32

Curtius, E., op. cit., especially, Ch. 4, "Rhetoric", 62-78; Ch. 5, "Topics", 79-105; Ch. 7, "Metaphorics", 128-144; Ch. 8, "Poetry and Rhetoric", 144-166

Crosby, R., "Oral Delivery in the Middle Ages", Speculum 11 (1936) 88-110

Quain, E. A., S. J., "The Medieval Accessus ad Auctores", Traditio 3 1945), 215-264 (On accessus, see also Curtius, op. cit., 226 ff.)

Huygens, R. B. C., Accessus ad Auctores. Édition critique (Berchem-Brussels 1954; Collection Latomus 15); id., Conrad de Hirschau Dialogus super Auctores. Édition critique (ibid. 1955; same series 17)

Arbusow, L., Eine Auswahl rhetorischer Figuren und Gemeinplätze als Hilfsmittel für akademische Uebungen an mittelalterlichen Texten (Göttingen 1948; 2nd ed. revised by H. Peter, 1963)

Howell, W. G., The Rhetoric of Alcuin and Charlemagne. A Translation with an Introduction, The Latin Text, and Notes (London 1941)

Wallach, L., "Onulf of Speyer, A Humanist of the Eleventh Century", Mediaevalia et Humanistica 6 (1950) 35-56; a good treatment of the colores rhetorici

Ogle, M., "Some Aspects of Mediaeval Latin Style", Speculum 1 (1926 170-189

N. B.: See also the works on literary genres listed under Literature in 4 above.

On the ars dictaminis see especially:

Baldwin, C. S., Mediaeval Rhetoric and Poetic, Ch. VIII, "Dictamen", 206-227

McKeon, R., "Poetry and Philosophy in the Twelfth Century: The Renaissance of Rhetoric", Modern Philology 43 (1936) 217-234

Poole, R. L., Lectures on the History of the Papal Chancery down to the Time of Innocent III (Cambridge [England] 1915)

Rockinger, L., "Briefsteller und Formelbücher des XI. bis XIV. Jahrhunderts", Quellen und Erörterungen zur bayer. und deutschen Geschichte XI (Munich 1863-1864; reprinted 1961)

Iguanez, M., and H. M. Willard, edd., Alberici Cassiniensis Flores Rhetorici, in Miscellanea Cassinese 14 (Monte Cassino 1938. See also the review by E. Franceschini, Bolletino di filologia classica 45 [1938] 124-134.)

Heller, E., "Die Ars dictandi des Thomas von Capua", Sitzungsber. Heidelberg Acad., 4. Abh. (1929)

Wieruzowski, H., "Ars dictaminis in the Time of Dante", Mediaevalia et Humanistica 1 (1943) 95-108

Erdmann, C., Studien zur Briefliteratur Deutschlands im elften Jahrhundert
(Leipzig 1948; Schriften des Reichsinstituts für ältere deutsche Ge-
schichtskunde 1).

On literature in verse, and especially on the ars versificatoria, see,
especially:

Baldwin, op. cit., Ch. IV, "Poetic, Old and New (Fifth to Seventh Centuries)", 99-125; Ch. V, "The Carolingians and the Tenth Century",
126-149; Ch. VII, "Latin Poetic in the Twelfth and Thirteenth Centuries", 183-205; Ch. X, "Poetic Achievement in the Vernacular",
258-301

Raby, Christian Latin Poetry, and Secular Latin Poetry (standard general
works, with excellent bibliographies. See 4 above.)

De Ghellinck, J., L'Essor de la littérature au XII siècle (see 4 above).
2, Ch. VI, "Poésie profane et poésie religieuse"

Peebles, B. M., "O Roma Nobilis", American Benedictine Review 1
(1950) 67-92

Faral, E., Les arts poétiques du XIIe et du XIIIe siècle. Recherches et
documents sur la technique littéraire du moyen âge (Paris 1923); id.,
"Le Ms 511 du Huntonian Museum de Glasgow. Notes sur le mouvement
poétique et l'histoire des études littéraires en France et en Angleterre
entre les années 1150 et 1225", Studi Medievali, N.S., 9 (1936) 18-119

Sedgwick, W. B., "Notes and Emendations on Faral's Les Arts poétiques
du XIIe et du XIIIe siècle", Speculum 2 (1927) 331-343; id., "The Style
and Vocabulary of the Latin Arts of Poetry of the Twelfth and Thirteenth Centuries", ibid., 3 (1938) 349-381

Brittain, F., The Medieval Latin and Romance Lyric to A.D. 1300 (2nd
ed. Cambridge [England] 1951; with good introduction, excellent selection of texts, and bibliography)

Spanke, H., Beziehungen zwischen romanischer und mittellateinscher
Lyrik, mit besonderer Berücksichtigung der Metrik und Musik (Berlin
1936)

De Lage, G. R., Alain de Lille. Poète du XIIe siècle (Paris 1951), especially Part III, "Structure et formes littéraires des poèmes", 103-168

Wilson, E. F., "Pastoral and Epithalamium in Latin Literature",
Speculum 23 (1948) 35-57

Munari, F., "Tradition und Originalität in der lateinischen Dichtung des
XII. Jahrhundert", Romanische Forschungen 69 (1957) 305-331.

N.B.: On hymnology and on religious and secular drama in the Middle
Ages, see the works listed under 4 above. On the Romance and
Germanic lyric and the relations between vernacular and Medieval
Latin poetry, see also the works on the vernacular languages and
literatures in the Middle Ages listed under 6 above.

On the ars praedicandi, see especially:

Baldwin, op. cit., Ch. IX, "Preaching", 228-257

Charland, T. M., O. P., Artes praedicandi. Contribution à l'histoire de la rhétorique au moyen âge (Paris 1936)

Owst, G. R., Preaching in Medieval England. An Introduction to Sermon Manuscripts of the Period c. 1350-1450 (Cambridge [England] 1926; id. Literature and Pulpit in Medieval England (ibid. 1933; reprinted 1960)

Schian, C. M., "Geschichte der christlichen Predigt", Realencyclopädie der protestantischen Theologie 15 (1904) 623-747, especially 639-649; ibid. 24 (1913) 333-346

Niebergall, A., et al., "Predigt", Religion in Geschichte und Gegenwart 4 (3rd ed. 1961) 516-539

Gilson, E., "Michel Menot et la technique du sermon médiéval", Revue d'histoire franciscaine 12 (1925) 301-360; reprinted in E. Gilson, Les idées et les lettres [Paris 1932] 93-154

Wilmart, Dom A., O. S. B., "Les Sermons d'Hildebert", Revue Bénédictin 47 (1935) 12-31

Davy, M., Les sermons universitaires parisiens de 1230-1231. Contribution à l'histoire de la prédication médiévale (Paris 1931)

Mourin, L., Jean Gerson, prédicateur (Bruges 1952)

Cantini, G., "La tecnica e l'indole del sermone medievale ed i sermoni di s. Antonio di Padova", Studi franciscani 6 (1934) 60-80, and 195-224

Caplan, H., "Rhetorical Invention in some Mediaeval Treatises on Preaching", Speculum 2 (1927) 284-294; id., "The Four Senses of Scriptural Interpretation and the Mediaeval Theory of Preaching", ibid. 4 (1929) 282-290; id., Mediaeval Artes Praedicandi: A Hand-List (Ithaca 1934; Cornell Studies in Classical Philology 24); id., Mediaeval Artes Praedicandi: A Supplementary Hand-List (1936; same series 25); id., "Classical Rhetoric and the Mediaeval Theory of Preaching", Classical Philology 28 (1933) 75-96; id., "Henry of Hesse on the Art of Preaching" PLMA 48 (1933) 340-360

12. Mediaeval Aesthetics

N. B.: Aesthetics, Literary Theory, etc., are covered also in many of the works listed in the sections of this Bibliography devoted to Philosophy, Latin and Vernacular Literature, Art and Music, Rhetoric and Poetic.

De Bruyne, E., L'Esthétique du moyen âge (Louvain 1947); id., Études d'esthétique médiévale. 1, De Boèce à Jean Scot Erigène; 2, L'Époque romane; 3, Le XIIIᵉ siècle (Bruges 1946)

Svoboda, K., L'Esthétique de Saint Augustin et ses sources (Paris 1933)

Biese, A., The Development of Feeling for Nature in the Middle Ages. English trans. (New York 1905; reprinted 1963)

De Wulf, M., "L'Histoire de l'esthétique et ses grandes orientations", Revue Néo-Scolastique 16 (1909) 237-259

Maritain, J., Art and Scholasticism and the Frontiers of Poetry. English trans. by J. W. Evans (New York 1962; id., Creative Intuition in Art and Poetry (New York 1953; Bollingen Series 35. 1. It is also available -- but without plates -- in Meridian Books.)

Grabmann, M., Des Ulrich Engelberti von Strassburg, O.P. (1277), Abhandlung De pulchro. Untersuchungen und Texte (Sitzungsber. d. Akad. d. Wiss. 5. Abh., Munich 1925)

Boving, R., "St. Bonaventura und der Grundgedanke der Disputa Raffaels", Franziskanische Studien 1 (1914) 1-17

Curtius, E. R., "Zur Literarästhetik des Mittelalters", Zeitschrift für romanische Philologie 58 (1938) 1-50; 129-232; 433-479; id., "Mittel-alterliche Literaturtheorien", ibid. 62 (1942) 417-491; id., European Liter-ature and the Latin Middle Ages (New York 1953) passim. The basic ideas of the articles just mentioned, along with those of many others, are incor-porated in this work of solid and comprehensive scholarship.

Atkins, J. W. H., Literary Criticism in Antiquity (2 vols. Cambridge [England] 1934); English Literary Criticism: The Medieval Phase (1943; revised ed. 1952); id., English Literary Criticism: The Renaissance (1947)

Marti, B. M., "Literary Criticism in the Mediaeval Commentaries on Lucan", TAPA 72 (1941) 245-254

Wellek, R., and A. Warren, Theory of Literature (New York 1949; a stimu-lating introduction to the theory of literature and to the methodology of literary scholarship, with valuable notes and bibliography)

Weinberg, B., A History of Literary Criticism in the Italian Renaissance (2 vols. Chicago 1961)

Hatzfeld, H., Literature through Art. A New Approach to French Literature (New York 1952), especially 1-62

Kayser, W., Das sprachliche Kunstwerk (7th ed. Bern 1961)

Stil und Formprobleme in der Literatur. Papers of the 7th Congress of the International Federation for Modern Languages and Literatures, ed. by P. Böckmann (Heidelberg 1959. See especially the sections "Methodische und prinzipielle Fragen", and "Zur Literatur des Mittelalters", 11-188.

13. Periodicals

N.B.: Those marked with an asterisk are especially important for Mediaeval Latin Studies. If there is a widely employed abbreviation, this abbre-viation is indicated.

Aevum. Rassegna di scienze storiche linguistiche e filologiche (Milan 1927 ff.)

American Historical Review (New York 1895 ff.) AHR

*Analecta Bollandiana (Brussels 1882 ff.) AB

Analecta Franciscana (Quaracchi 1885 ff.) A Franc

*Analecta sacra Tarraconensia (Madrid 1925 ff.) AST

*L'Année philologique (Paris 1924 ff.) A Ph
*L'Année thélogique augustinienne (Paris 1951 ff.) A Th A
Archiv für Liturgiewissenschaft (formerly Jahrbuch für Lit. [JLW]
    (Regensburg 1951 ff.) ALW
*Archiv für Diplomatik, Schriftgeschichte, Siegel und Wappenkunde (Münster-
    Köln 1955 ff.) A Dipl
Archiv für Studium der neueren Sprachen (Braunschweig 1846 ff.) AfnSpr
*Archives d'histoire doctrinale et littéraire du moyen âge (Paris 1926 ff.)
*Archivio-storico italiano (Florence 1842 ff.; 5th series 1900 ff.; 6th series
    1913-1923; 7th series 1924 ff.) A St It
*Archivum Franciscanum historicum (Quarrachi 1908 ff.) A Fr H
*Archivum Fratrum Praedicatorum (Rome 1931 ff.) AFP
Archivum Historiae Pontificiae (Rome 1963 ff.)
*Archivum Latinitatis medii aevi. Bulletin du Cange (Paris 1924 ff.) ALMA
Augustinianum (Rome 1961 ff.)

*Bibliothèque de l'École des Chartes: Revue d'érudition consacrée spéciale-
    ment à l'étude du moyen âge (Paris 1839 ff.) BECh
Bibliothèque d'Humanisme et Renaissance (Paris 1941 ff.)
Bulletin of the Institute of Historical Research (London 1923 ff.)
Bulletin of the John Rylands Library (Manchester 1903 ff.) BJRL
*Bulletin de la Société Internationale pour l'Étude de la philosophie médiévale
    (Louvain 1959 ff.) Bull SIEPM
*Byzantinische Zeitschrift (Leipzig and Munich 1892 ff.) BZ
*Byzantion: Revue internationale des études byzantines (Brussels and Paris
    1924 ff.) Byz

*Cahiers de Civilisation médiévale X^e - XIIe siècles (Poitiers 1958 ff.)
Catholic Historical Review (Washington 1915 ff.) CHR
*Celtica (Dublin 1955 ff.)
*Classica et Mediaevalia, Revue danoise d'histoire et de philologie (Copenhagen
    1938 ff.) C et M
*Collectanea Franciscana (Rome 1931 ff.) Coll Fr

*Deutsches Archiv für Erforschung des Mittelalters (Köln-Graz 1950 ff.
    It continues Deutsches Archiv für Geschichte des Mittelalters [1937-1943],
    Archiv der Gesellschaft für ältere Geschichtskunde 1-12 [1820-1874], and
    Neues Archiv der Gesellschaft für ältere deutsche Geschichtskunde [1876-
    1935].) DA
Deutsche Vierteljahresschrift für Literaturwissenchaft und Geistesgeschichte
    (Halle 1923 ff.) DVSLGG

*Ephemerides liturgicae (Rome 1887 ff.) E Lit
English Historical Review (London 1886 ff.) EHR
Eriu (Dublin 1904 ff.)
*Ephemerides Theologicae Lovanienses (Bruges 1924 ff.) EthL
Études celtiques (Paris 1936 ff.)

*Franciscan Studies: A Quarterly Review (Saint Bonaventure N.Y.) F Studies
*Franziskanische Studien ([Münster] Werl 1914 ff.) F Stud

Germanisch-Romanische Monatschrift (Heidelberg 1909-1942 and 1951 ff.) GRM
*Greek and Byzantine Studies (Cambridge [Mass.] 1958 ff.)

*Hispania Sacra, Revista de Historia ecclesiástica (Barcelona and Madrid 1948 ff.)
Historische Zeitschrift (Munich 1859 ff.) HZ
Historisches Jahrbuch (Munich 1880 ff.) HJ
History (London 1912 ff.)

*International Guide to Medieval Studies (American Bibl. Service [Darien, Conn.] 1961 ff.)
International Philosophical Quarterly (New York 1961 ff.)
The Irish Ecclesiastical Record (Dublin 1864 ff.) IER
Isis: International Review Devoted to the History of Science and Civilization (Brussels 1913 ff.)
*Italia Medioevale e Umanistica (Padua 1958 ff.)

Jahrbuch für Liturgik und Hymnologie (Kassel 1955 ff.) JLH
Journal of Ecclesiastical History (Manchester 1950 ff.) JEH
Journal of English and Germanic Philology (Urbana [Ill.] 1897 ff.)
Journal of the History of Ideas (New York 1937 ff.)
Journal of Theological Studies (London 1899 ff.) JTS
Journal of the Warburg and Courtauld Institutes (London 1939 ff.)

Latomus: Revue des études latines (Brussels 1938 ff.)
*Literaturblatt für germanische und romanische Philologie (Leipzig 1880 ff.)
Liturgisches Jahrbuch (Münster i. W. 1951 ff.) LJ

Manuscripta (St. Louis 1957 ff.)
*Medievalia et Humanistica. An American Journal of the Middle Ages and Renaissance (Boulder [University of Colorado] 1942 ff.) M et H
*Medieval and Renaissance Studies (Warburg Institute, London, 1941 ff.)
Modern Philology (Chicago 1903 ff.) MP
*Le moyen âge: Revue d'histoire et de philologie (Paris 1888 ff.) MA
*Mediaeval Studies (Toronto 1938 ff.) MS
*Medium Aevum (Oxford 1932 ff.) M Aev
*Miscellanea francescana (Foligno, Assisi, and Rome 1886 ff.) MF
Modern Language Notes (Baltimore 1886 ff.) MLN
Modern Language Review (London 1905 ff.) MLR
The Musical Quarterly (New York 1915 ff.) MQ

*New Scholasticism (Washington 1927 ff.)
*Nouvelle Revue Théologique (Paris and Louvain 1869 ff.) NRT
*Nuovi studi medievali (Bologna 1923-1927)

*Progress of Medieval and Renaissance Studies in the United States and Canada (Boulder [University of Colorado] 1923-1934; biennially 1935 ff.) PMRS

*Publications of the Modern Language Association of America (New York 1884 ff.) PMLA

*Quarterly Check-List of Medievalia (American Bibl. Service [Darien, Conn.] 1958 ff.)

Quarterly Check-List of Renaissance Studies (ibid. 1959 ff.)

Quarterly Check-List of Literary History (ibid. 1958 ff.)

Recherches de Science religieuse (Paris 1910 ff.) RSR

*Recherches de théólogie ancienne et médiévale, with Bulletin de théologie ancienne et médiévale (Louvain 1928 ff.) RTAM

*Répertoire des médiévistes européens (Portiers 1960 ff.)

*Revue d'ascétique et de mystique (Toulouse 1924 ff.) RAM

*Revue belge de philogie et d'histoire (Brussels 1922 ff.) RBPh

*Revue Bénédictine (Maredsous 1884 ff.) RB

*Revue des bibliothèques (Paris 1891 ff.)

Revue des Études Augustiniennes (Paris 1955 ff. It continues L'Année Théologique Augustinienne.) Rev E Aug

Revue des études juives (Paris 1880 ff.) REJ

*Revue des études latines (Paris 1923 ff.) REL

*Revue des études byzantines (Paris 1946 ff. It continues Échos d'Orient.) REB

*Revue de l'histoire littéraire de la France (Paris 1894 ff.)

*Revue d'Histoire ecclésiastique (Louvain 1900 ff.) RHE

*Revue d'histoire franciscaine (Paris 1924 ff.)

*Revue du moyen âge latin: Études, Textes, chronique, bibliographie (Lyons 1945 ff.) RMA

Renaissance News (New York 1948 ff.) RN

Revue historique (Paris 1876 ff.) RH

Revue historique de Droit français et étranger (Paris 1855 ff.)

*Revue néo-scholastique de philosophie (Louvain 1894-1945) RNPh

*Revue des sciences philosophiques et théologiques (Paris 1907 ff.) RSPhTh

Revue des Sciences Religieuses (Strasbourg 1921 ff.) RSR

*Revue Mabillon (Paris 1906 ff.)

*Revue philosophique de Louvain (Louvain 1945 ff. It continues the Revue Néo-Scholastique) RPhL

*Revue Thomiste (Paris 1893 ff.) RT

*Rivista di filosofia neo-scholastica (Milan 1909 ff.) RFN

Romance Philology (Berkeley 1947 ff.)

*Romania (Paris 1872 ff.)

*Romanische Forschungen (Erlangen 1885 ff.)

*Römische Quartalschrift für Kirchengeschichte (Rome 1887 ff.) RQ

*Sacris Erudiri. Jaarboek voor Godsdienstwetenschappen (Steenbrugge
  [Belgium] 1948 ff.) SE
*Scholastik: Vierteljahrschrift für Theologie und Philosophie (Freiburg i.
  Br. 1926 ff.)
*Scriptorium. International Review of Manuscript Studies (Brussels 1947 ff.)
  Slavonic Review (London 1922 ff.)
*Speculum: A Journal of Mediaeval Studies (Cambridge [Mass.] 1926 ff.)
*Studia Anselmiana (Rome 1933 ff.) SA
*Studi Medioevali (Turin 1904 ff., N.S. 1928 ff.)
*Studia Monastica (Montserrat [Barcelona] 1959 ff.)
*Studi e Testi (Rome 1900 ff.)
*Studien und Mitteilungen aus dem Benediktiner-und Zisterziensorden bzw. zur
  Geschichte des Benediktinerordens und seiner Zweige (Munich 1880 ff.;
  N.F. since 1911) SM
  Syria: Revue d'art oriental et d'archéologie (Paris 1920 ff.)

*Theological Studies (Woodstock [Md.] 1940 ff.)
  Theologisches Literaturblatt (Leipzig 1880 ff.) ThLBl
*Theologische Revue (Münster i. W. 1903 ff.) ThR
*The Thomist: A Speculative Quarterly Review (Washington 1937 ff.)
*Traditio: Studies in Ancient and Medieval History, Thought and Religion
  (New York 1943 ff.)

*Vigiliae Christianae: A Review of Early Christian Life and Language
  (Amsterdam 1946 ff.) VC
*The Year's Work in Modern Language Studies (Cambridge [England] 1931 ff.)

  Yearbook of Liturgical Studies (Notre Dame [Ind.] 1960 ff.)

  Zeitschrift für deutsche Philologie (Stuttgart 1869-1946) ZDP
*Zeitschrift für romanische Philologie (Halle 1875 ff.) ZRPh
*Zeitschrift für deutsches Altertum und deutsche Literatur (Berlin and
  Wiesbaden 1841 ff.)
  Zeitschrift für Kirchengeschichte ([Gotha] Stuttgart 1876 ff.)
*Zentralblatt für Bibliothekswesen (Leipzig 1884 ff.) ZBB
  Zeitschrift der Savigny-Stiftung für Rechtsgeschichte. Germanistische
  Abteilung (Weimar 1880 ff.); *Romanistische Abteilung (1880 ff.);
  *Kanonistische Abteilung (1911 ff.) Z Sav RG germ, Z Sav RG rom, and
  Z Sav RG kan

I. Index of Ancient and Mediaeval Authors, Collections of Texts, and Related Works

II. Modern Scholars, Reference Works, Etc.